72190

R. A. TORREY

R. A. TORREY

Apostle of Certainty

By
Roger Martin

072190

SWORD OF THE LORD PUBLISHERS
Murfreesboro, Tennessee 37130

Printed and bound in the United States of America.

This volume is affectionately dedicated to my loving wife Joy, who has been a constant source of inspiration and encouragement in the completion of the biography. She has given many hours to the proofreading of the manuscript and has offered valuable suggestions in the writing of it.

Dr. R. A. Torrey

Preface

"There are some men whose lives it is impossible to study without perceiving the impression that they were expressly sent into the world to do a work required by the juncture of history on which they fell."[1] Is it possible to conceive of the rise and spread of Christianity apart from Paul? How would Christianity have fared without an Augustine? What would the Reformation have been without a Luther, a Calvin, a Zwingli, or a Knox? How could the great Evangelical Revival have transpired without a Wesley or a Whitefield? How would early American revival movements have fared without an Edwards or a Finney? Would the great awakening of the late nineteenth century have been possible without D. L. Moody?

In similar fashion Reuben Archer Torrey was called as an apostle for the hour in which he lived. It is remarkable to note some of the parallels in the lives of Paul and Torrey. Both were well-educated and converted from skepticism. Both labored for some time in a rather insignificant ministry and were eventually thrust into a global evangelistic effort. Both were peerless preachers and teachers, and their writings made an indelible imprint on the generations which followed. One of Torrey's students and close associates, William Evans, also observed this same comparison. He saw the two as "cultured in the classics of the Greek, dominated by the Hebrew passion of religion, and commandeered by the Roman dream of world domination."[2]

Torrey did not desire that his biography be written. An humble man who sought to give Christ the preeminence, he feared excessive eulogizing. He considered writing an autobiography—how we wish that he had!—but the project did not materialize. His time was at a premium, and he felt more glory could be brought to God through his sermons than in an autobiography. Further, he did not believe anyone could really write his biography except himself. In line with this latter statement a bit of hesitation and awe has attended the efforts of this author to attempt such a work.

It is, however, my firm conviction that just such a work is needed. First, it has been a source of amazement to find over forty-five years after his decease the number of prominent Christians who have been signally influenced by Torrey. Some of these appraisals are to be found in the section entitled "He Being Dead Yet Speaketh." Second, I personally owe a debt to Torrey for his theological influence, particularly in the areas of inspiration of Scripture, the work of the Holy Spirit and personal evangelism. Third, there has been a great increase in the printing and circulation of Torrey's works, indicating the demand for his writings on the contemporary scene. It would appear that an adequate biography would be a welcome addition in view of his past prominence and continuing influence.

A thorough biography of Reuben Archer Torrey is long overdue. It was the request of the immediate family for years, however, not to divulge information concerning him except for brief biographical sketches or magazine articles. This was out of respect for Torrey's wishes. Happily the situation has changed, and the late Dr. Reuben A. Torrey, Jr., as well as other family members, was very kind and cooperative in contributing valuable facts and insights for this volume.

However, the writing of a biography of Torrey has been hampered somewhat because of the lack of source materials. Many of the most important sources such as personal letters, diary entries and private notes have been either misplaced or destroyed. I have endeavored to locate as much as possible in the way of primary source materials. Dr. Torrey, Jr., who read and corrected the first draft of this manuscript, commented: "Mrs. Torrey and I have read through the manuscript with keen interest and pleasure. We feel you have done an excellent job. It should be inspiring as well as interesting to all."[3]

The only works extant which deal with Torrey's life are four. There are the extended sketches of his life in *Torrey and Alexander* by J. K. MacLean and in *Around the World with Alexander* by G. T. B. Davis. The latter gives important information concerning the first phase of the worldwide evangelistic tour. His co-worker, Robert Harkness, wrote the Colportage book, *Reuben Archer Torrey*, in 1929; however, it in reality only gives some biographical glimpses of his person and ministry. The only attempt at an actual biography was by a student of Torrey at Biola, the late Dr. O. E. Sanden, who produced two unpublished typescripts. They are entitled *God's Marked Man* and *What R. A. Torrey Meant to Me*. Both are based largely on personal reminiscences.

The aim of this volume is not to diminish but rather to exhibit the glory of God as it was manifest in the life of His servant. As Torrey said in connection with his lecture on the life of D. L. Moody:

> I learned years ago, to go to one place for the deepest lessons of life. That one place is the Bible. But the truth of the Bible is illustrated in the lives of men; and many of its most precious teachings were illustrated in the life of Dwight L. Moody. The purpose of this lecture is not, however, to glorify Mr. Moody, but to glorify God, whose power and grace and love were so wonderfully magnified in this man.[4]

My aim could not be better expressed.

There are many dominant characteristics in the life and ministry of R. A. Torrey. He has been called "a giant for God," "tower of strength," "apostle of rare power," "rock of Gibraltar," "man with God a'back of him," "a faithful servant," and many others. The quality which has impressed me the most is his unshakable faith and conviction in the Word of God and its message. When Torrey said, "I know," few doubted him. It was this

underlying quality of his life which God used to move men
to decision and to shape the thinking of future generations
of Christians. He was indeed an "apostle of certainty."

A great in literature has said,

> Lives of great men all remind us
> We can make our lives sublime,
> And, departing, leave behind us
> Footprints on the sands of time,
>
> Footprints, that perhaps another,
> Sailing o'er life's solemn main,
> A forlorn and shipwrecked brother,
> Seeing, shall take heart again.

"A Psalm of Life"

—H. W. Longfellow

[1]James Stalker, *Life of Paul* (New York: Revell, 1912), p. 7.

[2]William Evans, "Dr. Torrey As I Knew Him," *King's Business,*
XXVII (January, 1936), p. 7.

[3]Reuben A. Torrey, Jr., personal letter, April 7, 1969.

[4]R. A. Torrey, "Dwight L. Moody: His Life Lesson," *The Southern
Cross,* (September 10, 1902).

Introduction

We have waited far too long for this thorough, adequate, scholarly story of the life of the famous evangelist, R. A. Torrey. It is a great joy to give a brief word of introduction to this very valuable, documented, researched and sympathetic biography of the tremendous evangelist-educator-Bible teacher.

Dr. Torrey died in 1928. I was 32. I never saw him and my early ministry had been largely in Texas and Oklahoma. But I was tremendously influenced by his writings. First came the little Moody Colportage book, *How to Pray*, by Dr. Torrey, costing then fifteen cents. How seriously I took it to heart! I would read awhile, then go to my secret place of prayer, in the West Texas cow country, and pray. Not simply that I learned some of the essentials about prayer but that my heart was stirred to deep concern on the subject may have had some part in the remarkable ministry of my own book, *Prayer—Asking and Receiving*.

Then came others of Dr. Torrey's books: *How to Work for Christ*, including the very useful book on personal soul winning; *What the Bible Teaches, The Baptism of the Holy Spirit*, and to me more thrilling than all, his *Soul-Winning Sermons*, prepared from notes as used in sermons in great campaigns in Australia and England. My, what Bible preaching!

Dr. Torrey not only believed the Bible but he took it literally, trying its promises and proving them. He risked everything to follow Jesus. When Mr. Moody died, he took on the world-girdling revival campaigns in Australia, New Zealand, England and America. He had set up the curriculum for Moody Bible Institute, then later did the same for Biola and in a strong sense is really the father of the Bible institute movement in America.

Torrey's position on the Holy Spirit enduement of power was simple, explicit and glorious, like that of Moody. Every Christian could have the mighty enduement of power for witnessing and winning souls. Dr. Torrey called it "filled with the Spirit," or, "baptized with the Spirit," or, "anointed with the Spirit," as the terms are used in the New Testament, and I think, was right. His emphasis on the Holy Spirit, as was that of Moody, was a little displeasing to those more interested in scholarly fame and popular Bible teachers like Dr. Gray, Plymouth Brethren teachers, etc. But it was like that of all the other great soul winners, like Spurgeon, Moody, Finney, Bill Sunday, Dr. Lee Scarborough, etc.

Here is a book well written by my scholarly son-in-law, Dr. Roger Martin. We trust it will have a tremendous impact for God. It is a joy to add our prayer, our testimony to the book about R. A. Torrey.

                                    John R. Rice
                                Murfreesboro, Tennessee

1976

Acknowledgments

There are a number of individuals and institutions to whom the author is greatly indebted in the research for this volume. Both the libraries of the Moody Bible Institute and the Bible Institute of Los Angeles have freely and generously offered their facilities and materials. Special thanks must be offered also to Dr. Wilbur M. Smith, who sent me invaluable materials from his files, and also to the late Dr. O. E. Sanden, who just before his death sent me all of his voluminous materials about Dr. Torrey.

The greatest help of all was the invaluable assistance, both through extensive correspondence and personal interview, of the late Dr. R. A. Torrey, Jr. Dr. Torrey also read and edited two rough drafts of the present work before he died. Important insights have been gained as well from other members of the Torrey family, particularly from the Rev. R. A. Torrey, III, and Mrs. Fred Renich.

There have also been important contributions from friends, associates and students of the late Dr. R. A. Torrey. Further, church clerks and historians and library assistants have also aided my research labors.

Contents

30,000 Conversions in 18 mos - 164

PART V. "HOLDING FORTH THE WORD OF LIFE"
(1906-1928) *see pg. 192 Conversion report.*

Index of Illustrations

PART I

Called to Be an Apostle (1856-1878)

1. A Determined Young Man

Lightning flashed! Thunder crashed with a resounding din! Large raindrops began to spatter on the windowpane. A storm was fast approaching. At the lovely country estate on Seneca Lake a worried mother awaited the arrival of her son. "Oh, where is Archie? I wonder if he is all right." She peered again through the window hoping to see the familiar carriage turn into the driveway. But it was nowhere to be seen.

At that moment a speeding team of sweaty, ungovernable horses traveled down a country road at breakneck speed with a husky, confident teenage lad at the reins. He relished the excitement of the race with the approaching storm, but this time he had more than he bargained for. Suddenly as if from nowhere a train shot across the trestle directly in front of him. Sensing the imminent danger, he pulled on the reins of the nervous team, straining every muscle in his powerfully-built body. It seemed as if they could not stop, but they did—just short of the crossing and certain tragedy.

Such narrow escapes were typical of young Reuben Archer Torrey and caused his parents, particularly his mother, many an anxious moment.[1] Even in his childhood in Brooklyn he had had little fear and early steeled himself not to cry. Almost from the beginning his parents had noticed his strong will.

Archie had been born in Hoboken, New Jersey, on January 28, 1856, when the slavery issue was at fever pitch. He was the third of five children; Albert and Nora were older; Edith and Swift were born subsequently.[2] His parents were Reuben Slayton and Elizabeth A. (Swift)

Torrey. Mr. Torrey was of Puritan stock and traced his ancestry back to Captain William Torrey, the fearless and respected leader who brought the Torreys from England to America in 1640. Captain Torrey was a man of real prominence in military and political affairs in Weymouth, Massachusetts, and his son was twice invited to become president of Harvard University.

The family line included a very generous sprinkling of ministers, doctors, scientists, journalists, educators, senators, governors, and statesmen of cabinet rank. Two of the most prominent were Dr. John Torrey, noted Harvard botanist, and Dr. Joseph Torrey, learned professor of church history at Vermont University. It should also be noted that the mother of President William Howard Taft was a Torrey. Mrs. Torrey's ancestors also came from England in about 1630. Both Reuben and Elizabeth were proud of their early New England ancestry.[3]

Reuben Slayton Torrey was a man of wealth. When Archie was born, he held the position of a New York banker in a time of great prosperity in the United States. Eastern bankers, financiers, and manufacturers benefited greatly from the great increase of production in the grain of the Middle West and the cotton of the South with its corresponding demand by both foreign and home markets. Such times of prosperity, however, elicited fantastic speculation in industrial and commercial enterprises, and the toll for such wanton indebtedness came in the financial panic of 1857. In this disaster Mr. Torrey lost his fortune.

But two years later he moved from Hoboken to Brooklyn, and with typical industry and ambition Mr. Torrey established himself in a prosperous box manufacturing business. He became even wealthier in this enterprise. Mr. Torrey also rose in the public life in New York State and was a leading member of the Democratic party in Brooklyn. At one time the nomination to the post of mayor of Brooklyn was offered him, but he declined it.

The political and religious atmosphere was electric in Brooklyn during the time of the Torrey's residence there.

The antislavery movement had already reached a peak before they arrived, and the tension increased during the Civil War era of 1861-65. Dr. Henry Ward Beecher, famed pastor of the Plymouth Congregational Church in Brooklyn, was one of the most fiery and outspoken political and religious figures in the North. People came from far and near to hear him speak on the crying issues of the day, particularly his vicious denouncements of the evils of slavery. It used to be said to the great throng coming from New York to the Brooklyn church, "Cross the ferry and follow the crowd."

No one in Brooklyn could have been unaware of his ministry, (although Mr. Torrey was a Congregationalist) but it is not too likely that the Torreys ever attended Plymouth Church. Beecher was not only a staunch Republican; he had deliberately left the Democratic party to endorse Abraham Lincoln in 1860. The Torreys regularly attended the Old South Congregational Church in Brooklyn Heights.

Mr. Torrey's presence commanded attention. Tall, powerfully built, with a large head, he had a striking physical appearance. When he spoke, others listened. He once ended a passenger panic during a railway accident by thundering in stentorian tones,"Sit down!" The awestruck passengers meekly sat down in their seats and remained virtually motionless until the excitement was over. Archie inherited his father's striking appearance and came to exhibit the same type of authority in similar situations.

Religiously Mr. Torrey called himself a Universalist because he sincerely believed that no one would be ultimately condemned. Nevertheless, he retained his membership in the Congregational denomination and refused to join a Universalist church because he believed in the deity of Christ. When a Universalist pastor called in the Torrey home and stated that he did not believe in the deity of Christ, Mr. Torrey promptly asserted the pastor was not a Christian. Reuben Slayton Torrey attended and supported both Congregational and Presbyterian churches during his lifetime.[4]

Elizabeth Torrey was a woman of culture. As was true of many gentlewomen of the era, reading and letter writing were among her favorite pastimes. Archie always spoke of his mother as a very beautiful woman and loved her dearly. Mrs. Torrey was an earnest Christian and a member of the Presbyterian church. Her most outstanding spiritual quality was persistence in prayer, and like Hannah with Samuel she dedicated Archie to the Lord's service even before he was born.[5] Truly she must have possessed that "unfeigned faith" of Lois and Eunice, the grandmother and mother of Timothy (II Tim. 1:5).

The Torrey family was religious but not overly strict with the children. They were allowed to participate in a number of worldly amusements, but Sunday was strictly observed as a day of rest and worship. The family attended Sunday services, and then Mrs. Torrey read the Bible and religious books to the children in the afternoon. She took a special spiritual interest in each child and taught them to pray at a very early age. Archie began praying at three years of age and, as soon as he was old enough, was taught to read the Bible daily.

The Torrey home was a lively household. They did considerable entertaining and frequently enjoyed house guests. Family life was happy, and a delicious sense of humor in both parents and children provided much hilarity and wholesome fun. Archie in later years enjoyed telling of the pranks and practical jokes they played on one another as well as on visitors and friends. Although later regarded as a stern man, Archie displayed this family sense of humor with delightful frequency throughout his life.

Just after the Civil War Mr. Torrey purchased a beautiful Geneva, New York, estate. His decision was prompted by his children, who with their unusual vigor and flair for adventure, had grown tired of the city. Mr. Torrey had been brought up in the country—actually some twenty miles from the spot he purchased—and was just as eager as the children to locate there again. So he decided to retire from business and purchased the 200-acre estate when Archie was ten years of age.

Their new home was ideally located. They had a lovely view of Seneca Lake from the little city of Geneva which was located at the head of the magnificent sheet of water. Pine trees, orchards, spacious lawns and gardens made it a scenic spot indeed. The estate was a splendid place for adventure and sports activity of all sorts. Horseback riding, hiking, skating and swimming became Archie's favorite pastimes.

When the family first arrived in Geneva, he did not know how to swim. His companions enjoyed their plunges, while he stood on the shore and shivered. He soon decided, "This will not do. I am going to teach myself to swim." So getting a book on the art of swimming, he read it through and began to practice. He lay down on the floor of his room and learned the strokes and motions perfectly. Then the long-awaited day came. Arriving at the shore Archie astounded his fellow swimmers by immediately plunging into the water and swimming—straight to the bottom!

Much discouraged, he thought he would never learn. But his oldest brother, Albert, said to him, "Archie, if you would just lie still on the water, with your build you would float." He tried it and found he floated with ease. He forgot about the book and began paddling in dog-like fashion. In no time he was swimming, and, as was usually the case, he soon became more expert than all the rest.[6]

His father raised and trained valuable horses for the racetrack, and Archie delighted in taming and exercising the wildest in the stables. It was not uncommon for Archie to be thrown, bitten or kicked, but he always proved more than a match for them. He boasted that he could handle anything on four legs, and often proved it by breaking horses that grown men could not handle. When Thunder came to the estate, however, it seemed that no one could break him. A spirited black stallion, he had been taught the dangerous habit of rearing up on his hind legs just before going through the barn door. After repeated tries at controlling the animal, in desperation Archie literally jerked him by the reins onto his back into the carriage. Thunder was cured.[7]

His natural propensity for the daring and exciting is illustrated in another incident during his teenage years. In the barn on the estate was a hayloft with windows directly above one another on each of the three stories. Young Archie thought it would be delightful adventure to return to the ground from the top by dropping from one window sill to the other. With accustomed daring the plan was executed, but one of the sills had a jagged piece of glass. When he caught hold of it, it cut a tendon in his finger which remained slightly crooked the remainder of his life.[8]

Archie's flair for the daring, however, did not indicate an outgoing personality. Quite the contrary, he was very bashful—even painfully so. He remarked in later years,

> A stranger could scarcely speak to me without my blushing to the roots of my hair. When I went away from home visiting with other members of my family, I could not eat enough at the table, I was so frightened to be among strangers. Of all the tortures I endured at school there was none so great as that of reciting a piece. To stand on the platform and have the scholars looking at me, I could scarcely endure it; and even when my own father and mother at home asked me to recite the piece to them before I went to school, I simply could not recite it.[9]

This characteristic persisted even after he was a student in college. When he was home on vacation and his mother would ask him to greet callers in the home, he could not say a word. After they were gone his mother would say, "Archie, why didn't you say something?"

"Why, Mother, I did."

"You did not utter a sound!" His attempts to speak got no further than his throat.

On the other hand, Archie possessed a remarkable ability to concentrate. He would frequently situate himself under a gas lamp in the corner of their large living room to read. At such times he was totally oblivious to the conversation of other members of the family. He so utterly lost himself in his reading that he never heard others call his name. His parents had to shake him to get his attention!

Archie was a person of strong ambition, and it was only natural that he planned to attend college. Many noted men in professional fields were among his ancestors, his mother was strongly inclined to literary and cultural pursuits, and his father had the means to provide him with a fine education. So Archie decided to be a lawyer. After his graduation from Walnut Hill, an Episcopalian school in Geneva, he was ready for college. But since he was only fourteen, it was necessary to wait a year before he could matriculate.

One of his favorite pastimes during this interlude was to browse through the attic of his home where the old books from the library were stored. One day he discovered one of his mother's books, the *Covenant of the First Presbyterian Church* in Geneva, and curled up in a corner to read it. He quickly became absorbed in it. "I wonder if I could become a church member." He readily assented to most of the propositions in the book until he came to a portion which said that a Christian must be willing to do exactly what God wanted him to do. At this point he closed the book abruptly and cast it aside. "If I say 'yes' to that, God will just as likely call me to preach the Gospel, and I have determined to be a lawyer. I will not become a Christian."[10]

Despite this determined decision, the thought came to him time and time again that he must preach the Gospel. From his birth his mother had been praying that he would become a minister, and Archie was well aware of this. It affected him considerably although he tried to dismiss the matter from his mind. A vivid dream haunted him for years.

> One night I dreamed that my mother was dead—though she was still living—and that I was sleeping in my old room, when she came in as an angel, and besought me to become a minister of the Gospel. I promised her that I would. I could never get away from that promise.[11]

But the exciting prospect of entering Yale College now enveloped his mind. Perhaps his pursuits at Yale would end these disturbing thoughts about the ministry.

[1]Interview with Reuben A. Torrey, Jr., December 22,23, 1965.

[2]There is little information about the members of the family. Both brothers eventually went into newspaper work. Nora later married a banker in Brooklyn; Edith, who never married, lived with her sister Nora all of her life. Personal letter from Reuben A. Torrey, Jr., April 7, 1965.

[3]Ibid.

[4]Ibid.

[5]Letter from Miss Edith Clare Torrey to Mr. Gaylord Perry, November 14, 1958.

[6]*Winona Echoes* (Winona Lake: Winona Lake Institutes, 1906), pp. 137,138.

[7]Torrey, Jr., interview

[8]Torrey, Jr., personal letter, April 7, 1965

[9]R. A. Torrey, *The Holy Spirit, Who He Is and What He Does* (New York: Revell, 1927), pp. 36, 37. Perhaps related to this natural reticence was his penchant for putting his foot in his mouth. He regarded himself as "born a bungler" with a tendency to say the wrong thing when he did speak.

[10]R. A. Torrey, autobiographical notes in *Moodyanna* collection, p. 1.

[11]George T. B. Davis, *Torrey and Alexander* (New York: Revell, 1905), pp. 22, 23.

2. *Lux et Veritas*

Yale College in New Haven, Connecticut, was one of the finest educational institutions of the day. From this time-honored and respected institution many a famous American had received his diploma. There were Eli Whitney and Samuel F. B. Morse in science and invention; John C. Calhoun in politics; William M. Evarts in law; Noah Webster in education; James F. Cooper in literature; and Jonathan Edwards, Lyman Beecher, and Horace Bushnell in theology. For many, to be a graduate of Yale was synonymous with success.

But Yale was more than just an educational institution. It was steeped in religious and classic traditions. Founded in 1701, the college still adhered more rigidly to its founders' convictions than any other major American college. Religiously it was Congregational. Educationally, with the motto *Lux et Veritas* (light and truth), it sought to train its students in scholarly research and to ground them thoroughly in the various fields of knowledge.

Equally important was the social life at Yale. The common college life was recognized by faculty and student alike as a vital part of learning. The activities in the classroom, chapel, dormitory, and on the campus were all necessary to fashion the complete Yale graduate. These ingredients of college life, harnessed to a strong sense of class consciousness, were geared to develop character and achievement in the students. As Pierson has noted:

> In the final analysis Yale College was not just a collection of students and professors, of laws and customs, of buildings and of books, but an organic society of enormous vitality and power. It was a generous and enthusiastic community with its own memories,

discipline, and ambitions—perhaps in its peculiar way as effective and successful a society as was to be found anywhere on this earth.[1]

Into this atmosphere Reuben Torrey was plunged when he entered Yale in 1871 at the youthful age of fifteen—the second youngest man in his class. His going to Yale was partly prompted by his mother since she knew of the strong religious orientation there and was praying that he might become a minister. Probably the strongest motivation for Reuben, however, was Yale's reputation for graduating successful men who made their mark in the highest positions of responsibility in American society. What better place to go to become a successful lawyer?

Reuben's appearance on the Yale campus coincided with the beginning of the administration of Professor Noah Porter as the new president. The twenty-five-year administration of Dr. Leonard D. Woolsey had concluded the previous spring, and the college had both expanded and gained in prestige under his wise administrative leadership. Porter was quite capable although much less personally appealing than his predecessor, and was more adept at teaching than administration. Professor Porter strictly followed the traditional Yale ideals.[2]

One of the initial challenges for the Yale freshmen was a hiking expedition up the imposing hillsides of New Haven. On the first Saturday or Sunday it was common to climb the red cliffs of East Rock and walk along the edge as closely as one dared. The following week the more strenuous journey up West Rock and Judge's Cave was attempted. Knowing Reuben's flair for adventure, one can easily visualize him energetically leading the pack.

The Yale freshmen suddenly became aware of the rigid class system on the campus, if they had not known of it before coming. Everything was done according to classes—society meetings, studies, athletics, and religious activities. Freshmen did not mingle with the "more mature" sophomores, and certainly not with the grave and revered upperclassmen.

The upperclassmen were careful to spell out carefully

delineated lines of privilege. Freshmen could not smoke a pipe on the street or campus, carry a cane before Washington's birthday, or dance at the Junior Promenade—the greatest social event of the year. Neither could they play ball, spin tops, or roll hoops on the campus. These latter were strictly pastimes for the revered seniors!

The apex of privilege and prestige, however, was centered in "The Fence." In the autumn and spring the students migrated here toward evening. Reserved for the upper three classes, "The Fence" consisted of a generous stretch of rails each for the seniors and juniors facing Chapel Street, and a short stretch facing the Green for the sophomores. There was also a little section at the very end for the freshmen if and when they overcame the Harvard freshmen at baseball in May. If they won, they had the coveted eight rails for the remainder of the year.

Imagine the excitement when the Yale frosh won! Bedlam immediately broke out, and the famous "shirt rush" was on. In the rush the Yale freshmen and sophomores tackled each other. Hats were crushed, coats ripped, and shirts shredded as the freshmen prepared to march to "The Fence." Then in a moment the hassle ceased as suddenly as if it had been prearranged, and the juniors herded the victors along the walk to the coveted rails.[3]

The gleeful freshmen won when Reuben was a member of the class, and after the initial excitement, the juniors began marching them down the walk. Suddenly a husky sophomore grabbed Reuben, intending to pull him off into the street. Undaunted, Reuben picked up the powerful sophomore in an instant and threw him to the ground. To Reuben's great surprise the juniors cheered and lifted him up on their shoulders and carried him on to "The Fence." The young man he had thrown was the champion wrestler of the college, who had trounced the junior classmen the previous year.[4]

Reuben, who loved sports, entered vigorously into tennis, swimming, boxing, and wrestling at Yale. He

especially excelled in the latter two because of his great
strength and long arms. Team sports had little attraction
for his individualistic nature. In addition, team sports,
such as baseball and boat races, were not as strongly
emphasized then. It was only during his final year at the
college that the first Yale-Harvard football game was
played.

The course of studies at Yale followed the traditional
lines with lessons in the Greek and Latin classics, rhetoric,
and mathematics for the first two years. The works of
Homer, Herodotus, Livy, and Horace were read and
recited, and students were thoroughly exposed to geometry,
algebra, and trigonometry. These foundation studies
lessened in the junior year, and physics (then called
natural philosophy), logic, and a choice of German or
French were added. In the senior year no less than eighteen
courses were taught by ten different professors. These
included linguistics, history, law, economics, geology,
history of philosophy, mental and moral philosophy,
natural theology, and evidences of Christianity.[5]

Reuben was especially fond of mathematics, philosophy,
and the natural sciences. Considering his remarkably
retentive and logical mind, it is not surprising to learn that
he excelled in mathematics. Logic and epistemology also
had a peculiar fascination for him, and he was enamored
with the Baconian method of inductive reasoning. In the
natural sciences astronomy and geology attracted him. He
gained his interest in astronomy one clear night while
watching a meteor shower with his professor on the Yale
campus.

The ideas which captivated him most, however, were
stimulated by the spiritual and scholarly discussion of Dr.
James D. Dana in the field of geology. Dr. Dana, one of the
most eminent geologists America has ever produced, did
not accept the Darwinian theory of evolution, and instilled
in his students his conviction of the essential agreement of
geology with the Genesis creation account.[6] This
distinguished professor took his students on long hiking

tramps around New Haven to illustrate various geological phenomena. These were a high point for Reuben, kindling in him a lifelong interest in geology. On hiking trips in later years he enjoyed pointing out to his son the history of rock formations, and kept a collection of rocks as one of his few hobbies.

But his consuming ambition was not necessarily to learn but to be a success. In this regard he was no different than many Yale men. This attitude, so prevalent among the students, caused Henry Canby to remark that New Haven was divided into "town, gown, and sweater"—rather than merely "town and gown." [7] Yale students graduated as well-informed and scholarly men, but their book learning was mostly secondary to other pursuits.

It was no secret to Reuben or to others that he was in school for a good time and for the prestige he might gain. Studies came easily for him, and he had plenty of time on his hands. His father paid all of his bills without ever asking a single question as to how he spent his money. His conscience was not overly sensitive about the worldly pleasures that came naturally to a fraternity man. Especially adept at winning card games because of his keen memory, he spent many an afternoon in this pastime. He enjoyed dancing so much that he often spent as many as four evenings a week in this entertainment. Smoking and social drinking were common habits on the Yale campus, and they held an attraction for Reuben as well. All the ingredients for having a "good time" presented themselves to Reuben, and he took full advantage of them.

He found campus life at Yale exciting and geared to youthful pleasure. One of the most popular meeting places then as today was the college dormitory room. Students commonly crowded into the small rooms for stirring "bull sessions." Sitting on chairs, beds, window sills, and on the floor, they conversed for hours with cigarette or pipe in hand. Or they congregated in some of the rooms especially reserved for card games.

One gala social activity was the eating club. Members

migrated from one landlady-cook to another in New Haven in quest of the most exquisite dishes. Many delightful hours were spent as they talked and sampled their choice menus. Reuben belonged to "The '75 Eating Club" with the motto, "Here's Richness."[8]

Life in the dormitories was pleasant, but it also had its drawbacks. The dormitories, of which the noted Old Brick Row was typical, contained numerous two-room suites—a study and a bedroom. The latter was a narrow, oblong room with two bedsteads foot to foot. There was a washstand but no running water. Water had to be brought from a lavatory on the first floor, and even the best dormitory had no shower for undergraduates. Students who desired greater cleanliness were given a special lecture on how to take a sponge bath from their washbowl!

There were tubs available in the gymnasium for the nominal fee of twenty-five cents per bath on the rare occasions when they were not being used by the athletes. There were also two tubs in the divinity school for the ministerial students. It was possible to steal a bath without being caught since the tubs were not often used by the ministers! Reuben, known throughout life for his immaculate cleanliness, probably found a sponge bath unsatisfactory and availed himself of the tubs in the gymnasium when he could. And with his penchant for fun and adventure, it is not hard to imagine his sneaking a Saturday night bath among the pious divinity school students.

But lest one think Yale was only geared to pursuits of pleasure it should be noted that religious exercises were also given a pronounced emphasis. Students often gathered into Bible study and prayer groups, but the central part of their religious life was Battell Chapel. Seven a.m. was rising time in order for students to be in the chapel for prayer by ten minutes after eight. Chapel was compulsory, and tutors were strategically stationed in high seats where they could spot inappropriate behavior among the students. Especially was it a temptation to take a last-minute peek at class notes during President Porter's five-minute prayer.

Offenders were sent to the dean's office to be given a brief lecture and an appropriate number of black marks.

It must have caused quite a commotion in the chapel the day Reuben sent his pocketknife flying blade first toward a fellow student. The thoughtless student had not reckoned with such a quick temper when he smiled at the way Reuben sang in the service. Fortunately the blade produced only a minor flesh wound. As it was, the incident was serious enough to merit expulsion from the college. Instead Reuben escaped with a generous supply of black marks and no doubt a longer than usual lecture on conduct.[9]

Reuben had not yet become a Christian, but he kept up religious appearances. He regularly attended Sunday services, read his Bible and prayed daily as a matter of course. These habits had been ingrained in him from childhood, but he had never attended a religious service that made any lasting impression on him. At this juncture his strong bent toward worldly pleasure completely dominated his thinking and living.

> I can hardly believe what I know to be true about my own affections and about my likes and dislikes. . . . In those days I hated the Bible. I read it every day, but it was to me about the most stupid book I read. I would rather have read last year's almanac any day than to have read the Bible. . . . In those former days. . .I loved the card table, the theater, the dance, the horse-race, the champagne supper, and I hated the prayer-meeting and Sunday services.[10]

Periodically, however, Reuben was still haunted by the thought that God was calling him to become a minister. This was forcibly impressed upon his mind one day in Dr. Cyrus Northrop's class in rhetoric. A very popular professor, who later became president of the University of Minnesota, he made his class into a kind of forum for the discussion of everything from politics to religion. Demonstrating how to outline a speech in one class, the professor chose as his topic "A Call to the Ministry." Everything he said made Reuben uneasy, and the troubled student tried desperately to persuade himself that he was not so called. But he found it impossible to dismiss the thought.[11]

In this frame of mind Reuben approached the end of his junior year. Although he had been elected to the Delta Kappa Epsilon society in the end of his sophomore year, the traditional Tap Day ceremony in the spring did not yield the coveted election to a senior society. This was a great disappointment to him. To make matters worse Reuben had not found the rich satisfaction he had expected in his quest at the fountain of worldly pleasure. Even his high ambition to become a lawyer had dimmed. With his "confidence in the flesh" sadly shaken the crisis came.

In the middle of the night he awoke smothered with a feeling of great despondency. Life seemed to hold no hope. In desperation he sprang from his bed to the washstand and opened the drawer. "I am going to end this whole miserable business. Where is that razor?"[12] But God held his trembling, fumbling fingers. And in that moment's lapse he dropped to his knees in the darkness beside the open drawer and began to pray. "God, if You will take away this awful burden, I will preach." Immediately a strange peace settled over him, and he fell into a restful sleep.[13] "Light and truth" at Yale had come from a totally unexpected quarter.

As he remarked subsequently, "I had gone to bed with no more thought of becoming a Christian than I had of jumping over the moon." Since there was no preliminary conviction, he thought no living being had anything to do with his conversion. But afterward it came to him. "My mother, four hundred and twenty-seven miles away, was praying, and praying that I would become a minister of the Gospel. And though I had gotten over sermons and arguments and churches, and everything else, I could not get over my mother's prayers."[14]

The full realization of his conversion did not dawn upon him, as it had centered in his surrender to preach. And although there was no marked change in his life, nevertheless, he told his classmates of his decision. They thought he was joking. His roommate remarked, "You are making an awful mistake; you are spoiling a good businessman"—his aptitude for business was such that he even handled his roommate's affairs—"to make a poor preacher." The response of his sister was hardly more gratifying. She felt his decision for the ministry had "spoiled a good waltzer to make a bad preacher."[15]

It was not until the end of his senior year at Yale that he made a public profession of his faith and united with the church. *The Scarlet Letter* by Nathaniel Hawthorne and *Bay Path* by J. G. Holland made strong religious impressions on him; however, it was *Ecce Homo* by J. R. Seeley that convinced him he should identify himself openly with the church.

Ecce Homo is not a book written in the orthodox tradition, but it had an appeal to young Torrey. Seeley stressed that a person had a valid title to citizenship in the kingdom of Heaven if he were prepared to obey God and sacrifice something for Him. Entrance into the kingdom was by faith, but this was interpreted as the capability for better things. The author's further stress was that a person might legitimately become a Christian without a full and final belief in Christ, and that progress in the things of Christ might be almost imperceptible.[16] Reuben could readily assent to these propositions. Thus his initial hesitation about uniting with the church because of his slow progress spiritually was overcome, and he decided to make an open confession of Christ.

There was no pastor of the college church at the time, so he approached President Porter as they went to the latter's class in moral philosophy and ethics.

"President Porter, I wish to unite with the church."

"Are you clear about it?"

"I am."

"Well, you are a clear-minded man."[17]

Although a most careless way to receive a member, this proved to be all the examination necessary for his admission to the college church. Thus he made a public profession of his faith in Battell Chapel and was officially received into the college church.

In the spring of 1875 Reuben was graduated from Yale with the rank of "second dispute," which was sixth rank out of eight groups of honors. But now instead of going to law school he made preparations to study in Yale Divinity School the following fall.

[1]George W. Pierson, *Yale College: An Educational History, 1871-1921* (New Haven: Yale University Press, 1952), II, 43.

[2]There was a controversy raging at the time between certain of the alumni and the college over the issue of elective courses. Yale's academic program was accused of being backward and nonprogressive, especially compared with Harvard's fully elective system under President Eliot. A limited elective system for Yale began the year after Reuben's graduation.

[3]Wilbur L. Cross, *Connecticut Yankee* (New Haven: Yale University Press, 1943), p. 84.

[4]Torrey, Jr., personal letter, April 7, 1965.

[5]Pierson, *Yale College.* . . , II, 70.

[6]Dana accepted natural selection within a theistic framework and believed in a progressive creationism in the creation week of Genesis.

[7]Pierson, *Yale College.* . . , II, 25.

[8]Letter from Mrs. Phillip Crane, Library Assistant, Yale University Library, October 12, 1965.

[9]Torrey, Jr., personal letter, April 7, 1965.

[10]Torrey, *Holy Spirit*, p. 78. Some writers have tended to exaggerate regarding the depth of his sin. He was thoroughly worldly but not a derelict.

[11]Torrey, *Moodyanna*, p. 1.

[12]Torrey never mentioned what was in the drawer. Many have thought it was a revolver, but it appears more likely to be the razor which he regularly kept in his washstand drawer. Torrey, Jr., personal letter, April 7, 1965.

[13]Davis, *Torrey and Alexander*, p. 23. Torrey joined several other prominent figures who turned from ambitions in law to the ministry—Martin Luther, Charles G. Finney, J. H. Jowett and Sam Jones.

[14]R. A. Torrey, *Great Pulpit Masters* (New York: Revell, 1950), III, 195, 196.

[15]R. A. Torrey, "Making the Most of Life," *King's Business*, IX (November, 1918), p. 938. He freely told others on the campus what God did for him. In later years he attended a class reunion and spoke to judges, senators, governors, and other leading citizens of Christ. He was convinced he could not have done so if he had sneaked out of Yale without confessing Christ openly.

[16]J. R. Seeley, *Ecce Homo* (Boston: Roberts Brothers, 1890), pp. 75, 91-94.

[17]Torrey, *Moodyanna*, p. 2.

3. Bramble Bush

Reuben's seminary career, however, did not progress as one might expect. In his final year of college he drank deeply from the well of philosophy and revelled in the speculations of Descartes, Locke, Spinoza, Fichte, Schelling, Schopenhauer, Kant, and above all, Hegel. In his spiritual immaturity he saw no essential conflict with Christianity, but the situation changed in the seminary. Speaking of his philosophical studies, he remarked, "I jumped into a bramble bush (the bramble bush of metaphysics), and scratched out both my eyes."[1]

As he came into contact with agnostic literature, especially that of the celebrated Edward Gibbon, for the first time he was afflicted with doubt. "I became utterly unsettled in my faith, and doubted whether the Bible was the Word of God, whether Jesus Christ was the Son of God and whether there was any God. I was utterly at sea."[2]

Slowly, however, Reuben began to move from his skeptical position. The principle which set young Torrey free is that enunciated in John 7:17, "If any man willeth to do his will, he shall know of the teaching, whether it is of God, or whether I speak from myself" (ASV). Reuben saw that the key to knowledge of the Divine is found in the will. If a person is *willing* to do the will of God once he is shown, then he shall *know* of the Divine truthfulness of that will—whether Christ's teaching was truly from God or merely that from a human teacher.

To him this was squarely in line with the Baconian method of inductive reasoning. It did not ask that he be committed to a proposition without investigation, but to be committed to accept it if it was the truth. Thus Reuben set out by earnest investigation of the Scriptures and Christian evidences and through prayer to find the truth, and it was not long before he was convinced of the essential truth of Christianity.

During this pilgrimage from doubt to faith Reuben found great help in the brilliant writings of the celebrated and learned Unitarians—Channing, Parker, Hale, and Clark. At this juncture in his thinking they were more advanced in their teaching than he was. "I saw that Christ was my Brother, a Real Man, tempted in all points as I was, and that if He got the victory, I could, too, the same way He did." [3] He found on further investigation, however, that the orthodox doctrine of the person and work of Christ embraced all of value that Unitarianism taught and much more. It led to his abandonment of their truncated Unitarian teaching concerning Christ.

Even after his deliverance from agnosticism Reuben still had lingering doubts about some of the orthodox doctrines, namely, the inerrancy of Scripture and the everlasting punishment of the lost. In fact he became the leader of the new theology and destructive criticism wing in the seminary, and influenced by W. Robertson Smith, even wrote an unpublished work on the importance of the higher criticism of the Bible. He had influential teachers of decidedly orthodox stamp such as Dr. Leonard Bacon and Dr. Samuel Harris in theology and apologetics, but his strongly independent turn of mind would accept nothing on the mere word of others. His continuing interest in philosophical studies was reflected in his choice of the BD thesis topic. It dealt with transcendentalism. [4]

In the Divinity School Reuben registered marked achievement in Greek and Hebrew. His retentive mind aided his linguistic studies greatly, and on one occasion in a "read down" contest in Hebrew class he read too fast for his instructor to follow! [5] And although he won the coveted Hebrew award at Yale, his main interest was in Greek. And it was in this language, under the tutelage of the recognized Greek scholar, Dr. Lewis Packard, that he excelled.

While Reuben was in the seminary, he was licensed to preach by the Association of the Western District of New Haven County (Congregational). It must have been a little disconcerting to his questioners to find that the young scholar had to rack his brain to give the basic proof texts for the deity of Christ. [6] But despite his immature knowledge and his chronic fear of speaking in public, Reuben now decided that if he was going to be a minister, he had best learn to preach.

His first speaking engagement was a prayer meeting service in a little Methodist church. So he learned a piece by heart and delivered his first "sermon" to the congregation.

> As soon as the meeting was open, I grasped the back of the settee in front of me and pulled myself up to my feet and held on to it lest I should fall. One Niagara went rushing up one side and another down the other, and I tremblingly repeated as much of my little piece as I could remember, and then dropped back into the seat. [7]

Reuben felt quite dejected at the conclusion of the meeting—as many young ministers do when they make their first attempt to preach. But there was one bright spot. A sweet, elderly lady came up to him, saying, "It did me so much good. You spoke with such feeling."

"Feeling," he mused, "the only feeling I had was that I was nearly scared to death!"

During the summer Reuben went to various places in Ohio to preach. An unexpected occurrence took place when he arrived in the little village of Mesopotamia. At the time a temperance revival was in progress, and he was invited to speak at the meeting. His heart sank within him. Not only had he never attended a temperance meeting before, he had convinced himself that total abstinence was not necessary for a Christian. In desperate straits he groaned within himself and wished that he had not come to the village. But now he felt an obligation to attend the meeting.

He met the issue squarely, meditating and praying about the matter the rest of the day. Then he came to a certain conclusion. "I prayed it through, and it became as clear as day that if for nothing more than my influence, I ought to stand and sign the pledge." So he went to the meeting, and at the conclusion each person who had not signed the pledge was asked to stand. Reuben stood along with two others. "I felt in dreadfully bad company when I saw an old soaker stand, but I felt in very good company when a 'good looking' young lady also stood." [8]

It was during that same summer of 1877 a year before Reuben's graduation, that a twin sorrow befell the Torrey home. His mother and father died within three weeks of each other; his mother on July 15; his father on August 3. Reuben was very much attached to his parents, particularly his mother; and it was a great personal sorrow to lose them both in so short a time. It was a comforting thought to Reuben that his mother had lived to see her son begin preparations for the ministry. Although she lived only about three years after his conversion and call to the ministry, perhaps she glimpsed with the eye of faith the special place God had for him.

Mr. Torrey's passing was hastened by the death of his wife, but was also due to the financial strain caused by the loss of his second fortune four years earlier in the financial panic of 1873. In addition to the corruption and malpractices in the sordid Grant administration the cause was much the same as the 1857 crash—wild speculation and overexpansion in railroads, industry, and agriculture. Hundreds of Eastern industrialists and manufacturers, including Mr. Torrey, suffered great financial losses. What remained to Mr. Torrey dwindled, and the small inheritance he left after his death was badly mismanaged.

The death of his father left Reuben entirely on his own financial resources. All he received from his father's vast earnings were a leather matchbox and two gold sleeve buttons. This was a far cry from the time earlier in his life when he and his brothers and sisters gathered together in the home one evening to consider what they were worth. Their amused father sat listening and relating to them his income and the worth of his holdings. They had gone to bed

feeling very rich that evening. But Reuben felt it was
providential. "I'm glad I did not inherit a fortune. It would
have ruined me." [9]

His senior year was almost completed when President
Porter announced that D. L. Moody was coming to New
Haven for meetings and that he had been invited to speak
in Battell Chapel. He charged the students to have an
attitude of "unusual expectancy and respect" for Mr.
Moody as the "greatest evangelist of our time." [10]

Several of the young theologians, including Reuben, had
heard previously of the uneducated Moody and decided to
go to the town meetings, thinking their presence would give
him some encouragement. After all, had they not taken
their AB's and were they not on the threshold of receiving
their cherished BD's? To their amazement the evangelist
was not in the least impressed. His brusque advice to
Reuben was, "Young man, you'd better get to work for the
Lord!"

So, swallowing their pride, Reuben and some of the
others asked him to teach them how to lead men to Christ.
Moody then gave them a few Scripture texts and charged,
"Now, gentlemen, go at it." So Reuben went "at it."

His first convert was a Miss Smith, a young lady he used
to meet in the ballroom. He had not seen her since his
conversion during undergraduate days, but she was
attending the meetings. When he saw her, he reasoned with
himself, "Have you got enough religion to go over and talk
to that young woman about Christ?" Then he thought, "If
I haven't, I haven't got enough to talk about anyway!! So
he approached the young woman. "Miss Smith, I have
accepted the Lord Jesus Christ. I wish you would."

Reuben had not expected such a difficult encounter. She
brought up every excuse and objection that a worldly
person thinks of, and he tried his best to answer them. But
after two solid hours of dealing with her, she finally knelt
with Reuben and accepted Christ as her personal Saviour.
She made the decision because, as she said to Reuben
afterwards, "I thought if Jesus Christ could save you after
what I knew you used to be, He could save anyone."

This "first fruit" in his ministry had a more radical effect upon him than his conversion.

> When I went out of Dwight Place Church that afternoon it did seem as if there was a fairer light in the sunshine than I had ever beheld; it did seem as there was a new beauty in the grass and the flowers and the trees. It did just seem as if the whole face of this old world was transformed."[11]

When he graduated from the Divinity School later in the spring,[12] he had an entirely different slant on the Christian ministry. The youthful graduate began supplying for the Congregational Church in Nelson, Ohio.

[1] R. A. Torrey, *God Hath Spoken:* Twenty-Five Addresses Delivered at the World Conference on Christian Fundamentals, May 25-June 1, 1919, p. 142.

[2] Torrey, *Moodyanna,* p. 2.

[3] R. A. Torrey, *Christ of the Bible* (New York: George H. Doran, 1925), p. 74.

[4] Torrey, *Moodyanna,* p. 3.

[5] *Yorkshire Daily Observer,* May 14, 1904.

[6] R. A. Torrey (ed.), *The Higher Criticism and the New Theology* (New York: Gospel Publishing House, 1911), p. 241.

[7] Torrey, *Holy Spirit,* p. 37.

[8] Davis, pp. 32,33.

[9] Ibid., p. 19.

[10] Richard K. Curtiss, *They Called Him Mr. Moody* (Garden City, New York: Doubleday and Co., 1962), pp. 318,319.

[11] *Winona Echoes,* p. 127.

[12] William Howard Taft, who was to become the twenty-seventh president of the United States, was graduated with an AB from Yale in the same year. The two surely must have met since they were related to each other.

PART II

Shaping the Vessel (1878-1889)

4. Minority Call

"Our pastor has resigned, and we are authorized to extend to you a call to become our pastor." So said the committee from the Congregational Church in nearby Garrettsville to the young seminary graduate. Having been assured that the call was unanimous, Reuben accepted and began his duties in the new parish on November 9.[1]

Upon his arrival he learned to his chagrin that the call was a mistake—his mistake! The true state of affairs revealed that the congregation had had a row with the former pastor. The majority wanted to keep him, but the minority group was so strong that they succeeded in dismissing him and had issued the call to Reuben. His chief backer was the most cantankerous man in the community, and true to his reputation, shortly tried to have a row with the new pastor. Eventually he became a true friend, however, and was the only person who ever left him a legacy.

Since Reuben had only been licensed, an ordination council, made up of area Congregational pastors, convened approximately a month later. The council unanimously sustained the examination of the candidate and officially ordained him to the Congregational ministry. No doubt he fared better in his examination concerning the deity of Christ. Determined to make of himself what God wanted him to be, he decided to give five mornings a week exclusively to Bible study.[2]

Garrettsville, a community of 969 inhabitants, was a scenic little town nestled in the green hills of Northern Ohio. It was not, however, the most promising field of endeavor for a polished seminary graduate. He thought of it "as one of the most hopeless and hardened parishes that

a church was ever situated in." The town boasted of two
well-patronized saloons and was rampant with infidelity.
In addition, the three village churches—Methodist,
Baptist, and Congregational—were frequently involved in
quarrels. Reuben's charge had about 50 members, and most
of them were of the nominal variety.

An initial surprise confronted Reuben in his
Garrettsville charge. Imagine the new pastor's
astonishment when he saw in his congregation Clara Belle
Smith, the "good looking" girl he had met at the
temperance meeting over a year ago. The impression had
been mutual. For Clara had said on her way to hear the
new Congregational pastor, "I wish it were that young man
I met at Mesopotamia." How pleasantly surprised she was
when she found out that it was he!

Clara was the daughter of Orin B. Smith, a ship's
captain and part owner of a shipping company on the
Great Lakes. She had had considerable sadness during her
girlhood and lived a rather lonely life. Her mother had a
prolonged illness before her death, and her father was
absent for long periods of time because of his work on the
Lakes. Clara had attended Hiram College not far from
Garrettsville but did not graduate. After leaving college she
lived with relatives in Garrettsville and took up sewing as a
means of self-support. Her religious background on her
mother's side extended back to the Huguenot persecutions
in France when her ancestors fled to Wales. She belonged
to the Episcopal Church, but frequently attended the
Congregational Church in Garrettsville.[3]

Clara was indeed an attractive girl. A dark brunette with
wavy hair and brown eyes, her trim, well-groomed
appearance gave the impression of elegance and culture.
She was modest and of a quiet, even-tempered disposition.
Not given to much sentimentality, Clara was practical-
minded and rather matter-of-fact. In these latter respects
she was very much like the young pastor about whom she
was shortly to learn a great deal more.

Clara sought the young pastor's counsel about a number

of personal problems which she faced. They found themselves drawn to one another, and a pleasant courtship ensued. Friendship ripened into love, and not long afterward they were engaged. One day as he was walking her home, Reuben remarked, "Well, Clara, I guess we might as well call it engaged," and she agreed.

The decision, however, was really not quite as simple as that for Reuben. He had been very much enamored with Clara but was not sure that he should ask her to become his wife. But the time came to decide, and he sought an isolated spot outside of town to think and pray. "Lord, I will not leave this place until it is clear to me what Thy will is." Almost instantly it came to him that she was God's choice for him. He never regretted nor doubted the decision and always spoke in glowing terms of the prize he received in Clara Smith.[4]

It would be interesting to know just how the logical and scholarly Torrey wooed his wife. He was a tender but reserved lover, and his head played quite as vital a part as his heart in his romance. Perhaps if the details were known there would be some delightful incidents such as occurred in the romances of Spurgeon and Moody. The young couple was married in the church on October 22, 1879—approximately a year after his arrival in Garrettsville. Reuben was twenty-three; his bride, twenty. Church records describe the wedding as "a very pretty affair."[5] The congregation rejoiced with the pastor in his acquisition. Clara had been received into the membership of the church some six months earlier.

A glimpse of the young couple's early home life has been given by Dr. Reuben Torrey, Jr., spoken shortly after his father's death.

> Although a young and deeply devoted husband, he frankly counted the cost he must pay if he were to make of himself all that God would have him to be. Together he and his young bride agreed that he must put his work and study first; domestic demands must be made secondary; the enjoyment of the social side of the home life must be strictly limited. The hours devoted to study left little time for the home during those early years.[6]

This, in addition to extra hours tutoring German and geology to supplement his income, meant many lonely hours for the young wife. Often she would take her basket of sewing and quietly slip into his study and work in loyal silence just to be near the husband she adored.

Although he was dedicated to his work, Reuben had his limitations. As he noted years later, "I had taken my two degrees, but as to knowing about the truth of God, I do not know of anyone who undertook the conduct of a church who knew less about it than I did."[7] Not only was Reuben ignorant of the administration of a local church ministry, he was also handicapped with unorthodox views of Christian doctrine. He taught the errancy of Scripture and universalism in salvation—even though they were contrary to the creed of Congregationalism.

Further, his attitude toward the second coming of Christ fared little better. Virtually coinciding with his arrival in Garrettsville was the convening in New York of the first Premillennial Conference in America. It had awakened great interest in the subject, and the *New York Tribune* printed the addresses in full. The chorister of Reuben's new charge was the editor of the local paper, and he became much interested in the addresses. Consequently, he went to his new pastor and asked him, "Will you not speak on the second coming of Christ?" Reuben tried to put him off as best he could but thought to himself, "You will be a great deal older than you are now before you hear me speaking on so impractical and visionary a subject as the second coming of Christ."[8]

In addition, much of his preaching was theoretical, and he still had great difficulty speaking in public. He wrote out all his sermons in full, committed them to memory, but it was a crucifixion to deliver them. When he finished, he sank back into his chair with great relief saying to himself, "Well, that's over for another week." But then the thought that he must speak again next week immediately haunted him. "I am killing myself preaching three times on Sunday"—he still supplied in the afternoon for the Nelson Community.

His platform decorum was also marred by the very distracting habit of twisting the button of his coat as if he were grinding out the sermon. Clara thought as she watched, "I wonder what would happen if someone cut off the button!"

But despite these drawbacks, according to one of his members, "Through his efforts the attendance at Sunday services increased, and there was new enthusiasm in all church work." [9] Through the influence of Evangelist Charles G. Finney, he impressed upon his people the need for an evangelistic ministry. He noted later, "Before undertaking that church I had read the biography of Mr. Finney, and his *Revival Addresses*, and I had the idea that the normal state of a church was revival, so I started out on that line." [10]

Now Finney had been so signally blessed of God in evangelistic work that it would be most difficult for a person to read these two volumes and not catch some of his revival spirit. In concluding his section on "When a Revival Is to Be Expected," Finney wrote:

> In truth a revival should be *expected* whenever it is *needed*. If we need to be revived it is our duty to be revived. If it is a duty it is possible, and we should set about being revived ourselves, and, relying on the promise of Christ to be with us in making disciples always and everywhere, we ought to labour to revive Christians and convert sinners, with a confident expectation of success. Therefore, whenever the Church needs reviving, it ought and may expect to be revived, and to see sinners converted to Christ. [11]

Finney's logic appealed to Torrey. There was no question that the community *needed* reviving. If a revival is needed, then it should be expected. If it is a duty, then it is possible. He decided, "We shall have a revival."

He preached as earnestly as he could but at first there was little headway. Then, approximately a year after his arrival, there were two important decisions. One, an elderly backslider who was thoroughly reclaimed, commenced to pray for a revival in the village and received an inward assurance that God had heard her prayer. After a time the

lady moved to California but insisted that God would send
a revival. Sensing that God was beginning a work in their
midst, Reuben took two important steps.

Following the example of Moody, with whom he had
worked in the inquiry room both at New Haven and
Cleveland (he attended these meetings in late 1878), he set
out to train his people. So the young minister announced to
his startled congregation that classes in personal
evangelism would be conducted for the next three weeks,
six nights a week. For those who came Reuben hammered
into them the essentials of intelligent personal work.

His third step was a precarious one. He tackled the
Methodist and Baptist churches in town and tried to get
them to unite for meetings. Difficulty ensued, however,
when the pastors made conditions not agreeable to one
another. Reuben said affirmatively, "Gentlemen, I do not
care for any conditions. You can do all the preaching, or
either one of you can do it, but we are going to have united
meetings to pray that God will bless the town."[12]After some
seesawing back and forth finally it was decided that they
should meet in the Methodist church, and the Baptist
preacher's son should do the preaching. Apparently the
ministers took Reuben at his word about conditions—his
church was left out of it.

Further problems arose with his congregation. They
disapproved of union efforts because of the unfortunate
rows which had invariably followed previous ones. The best
man in his congregation, a man old enough to be his father,
met him the next day on the street after the arrangements
had been made. He was as mad as a March hare and said to
Reuben, "See here, you should have consulted us before
you arranged for a union meeting. We know the town; you
don't. We have tried to have union meetings, and every
time it has ended in a row."

Reuben replied, "You just mind your business, and don't
kick over the traces, but go to work for all you are worth."

"I don't propose to kick over the traces, but you should
have consulted us."

"If I had, we would never have had a union meeting at all."

Two weeks later in the midst of the revival the man came to Reuben and said, laughingly, "You were right, and I was wrong. If you had consulted us, we would never have had a revival."[13] The union meetings lasted nine weeks, but the impact of the meeting made an indelible impression on both the churches and the community. The spirit of revival continued throughout all of the remaining time Reuben was in Garrettsville.

The revival had its effect in numerous ways in the community. The spirit of evangelism transcended the denominational differences and cemented the relationship among the churches. As a result of their cooperative efforts, local option was eventually secured for the town and continued until the repeal of the 18th Amendment.[14]

The greatest result of the meetings was the significant number in the small community who were converted or reclaimed. Several were delivered from infidelity, and some infidel lecturers were subsequently brought to the village to stem the tide of revival. In Reuben's own church many were received into membership in the following months and years. On one Sunday, March 7, 1880, a total of 21 members were received. This was an exceptional number for a small community. In the annual report for the year 1881 the church minutes reveal 33 additions to the church—23 by profession of faith and 10 by letter. The increase in membership created a space problem for the old frame building, and in that same year a committee was selected to consider the matter of an addition to the church.[15] Another "member" of the congregation was Reuben and Clara's first child, Edith Clare, born on November 8 of that same year.

Reuben was very careful in his reception of inquirers into the church on profession of faith. Each one was dealt with extensively as to his belief in Christ, and he sought to ground them firmly in the faith. Some of his congregation were a little shocked, however, at his practice of baptizing converts so quickly after their conversion.

One of his members described him as "active, of keen
mental ability . . .a man of prayer, faith and action."[16]
Reuben, as he became more steeped in the Scripture
promises and teaching on prayer, began to experience some
notable answers.

One of the most remarkable of these was prayer for the
healing of a serious illness. A young dentist in his church
became violently ill with typhoid fever, and Reuben went
to see him. When he arrived, the patient was unconscious
and the pastor was told by the physician that there was no
hope whatever for recovery. But as Reuben sat by his
bedside, a sudden impulse came to him that he should
kneel and pray for the recovery of the young man. As he
prayed, a great assurance came into his heart that God had
heard his prayer. Arising from his knees, he said to the
doctor, "He will get well."

The doctor, who was a backslider, smiled and replied,
"Well, Mr. Torrey, that is all very well from your
standpoint, but he cannot get well. The crisis is past and he
has passed the wrong way, and he will die."

Reuben replied, "Doctor, that is all right from your
standpoint, but God has heard my prayer. The man will
not die; he cannot die at this time; he will get well." The
pastor returned home only to be told a short time afterward
that the man was now experiencing the certain last
symptoms of a man dying with typhoid fever. Reuben
confidently replied, "He is not dying; he cannot die now.
He will get well." And to the astonishment of the doctor
and others, he did live and led a normal life for over forty
years.[17]

As a man of "faith" and "action" he had some
interesting encounters with the two characteristic
Garrettsville maladies—intemperance and infidelity.

One morning as he was in his study preparing a sermon
for the following Sunday, a voice seemed to say to him, "Go
down to Thompson and Horton's saloon and speak there."
"No," I thought, "that is not what I took two degrees at
Yale for, to go and speak in a public house. I was trained to

prepare sermons according to the best homiletical methods and to deliver them with the best art of oratory which is at my command." But the voice persisted, "Go and speak at Thompson and Horton's saloon." Convinced that it was God's leading, he finally arose hastily from his desk, put on his hat and coat, and set out for the saloon—walking rapidly so as not to lose courage.

Upon arriving, he pushed open the door and said, "Gentlemen, please lay down those cards. I have come down to pray with you." The startled patrons dropped their cards and appeared a little frightened and subdued at his unexpected entrance. But they were not nearly so frightened as Reuben. The young pastor knelt in prayer, said a few words to them, and just as promptly left again for his study. One can be sure the incident caused a buzz among the saloon patrons of the village.

An unexpected rebound came a few days later when he chanced to meet a rival saloonkeeper, a wicked and dangerous man. The proprietor was leaning on a post in front of his business and glared at Reuben as the latter approached. He gruffly remarked, "See here! I hear you went in Thompson and Horton's saloon the other day and prayed."

"Yes, I did."

"Well, I would like to know if my saloon is not just as good."

Reuben promptly marched into the latter's saloon without hesitancy and conducted a similar service.[18]

Reuben also had frequent encounters with infidelity in the village. When infidel lecturers often came to the community, he made it a special point to hear them. It was his aim to let the people of the community know that he was thoroughly versed in the substance of infidel teaching. Their devastating opinions did not bother one who had passed through the fires of skepticism himself. Reuben also sought the friendship of infidels in the community, but it was for the single purpose of winning them to Christ.

An interesting incident took place over this issue of

infidelity. Subsequently to the revival stirrings in the town there was a concerted effort on the part of many to re-establish infidelity. As a result they invited a follower of the notorious Colonel Robert Ingersoll to lecture. Quite a number of townspeople, including Reuben, went to hear him. Reuben was pleased with the lecture as it had an adverse effect upon the listeners—many of them vowing never to be influenced by infidelity again.[19] In fact, the following day Reuben met the man and told him that his lecture had done the community a world of good. "After they heard the aimless prattle you exhibited on the lecture platform it will never be necessary to refute infidelity in the town again!"

One lady immediately joined the young pastor's church, vowing that she would never be fooled by infidelity again. She became one of the most useful members of his congregation.

As for Reuben, his bout with agnosticism was past, but he still had lingering doubts about some orthodox doctrines. He felt the need for advanced study.

[1]Notes on the minutes of the Congregational Church, Garrettsville, Ohio, October 22, 1878, to October 15, 1882 (compiled by Mrs. Georgia Lee Alford, Church Clerk), p. 1.

[2]Reuben A. Torrey, Jr., "Dr. R. A. Torrey in His Home," *Moody Monthly* XXX (February 5, 1929), p. 67.

[3]Torrey, Jr., personal letter, April 7, 1965.

[4]Ibid.

[5]Minutes, Garrettsville, p. 3.

[6]Torrey, "Home," p. 68.

[7]Davis, p. 27.

[8]R. A. Torrey, "The Second Coming of Christ," *King's Business,* V (August-September, 1914), p. 423.

[9]Minutes, Garrettsville, p. 3.

[10]Davis, p. 27.

[11]Charles G. Finney, *Revivals of Religion* (New York: Revell, n.d.), pp. 33,34.

[12]Torrey, *The Southern Cross,* (September 10, 1902), p. 76.

[13]Davis, pp. 28,29.

[14]A plaque in front of an old theater states that in 1886 saloons were abolished in Garrettsville.

[15]Minutes, Garrettsville, pp. 2,3.

[16]Ibid., p. 3.

[17]R. A. Torrey, *Divine Healing* (Chicago: Moody, n.d.), pp. 23,24.

[18]R. A. Torrey, *The Wondrous Joy of Soulwinning* (London: Morgan and Scott, n.d.), pp. 32,33.

[19]R. A. Torrey, *Revival Addresses* (New York: Revell, 1903), p. 209.

5. The Voice of God

"Tor, why don't you resign your pastorate and do graduate work in Germany? You know the language, and some of the world's greatest scholars are there." So said Howard Bell, well-to-do friend and Yale classmate, who had taken his BA with Reuben.

"I'd like to, Howard, but I have family responsibilities now. Besides it's too expensive?" (His salary was $650 a year and "as much more as can be raised".)

"Never mind the expenses. I will pay them for you."

Not inclined to accept charity, Reuben immediately responded, "No, I couldn't let you do that, Howard."

"Well, then, let me loan you the money. Take all the time you like to pay it back."[1]

At his continual urging, Reuben accepted the offer, but only on the condition that he take out a life insurance policy making Bell the beneficiary. So he resigned the Garrettsville pastorate, declining a unanimous—and it was unanimous this time—vote to retain him as pastor and grant him a year's leave of absence. But Reuben did not wish to obligate himself to the church since God might lead otherwise upon his return. He gave his reason for resigning as "ill health and a desire for further study."[2] Thus he set sail for Germany with his wife and little daughter in the fall of 1882.

Germany—the land of the Reformation. The country had been torn by wars and internal strife for years in the wake of the Reformation, and it had been united and stabilized as an important country slightly more than a decade when Reuben arrived. "The Iron Chancellor," Otto Von Bismarck, the architect of German unity, was still the

chief figure in the German state. As to education and
scholarship the German universities were held in great
esteem around the world. Reuben spent approximately a
year in study at the two Lutheran universities of Leipzig
and Erlangen, dividing his time equally among them.

Narrow, crooked streets and houses with high-pitched
roofs dating from the 16th century characterized the quaint
and beautiful city of Leipzig. It was steeped in tradition
and proud of its association with the composer Wagner and
the philosopher Leibnitz, who were natives of the city.
Bach and Mendelssohn also had once held musical posts
there, and Luther had debated in the city. As to the
university the philosophers Fichte and Schelling and the
philosopher-poet Goethe were some of the more illustrious
alumni. Goethe had called the great university a *Klein
Paris* ("Paris in miniature").

Reuben's special fields of interest were Biblical Studies,
Dogmatic Theology and Christian Evidences. At Leipzig
he studied under Franz Delitzsch, Ernst Luthardt and F.
A. Kahnis, although most of his time was given to the
former two. Their fields of study appealed to him the most.
Delitzsch was the leading authority on Old Testament
criticism and Hebrew in Germany and co-author of the
famous *Keil and Delitzsch Commentary on the Old
Testament.* Luthardt was a well-known authority in
Dogmatics; Kahnis, in Church History.

All three were representatives of the Erlangen theology,
which aimed at a synthesis of the Lutheran Confessions
with the newer learning—*eine alte Weise, neue Wahrheit
zu lehren* (to teach the old truth in a new garb.) The grand
concept of *Heilsgeschichte* ("holy history") was the
controlling principle for the entire system, which taught
revelation is centered in the acts of God. Scripture is the
record of those historical events.

Reuben especially profited from the lectures of Professor
Delitzsch in both the classroom and the private sessions
with select American students. The Old Testament scholar
had high regard for Reuben and, when he learned that his

pupil was going to Erlangen, said, "Well, you will need letters of introduction." The venerable professor bade Reuben goodbye with tears in his eyes.[3]

It was in the following year that Reuben arrived at Erlangen. A green, forested village, it was kept remarkably neat and clean—even to the sweeping up of the pine needles from the streets. Neither the city nor the university had the rich tradition and historical prominence as Leipzig, but some of the most prominent thinkers of the time taught there. Further, it was richly endowed with some of the finest educational facilities. The letters of introduction from Delitzsch proved to be far more valuable than Reuben could have dreamed. Professor F. H. R. Frank, rector of the university, to whom the letters were primarily directed, formed an intimate friendship with Reuben and Clara. He asked the young student to study under his own personal direction and gave him free rein in his private library. This was an invaluable help to Reuben.[4]

Professor Frank was one of the most outstanding thinkers of his day and the most original theologian of the Erlangen school of theology. He based the certainty of all the important truths of Christianity upon the experience of regeneration. Reuben had already read his well-known *System of the Christian Certainty* and eagerly anticipated his study with him. Theodor Zahn, foremost authority on the New Testament and author of the monumental three-volume *Introduction to the New Testament*, was also one of Reuben's instructors.

It was a very stimulating experience for young Torrey to interact with the most advanced theological thought of the day, but it also sharpened the dilemma of his own theological outlook. Was the critical and experimental approach of the *Heilsgeschichte* view correct? Does God's revelation center in the acts of God in history? Does Divine truth have to verified by Christian experience to be truly valid? Or does God's revelation center in the words of Scripture as infallible and inerrant?

Reuben came home from his classes one day feeling himself all at sea in his thinking. He sat down at his table and put his head between his hands. It seemed as if it would burst. As he pondered the issues, it seemed as if a real voice spoke, "Reuben, I know some things which you cannot know." [5]

From that moment on Reuben decided to accept by faith the hypothesis—and at this point it was just that, an hypothesis—that the Bible was the inerrant Word of God. Both practically and intellectually he decided, "I will follow the Bible wherever it leads me." Slowly but surely he moved away from the critical approach to the Scriptures, and accepted the "old truth" in the "old garb."

The year's experience abroad was a highlight for Reuben in other areas than the strictly educational. He visited historical ruins, caves, art galleries, museums and other places of interest. Quite often he saw things which made a profound impression on him. It was his custom to visit the ruins of one of the ancient German castles. While there he tried to visualize their former splendor, but his imaginative spell was easily broken by slimy snails dragging themselves over the crumbling ruins. It spoke to him forcefully of the fleeting glory of earth and helped to fix his mind upon spiritual values.

On another occasion he saw a picture in an art gallery at Munich which captivated him. The picture depicted the approach of a storm with black and ominous clouds and bending trees in the fierce wind. Frightened people and animals were frantically looking for shelter. To him it was a perfect representation of every person's need for a hiding place, and he later used the illustration in one of his most forceful sermons.

Reuben also enjoyed ice skating on the cold, clear German nights and hiking in the mountains. On one of his hiking expeditions he was subjected to a very severe test. He and a company of the beer-loving university students climbed to the summit of a high mountain on a very warm day. Upon reaching the top, he discovered to his dismay that there were no temperance refreshments available. Though tortured by thirst he did not yield. Upon the return

trip he drank from a spring which was supposed to be
poisonous, rather than sacrifice his convictions.[6]

His stay in Germany had been a pleasant one. Clara,
who set up housekeeping in both German villages and
provided a cozy home atmosphere, contributed not a little
to that pleasantness. Reuben had intended to spend
another year in Germany, but financial consideration and
Clara's second pregnancy made it inadvisable to remain.
So he returned to the States and was soon confronted with
an important decision.

[1] Faith Coxe Bailey, "R. A. Torrey's Most Persuasive Sermon," *Moody
Monthly,* LVI (February, 1956), pp. 15, 16.

[2] Minutes, Garrettsville, p. 4. The reference to "ill health" is curious.
Did he still fancy that he was killing himself in his ministerial duties? Or
was it the awful bout with hay fever which he invariably had in August,
the month of his resignation?

[3] Torrey, *Moodyanna*, p. 3.

[4] Ibid.

[5] J. H. Hunter, "A Faithful and Wise Steward," *King's Business,* XX
(January, 1929), p. 11.

[6] *The Southern Cross* (September 10, 1902), p. 75. He did not feel that
the drinking of beer in such an exceptional circumstance would cause him
any harm. It was solely for the sake of his testimony.

6. Benefit of a Doubt

Upon his return from Germany Reuben was confronted with a choice of one of two fields of service. One was a struggling, unorganized group of Christians in Minneapolis; the other, a prosperous, established congregation in Brooklyn. There was much to commend the latter opportunity for the scholarly and cultured young minister. It was an established church in the East which offered an attractive salary. Further, Brooklyn had been his previous home for almost eight years during his childhood, and his two sisters and a brother resided there. But despite the advantages of the Brooklyn pastorate, he felt that he should give God the benefit of a doubt and went to the pioneer work in Minneapolis.[1]

Minneapolis was a rugged Northwest frontier town located on the Mississippi River. It had been incorporated into a city less than twenty years when Reuben arrived. The winters were long and severely cold, which caused Easterners to remark that it was another Siberia unfit for human habitation. It was an alert, enterprising community, however, and the city rang with sleigh bells in spite of weather which dipped to as low as forty degrees below zero. In the summer, however, it was a place of scenic beauty and was a health resort for wealthy Southerners. The "city of water" (meaning of Minneapolis) was a place of beautiful falls, and twenty-two natural lakes were within the city limits.

Reuben and Clara came to especially enjoy the summers in Minneapolis. Many happy hours were spent together boating or swimming at Lake Minnetonka, driving through the scenic countryside or frolicking with their children at a

picnic.[2] Reuben still enjoyed ice skating in the winter, but
this exercise was a little strenuous for Clara and the young
members of his family. Reuben strictly observed a family
time although the duties of his new pastorate were to make
many pressing demands upon his time.

The struggling little congregation numbered eleven and
met on the outskirts of the city. It was a home mission
project of the Congregationalists, who had conducted a
census of the area to determine the prospects.
Unfortunately, the job was poorly done, and the list given
to him proved to be almost worthless. Further, in their
effort to attract a suitable pastor, the "census" list was
supplemented by names of prominent people taken from
the mailboxes and directories. When Reuben learned of
this deceptive maneuver, he was not a little disconcerted.

The outcome was inevitable as he began his calling.
Frequently doors were slammed in his face by insulted
Minnesotans. At one point the chagrined and indignant
Reuben decided to stop his calls. Was he not a member of
the prominent Torrey family and of better stock than these
Minnesotans? But the thought occurred to him, "Didn't
Christ belong to a better family than he did? How was He
treated? He was despised and rejected of men." That
settled it. Despite the rebuffs he continued his visits.[3] One
of those who slammed the door in his face Reuben
determined to win for Christ. It took three years to reach
him, but when he did the man became one of the most
active members in his church.

On the other hand, Reuben found that these
Minnesotans were generally very hospitable and easy to
interest in the public good. Minneapolis lumberjacks were
part of one of the earliest hospitalization plans in the
States. This social-mindedness led to his being invited to
assume places of responsibility in the local philanthropic
enterprises. Further, the Congregational Association also
sought his assistance in the denominational work both
local and state. It was felt that one with so much advanced
education could do almost anything. Thus Reuben became
aligned with seven organizations—Associated Charities,

Newsboy's Home, Finance and Printing Committee of the State Association, Congregational Club, and three others. These organizations took a great deal of time and responsibility and detracted from his directly spiritual labors. And although he was for these causes, he seriously questioned whether this was a part of his calling. He queried in soliloquy fashion with the Lord:

"What did I call you to do anyway?"

"Well, You called me to preach."

"What are you doing?"

At that point he looked up from his desk at the seven pigeonholes where he kept the materials for the organizations and promptly wrote out seven resignations. He decided, "I am going to give myself to the business God has called me to." From this time onward he had as his central aim the teaching and preaching of the Word of God. [4]

Reuben's dedication to the ministry, combined with his deep sense of obligation, often carried him into the most unlikely places to preach. Once in Northwest Minnesota he preached to a small group of people during a blizzard so blinding that people could hardly walk the streets. Eleven people were present—nine Christians and two unsaved. He gave his best to the crowd, who had come with such difficulty, and had the joy of winning the two unsaved to Christ. On another occasion he went three miles through a storm to a meeting. Only a backslidden caretaker was there. Satan said, "Don't have a meeting. No one is here but you, the preacher, and the caretaker, who had to come." Undaunted, he conducted the service and saw the caretaker restored to fellowship.

Reuben's aggressiveness in evangelism was greatly stimulated by the conversion of three very hardened individuals. One was a professional murderess so hardened in sin that when she heard Reuben preach she prayed to the Devil afterwards to take away her conviction. The second was a drunken shoemaker who tried to murder his own wife in one of his debauches and who went steadily from bad to worse after the incident. The third was the

brightest man in a certain university who in utter despair
tried to commit suicide five times. "They seemed to be the
most hopeless cases that I had ever met, and one day I told
my Heavenly Father that if He would give me those three
persons, I would never despair of another man or woman as
long as I lived."[5] Their conversions gave Reuben an
inextinguishable confidence in dealing with the most
derelict of cases.

One of his greatest tests was a drunkard of about fifty
years of age whom Reuben said, "I will see this man saved
no matter what it costs me in time, money or patience."
The man made a profession and was the pet to Clara of all
the drunks who came under their roof. Before long,
however, Reuben was notified that his "convert" was in a
drunken rage. Promptly he went to the man's lodging only
to find him in a nasty, fighting mood. Realizing the danger
of the man's leaving the room, Reuben lunged at him. For a
few brief moments there was a flurry of arms and legs, but
the minister landed on top. Reuben's great strength proved
to be advantageous in this "ministerial duty," and his
assailant stayed securely pinned until he regained his
senses.

This type of thing went on for months and years. Reuben
lost sight of him for awhile, but finally he turned up years
later in one of Reuben's services in Chicago. Immediately,
even though the service had started, Torrey stepped down
the aisle and cordially greeted his visitor. Noticeably
impressed by this gesture of continued concern and
friendliness, the man stayed for the after meeting and was
genuinely converted.[6]

The most significant personally of all his soul-winning
experiences, however, was that of his brother, Swift. Swift
had married into an ardent Roman Catholic family who
tried to separate him from his Protestant parents. Torrey
had prayed for his brother's conversion for years, but there
had been no visible change in his attitude. His wife died
soon after their marriage, and when his only child, Molly,
was quite young, Swift became critically ill, apparently
with tuberculosis.

Learning of his critical condition, Reuben hurried to Brooklyn to be at his bedside and urged his brother to accept Christ as his Saviour. At first Swift extended his hand, then pulled it back and turned his face to the wall. His only reply was, "Go away, Archie, I do not want to hear about it." Reuben was hurt and puzzled. He retired to another room to pray, but his prayer was mingled with complaint. Had he not prayed earnestly for his brother? Had he not taken the promise of Acts 16:31 for household salvation seriously? How could it be possible at this last hour that he would not be saved?

Presently there was a knock at the door, and the nurse informed him that his brother wished to see him. Immediately he went in, and his brother extended his hand, saying, "Archie, I can hold out no longer. Pray for me that I may know your Christ." Then and there Reuben led him into a glad acceptance of Christ. Swift also asked his brother to take his daughter Molly and rear her with his children. He promised that he would.[7]

After three years with the Open Door Church he organized the People's Church (Congregational) in the heart of Minneapolis with thirteen charter members. At the same time he also became the superintendent of the City Missionary Society (Congregational). Torrey was a diligent and vigorous worker, and his labors increased significantly with these twin responsibilities. During the three years he was connected with these works he taught or preached six nights every week—not once fancying that he was killing himself—and often returned home as late as twelve at night. Sundays were especially pressing as services were held continuously during the day—often numbering ten in the summertime. Most of the services of the little church were held in theaters, halls and places of public resort. His church was among the leaders in Minnesota in conversions and accessions to membership.

Other responsibilities also began to demand his time. He started teaching the Union Sunday School lessons in a public hall on Saturday afternoon. Four or five hundred Christian workers frequently crowded into the auditorium for these lessons. At the start the plan was to have a minister each month to teach the lessons; however, Reuben did such an excellent job that he continued in that position the remainder of the time he was in Minneapolis.

His outstanding work in personal evangelism brought him to the first meeting of the International Association of Christian Workers in Chicago. To his amazement he was elected chairman of the Association, a position he held throughout the life of the organization.

But despite the successes which attended his ministry there were still important issues, both doctrinal and practical, which needed settling. God had only begun to shape His vessel.

[1] In later years Torrey always counseled his students to give God the benefit of a doubt if they wavered between a "big" or "little" call.

[2] The Torrey family increased with the appearance of Blanche on April 8, 1884, less than a year after their arrival in Minneapolis. Reuben Archer, Jr., their only son, was born three and one half years later on September 16, 1887. Then there was Elizabeth Swift, who was named for Torrey's mother. She arrived on March 5, 1889, the last year of his ministry in Minneapolis.

[3] Bailey, p. 16.

[4] R. A. Torrey, "Stick to Your Proper Business," *King's Business,* VII (September, 1916), p. 772.

[5] J. Kennedy MacClean, *Torrey and Alexander* (New York: Revell, 1905), p. 77.

[6] R. A. Torrey, *Anecdotes and Illustrations* (New York: Revell, 1907), pp. 124-127.

[7] Torrey, Jr., personal letter, April 7, 1965. Unfortunately there were no witnesses to Swift Torrey's request about Molly, and Torrey was not allowed to take her. This was of lasting regret to Torrey. Although her grandmother tried to keep her from knowing about the Torreys, in later years she did make contact with them and was converted.

7. Fork in the Road

"I have come to the fork in the road more than fifty times, and in every instance where my reason and common sense differed from the Bible, the Bible had proved right and my reason wrong."[1] So Reuben wrote in later years concerning his experience with the Bible. Paralleling his active ministry in Minneapolis was an equally intense devotion to the study of Scripture. It was in connection with this study that most of the major "forks" were encountered.

One of those was the second coming of Christ. For some time he had regarded those who preached on the second coming as either visionary or outright cranks. While he was in Germany, however, Frank had recommended to him Bishop Martensen's *Dogmatic*. Martensen was a premillennialist, and through this reading Reuben became intellectually convinced of the essential truthfulness of this position. After his arrival in Minneapolis, he witnessed a debate between a premillennialist and a postmillennialist, and the former won hands down. Reuben was greatly impressed with the scriptural basis of the doctrine, but its practical reality still managed to elude him.[2] His ingrained prejudice against symbolism and typology caused him to remark, "I almost wished that Revelation were not even in the Bible."

It was while he was attending a meeting of the International Association of Christian Workers that a delegate gave him a little tract stressing the spiritual importance of the Second Coming. "It transformed my whole idea of life, it broke the power of the world and its ambition over me and filled my life with the most radiant optimism even under the most discouraging circumstances."[3] It became not only a cherished doctrine but a "blessed hope." He came to quote I Thessalonians 4:13-18 in each letter he wrote to those sorrowing over the death of a departed Christian.

A matter of more secondary importance concerned his view of baptism. He became convinced through a searching study of the Scriptures that immersion was the mode of baptism practiced by Christ and the apostles. Thus he and his wife were immersed though both had been sprinkled as infants. Reuben did not believe, however, that baptism by immersion was important enough to serve as a denominational divider. When once asked, "Do you believe in believer's baptism?" he replied, "I do, but I don't make a hobby of it."[4] Reuben simply desired to follow the Scripture pattern in baptism, but made no attempt to legislate for others in this regard.

A third area dealt with the subject of divine healing in answer to prayer. Reuben's first experience in praying for and expecting healing came in the previously recounted Garrettsville incident; however, it was only in Minneapolis that he began seriously to study the subject. A number of verses concerning bodily healing impressed him, but none more than James 5:14,15. Torrey believed the passage gave the divine plan for the healing of a serious illness (not a headache, simple pains or minor sicknesses).

Reflecting upon his conviction concerning these verses in later years, he gave both the positive teaching of the passage as well as what it opposes:

> He is to "call for the elders of the church, and let them pray over him" in the calm and quiet of the home; and "the prayer" of (Spirit-given) *faith* is to "*save* him that is *sick*," and not the *intense carnal excitement* which would temporarily *galvanize* him into brief activities from which there is an appalling reaction, often leaving the poor victim of the religious charlatan worse than ever, and not infrequently sending him to the insane asylum or the cemetery.[5]

Although Reuben was not opposed to medication and

had a family doctor in case of need, it was customary for him to pray for sick members of the family. The family came to depend upon his prayer of faith in time of illness. Once while he was away for a meeting, his daughter Blanche became seriously ill. Clara cared for her during the night, and in her distress Blanche expressed her yearning for her father to be there to pray for her. Shortly after saying this she felt greatly relieved and fell into a restful sleep. Soon she was completely well and able to return to school. A few days later a letter came from Reuben in a distant city inquiring what was wrong with Blanche. He further noted that he had been deeply impressed to pray for her in the middle of the night. It was later learned that she began to recover at the precise hour in which he prayed. 6

Reuben also experienced complete healing from an ear infection which had come as a result of scarlet fever when he was very young. An operation had been performed on the ear, but for years he suffered a discharge from it. Even in manhood he had to keep absorbent cotton in his ear most of the time. The drum was perforated, and it was with much difficulty that he could hear with the ear. Temporary relief came from an ear specialist in Cleveland, but soon the difficulty returned.

Then one day while in Minneapolis he suffered a severe pain in the ear. The thought came to him. "You pray for the healing of others, why not ask God to heal your own ear?" At once he knelt and asked for healing. It came instantly. The drum healed over, and the ear became just as sound as the other. Two ear specialists to whom he related the incident examined the ear and stated that the drum was evidently once perforated but was now healed. 7

In Minneapolis there were a number of cases of healing in answer to prayer, but two are notable. One was the case of an invalid woman who had been ill for four years and had been treated by nine different physicians. Her case was pronounced hopeless. She and her husband were formerly Roman Catholics but had been converted. The relatives were still Catholic, however, and one said when

Reuben came to see her, "If she is healed, we will all become Protestants."

Reuben prayed for her and received an immediate assurance that the healing was granted. It was not his usual custom to so speak, but he said, "I expect you as soon as I am gone to get up and go about your work." The woman did so, and came three miles for the Sunday service the following week.

Another instance was the case of a Methodist minister's daughter in one of the Dakotas. This two-year-old daughter had a backbone which was improperly formed. It was terribly misshapen and caused her constant pain. She was taken to Minneapolis specialists only to be told that she could not even live for more than three years. The distressed parents even tried Christian Science, but found no help whatever. Then they took her to Reuben. When he prayed for her, she received instant relief. The defective part of her body was made right, and she slept normally that night for the first time. She later grew into beautiful womanhood and became a candidate for the mission field.[8]

A fourth key area was the fullness of the Spirit, or as he referred to it, "the baptism with the Holy Spirit." He became convinced from a study of the book of Acts that every minister of the Gospel should be endued with power from on High. He went to a business friend of his and said to him in private, "I am never going to enter my pulpit again until I have been baptized with the Holy Spirit and know it, or until God in some way tells me to go."[9] Claiming the promise of I John 5:14, 15, Reuben shut himself up in his study and spent the time continually in prayer asking God to baptize him with the Holy Spirit.

Within a week he received what he had asked for. He later confessed that had he known his Bible better, it would not have been necessary for a single day to pass. But despite Reuben's lack of knowledge, God rewarded his seeking heart.

It was a very quiet moment, one of the most quiet moments I ever knew; indeed, I think one reason I had to

> wait so long was because it took that long before my soul could get quiet before God. Then God simply said to me, not in any audible voice, but in my heart, "It's yours. Now go and preach."[10]

His experience affected greatly his attitude toward preaching. What had been a fear and dread now became a rapturous joy. The abnormal bashfulness which characterized him since childhood vanished.

> I have no dread of preaching now; preaching is the greatest joy of my life, and sometimes when I stand up to speak and realize that He (the Holy Spirit) is there, that all the responsibility is upon Him, such a joy fills my heart that I can scarce restrain myself from shouting and leaping.[11]

Thereafter he exclaimed, "I have a perfect sense of freedom and absolute absence of fear."

Reuben gave a very carefully delineated definition of the baptism in the Holy Spirit in three propositions.

First, it is a definite experience which the believer may know he has received or not. Those in New Testament times knew it, so also should believers in the present day.

Second, it is an experience distinct from and additional to the work of the Spirit in regeneration. Both may occur simultaneously, and in a normal state of the church would do so; nevertheless, two distinct ministries of the Spirit are in view. Every believer has the Spirit, but not every believer has the fullness of the Spirit although it is his spiritual birthright to have it. He had no thought of a "second blessing."

Third, it is a work always connected with and primarily for the purpose of testimony and service. It is not primarily to make the believer happy or holy, although that may accompany the Spirit's work. Rather it is to make the believer useful and powerful in the ministry. Thus he experiences in his life the same enduement of power which proved to be the turning point in the ministries of such men as Wesley, Finney, Spurgeon, and Moody. At the time he was in a relatively obscure place of service, but from that time forward his ministry began wonderfully to enlarge.[12]

The fifth "fork" was the most difficult of all—the eternal punishment of the wicked. He had believed and taught that there was a real Hell and awful punishment, but that the punishment of the wicked was not eternal and that Hell would ultimately be abolished. Thus all creatures, including the Devil, would ultimately be saved. He had convinced himself that everlasting punishment could not and must not be true. "I thought that I was a Universalist for all time and that anyone who was not a Universalist was not well posted." [13]

But the more he studied the Scriptures, he became convinced of its teaching of eternal punishment. Further,

> It dawned upon me also that it was quite possible that a God of infinite wisdom might have a thousand good reasons for doing a thing, when I, in my infinite foolishness, could not see even one, and my fondly-cherished Universalism went up in smoke. [14]

His firm conviction of this as a clear Scripture truth is reflected in a statement written many years later:

> If anyone could produce me one single passage in the Bible that, fairly constructed, according to its context and the usage of the words and grammatical construction that clearly taught that the punishment of the wicked would not be absolutely endless and that somewhere, somehow all would repent and be saved, it would be the happiest day of my life. But no such passage can be found. I have searched for it from the first chapter of Genesis to the last chapter of the Revelation but cannot find it, it is not there. I am thoroughly familiar with the passages that men urge. I have formerly used them myself, but they will not bear the construction that is placed upon them if we deal honestly with them. [15]

Reuben took no special delight in preaching on an eternal Hell; nevertheless, he fearlessly proclaimed it. He often confessed that he had many heartaches over the destiny of the Christless dead but no longer any intellectual barriers. Reuben stated in connection with his acceptance of the doctrine of eternal punishment:

> Some men may be able to believe what they want to believe but to doubt or deny what they want to doubt or

deny. I am not built that way. My wishes play no part in my decision. I have to be governed by my intellect, but of course, I know that a will surrendered to the truth and to God does more than anything to clarify the intellect.[16]

Reuben's surrendered will was to encounter one other major "fork" in his final year in Minneapolis.

[1]*The Southern Cross*, (September 10, 1902), p. 12.

[2]Torrey, "Second Coming," pp. 423,424.

[3]R. A. Torrey, *Return of the Lord Jesus* (Los Angeles: Biola Book Room, 1913), p. 21.

[4]Torrey, Jr., personal letter, December 14, 1965.

[5]Torrey, *Healing*, p. 13. Reuben's convictions concerning divine healing remained virtually constant throughout his life although he gave lesser stress to it in later years. He considered it a private matter and never believed physical healing to be a vital aspect of his ministry. He only occasionally mentioned it publicly, and instances of divine healing in his ministry are less frequent after his Chicago ministry.

[6]Torrey, Jr., personal letter, April 7, 1965. He also indicated that his father, although recognizing that the anointing was symbolic and not a necessity, was accustomed to anoint with olive oil in his earlier years.

[7]Torrey, *Healing*, pp. 33-35.

[8]Ibid.

[9]Torrey, *Holy Spirit*, p. 198.

[10]Ibid.

[11]R. A. Torrey, *The Four Great Essentials* (Los Angeles: Biola Book Room, 1920), p. 11. Torrey believed in ecstasies and raptures, but these were never public. Further, he did not believe they were of primary importance. "I would rather go through my whole life and never have one touch of ecstasy but have power to witness for Christ and win others for Christ and thus save them, than to have raptures 365 days in the year." R. A. Torrey, *The Person and Work of the Holy Spirit* (New York: Revell, 1910), p. 182.

[12]Torrey, *Holy Spirit*, pp. 109-120.

[13]R. A. Torrey, *Great Pulpit Masters*, III (New York: Revell, 1950), p. 87.

[14]Ibid.

[15]R. A. Torrey, *The Destiny of the Christless Dead* (Glendale, California: Church Press, n.d.), p. 11.

[16]Ibid., p. 5. His acceptance of eternal punishment was not an overnight decision. Though he accepted it at this point as a Biblical teaching, it was only during his first winter in Chicago that it became an intense inner conviction. Torrey, *Person and Work*, pp. 92,93.

8. "Life of Trust"

There had been stirrings in the heart of Reuben Torrey concerning faith ever since Moody's meetings in New Haven. In one of his sermons Moody mentioned, "Faith can do anything." The thought lodged itself securely in Reuben's mind, and he said to himself, "That is so. No man has ever accomplished anything for God who did not have a mighty faith. I am going to have faith." He tried to work up a great faith but had little success and was forced to confess, "I am making no headway at all." [1]

But as he came into further contact with the Scripture, he learned that "faith cometh by hearing, and hearing by the word of God" (Rom. 10:17). It was only then that he began to discover the meaning of real faith. His thinking concerning faith was further stimulated by the reading of George Muller's *Life of Trust*. Muller drew his attention to absolute and direct trust in the promises of God for daily needs.

> I would just observe, that we never contract debts, which we believe to be unscriptural (according to Romans XIII. 8); and therefore we have no bills with our tailor, shoemaker, grocer, butcher, baker, etc.; but all we buy we pay for in ready money. The Lord helping us, we would rather suffer privation than contract debts. . . I am well aware that many trials come upon the children of God, on account of not acting according to Romans XIII. 8. [2]

Reuben confessed that Muller's book made a profound impression on him and completely took out of him all his ambition to be a world-renowned minister in a great metropolitan church. It radically altered his entire conception of the Christian life and ministry.

He became personally convinced in the fall of 1888 that

he should trust God directly for all of the needs of himself and his family. At that time he owed $600 to Howard Bell in connection with his European study and $100 each for his rent and groceries. He resolved to go no further in debt and to pay up the old debts as soon as possible. The decision was known only to his family, and the venture was marked by intense conflict.

> It was an awful struggle, but I settled it in my study that from that hour I would obey everything I found recorded as being Christian duty in the Word of God; that I would go wherever God told me to go; say whatever I thought God told me to say; and never ask anybody for a penny of money but just look to God to supply as he might see fit. And from that day to this I have been in Beulah Land. [3]

Fortunately, many of these first "Beulah Land" experiences have been recorded in his few extant diary entries. His first step in faith for daily needs came in the ordering of wood for the winter. It was past time to order, but he had no money. He asked God for the money by Saturday and made arrangements to have it delivered on Monday. On Saturday afternoon after his Bible class a layman, N. H. Pierce, handed him a check for $25, the first donation he ever remembered anyone handing him there. Reuben was almost overcome. It was the exact amount needed. The man told him that the money had been owed him for years, and coming unexpectedly as it did, he decided to give it to Reuben.

A week later he decided to ask the Lord for $100 to pay some of the old debts. By Thursday of that week he had received it. A deacon, Mr. Campbell, gave him an unexpected gift for the amount. It was most unusual since he had just given that amount to the Mission work, and it was four times the amount he had given in previous years. [4]

A short time later some unexpected money came. He pondered, "Shall I spend it all, or save for the future?" Then he thought, "God can provide for the future." So he went to the bank and drew out all that he had with the exception of two dollars. Within ten minutes of this

Good

transaction Mr. Dyer, the treasurer of the City Mission
Society, gave him $244! He wrote in his diary:

> These experiences are noticeable, as they were
> unknown to me until I stepped right out to trust the Lord,
> and at that time these persons (those who gave the gifts)
> did not know of the stand I had taken. 5

Such incidents prompted him to take a further gigantic
step of faith, which he felt clearly led to do.

> It soon became evident that the Lord wanted me to give
> up my salary, which had been paid with great
> irregularity. By His grace I did this January 1, 1889. I
> proposed to take the whole Mission work—rent, gas,
> everything—as a faith work. , . and on January 1 we
> began with no pledges for the future. 6

Because of a concurrence of circumstances, chiefly
financial, the Mission Society had been obliged to abandon
their initial reluctance and follow his proposal. In this
decision he was also taking the responsibility for the needs
of the six members of his family.

Reuben noticed that "the money came, but singularly
enough not from the old expected sources." At times he
personally went without a meal or had just a few pennies in
his pocket, but never did he fail to have the needs of his
family or of the Mission met. The circumstances were often
remarkable, and usually the money was just enough to care
for the present need. He testified that he never enjoyed
such a sense of security and freedom from care and anxiety
as he found at this time.

There were also some valuable corollary lessons which he
learned. One was that it was unacceptable to *lend* money to
the Lord. In a time of serious need he advanced $25 from
his own pocket to the Mission and thought to himself,
"When money comes, I will reimburse myself." But the
money did not come, and after prolonged heart searching
he saw that God did not want him to lend *Him* money. So
at great personal sacrifice he said of the "loan," "It is
yours, Lord." Inside of twenty-four hours $21 of the
original amount was back in his pocket, and more money
came for the Mission. 7

Another serious occasion involved the rent for the Mission building. It was soon to be due as also were the gas bills, and the money was not forthcoming. Reuben had taken the ground that he would close the Mission hall rather than allow it to incur debt for a single hour. It was a close call, for money was not in hand less than two days before the due date. But then the needs were met. Actually there were some sources from which the money seemed sure—in fact, had already been contributed to the Mission—but it had not come at the exact time needed. Reuben explained the precarious situation as looking to the promised source of income rather than to the Lord Jesus Himself.

There was another time of dire need for the Mission, and the necessary money had not come. He earnestly prayed about the situation, but had little faith for an answer when he retired late in the evening. In the middle of the night he was awakened in great pain and physical distress. He asked God for physical relief and again for the needed money, but there was no answer.

> Then I looked up and I said, "Heavenly Father, if there is anything wrong in my life anywhere, show me what it is and I will give it up." Instantly God brought up something that had often come up before to trouble me. . . I would say, "That's all right. I know it's all right. There is nothing wrong about that," but all the time in the bottom of my heart I knew it was wrong. I said, "Oh, God, *if* it is wrong in Thy sight I will give it up." There was no answer. Then I cried, "Oh, God, this is wrong; it is sin. I give it up now." Instantly God touched my body, immediately I was as well as I am this moment, and the money came and the work went on. 8

Thus Reuben learned by personal experience that no sin or barrier can be allowed to come between the soul that trusts and the living God who provides. He learned the same truth as Muller who said, "It is not possible to live in sin, and at the same time, by communion with God to draw down from Heaven everything that one needs for the life that now is." 9

These experiences in faith exhibited some remarkable

results. By mid-April, 1889, he could say that all of his past debts had been paid, with the exception of $200 remaining on his loan from Bell. That was soon to come. And although his income was much less than he originally received as a salary, he was able to do something he had never done before—pay for things as he got them. Further, there was a debt of $1,500 on the Mission when he started, and by this time it was paid in full. He wrote in his diary:

> Thus the Lord fulfilled His Word (Philippians 4:19). My faith has grown simply by stepping out on the bare Word of God and putting it to a test. Many times I had nothing else to look to, but it has never failed.[10]

Reuben's life of trust took him entirely out of the realm of the theoretical. His belief in God was placed in the crucible of a rigid, practical experiment, and he had been convinced beyond the shadow of a doubt that there was a Living God who answered prayer. He never fully understood the philosophy of prayer, but he was certain of the *fact* of answered prayer.

In this experience Reuben saw faith and prayer in an entirely new dimension. It underlay this startling statement:

> Prayer is the key that unlocks all the storehouses of God's infinite grace and power. All that God is, and all that God has, is at the disposal of prayer. But we must use the key. *Prayer can do anything that God can do, and as God can do anything, prayer is omnipotent.*[11]

Though Reuben did not publicize these marvelous experiences of faith, they did not go unnoticed. Eventually they came to the attention of Moody in Chicago.

[1] Davis, pp. 24,25.

[2] George Muller, *Life of Trust* (New York: Sheldon and Co., 1878), p. 89.

[3] R. A. Torrey, *How God Answered Prayer* (Chicago: Bible Colportage Assoc., n.d.), p. 3.

[4] Ibid., p. 4.

[5] Ibid., p. 6.

[6] Ibid., p. 5.

[7] Ibid., p. 8.

[8] R. A. Torrey, *Power of Prayer* (New York: Revell, 1924), pp. 201,202.

To the author's knowledge Torrey never mentioned what this barrier was in his public utterances. In a letter from his daughter, Miss Edith Clare Torrey, to Mr. A. P. Fitt, dated November 14, 1958, she stated: "He himself told me that the hardest thing he ever had to give up was coffee. This he was obliged to relinquish because it made him very nervous, and he was determined that there should be nothing in his life which would in any way lessen his efficiency in proclaiming the Gospel." He never regarded it as a standard for others, however.

[9]Muller, p. 88.

[10]Torrey, *How God*, p. 8. With a note of triumph he frequently recounted to students in later years, "I risked and I won!" It should be noted, however, that Reuben later reverted to a more conventional type of economic arrangement concerning his salary. But he did so only on the conviction that he had stood the test. He did not believe it was a matter of Christian duty for all time, or even that God led every person to do the same. Further, it sharpened his conviction that money was a sacred trust.

[11]Torrey, *Power*, p. 17.

PART III

Edifying the Body of Christ (1889-1901)

9. Wanted: a Man of God

"You make my mouth water for him!"

So said D. L. Moody to Congregational pastor E. M. Williams, as the latter described in glowing terms Torrey's faith work and aggressive evangelistic ministry in Minneapolis. Fleming H. Revell, Moody's brother-in-law, had also related to him Torrey's exceptional conduct of the large International Christian Workers Conventions. Moody was impressed. "A man who can control a group of people like that is a man I want." [1]

Moody had been searching for a superintendent to organize and direct a proposed Bible Institute in Chicago. He deemed it the largest thing he had yet undertaken, and felt it was going to accomplish more than anything he had yet been permitted to do. But he *must* have a capable superintendent. Could it be that young man whom he had set to work in the inquiry room at New Haven and Cleveland?

The first inkling Torrey had that Moody was considering him for the work came in a letter from a college and seminary classmate, Rev. John Collins, who was secretary of the International Christian Workers Convention. When the two met later, he asked Torrey, "Have your ears burned this summer?"

"No," Torrey replied.

"Well, I should think they would, for I have been talking about you a great deal to Mr. Moody," and passed on the import of their conversation. [2]

Presently Torrey received a letter from Moody inviting him to the preliminary conference in September for the establishment of the Institute. There was no suggestion,

however, of the place he might have in the work. Torrey left
for the conference and through a mistake in the dates
arrived a day early. He was immediately directed to Moody,
who dismissed the workers surrounding him, saying, "I
want to see you alone." They retired to a room by
themselves, and Moody laid out the whole plan of the
Institute. Then to Torrey's amazement, he said, "I want
you to take charge of this thing. Will you do it?"

Torrey could not give an immediate reply. Moody said,
"I do not want you to. Pray over it and as soon as you are
clear, tell me." Three days later on Friday, despite the
difficulty of leaving the Minneapolis work so quickly, it
became perfectly clear that the Lord was calling him to the
work in Chicago. He related his decision to the evangelist,
who said, "Get home just as quickly as you can, and get
back just as quickly as you can. I will need you more next
week than I do now." When asked when he thought he
could return, Torrey replied, "Tuesday morning at nine
o'clock."

Arriving in Minneapolis the next morning, Torrey told
his wife to have everything packed and ready to go to
Chicago by six o'clock Monday night. He speedily put his
affairs in order and left for Chicago Monday evening (his
family followed a short time later). On Tuesday morning he
arrived in Chicago and went directly to the Institute
building. When Torrey stepped into the door, Moody, who
was in the hall, looked up at him with a start.

"Where did you come from?"

"Minneapolis."

"How did you get here so soon?"

"What time did I tell you I would be here?"

"You said you would be here at nine o'clock, Tuesday
morning."

"Look at your watch."

It was exactly nine o'clock. He had Moody's confidence
from that time until the evangelist's death some ten years
later. [3]

The Chicago which greeted Torrey at the dawn of the

1890's was big and booming. It had come a long way since it had been incorporated as a town some sixty years earlier—this despite one of the most devastating fires in history less than two decades previous. Over 100,000 had been left homeless and 2,100 acres destroyed, but the energetic population quickly rebuilt. Now the rising metropolis had reached such prominence that it was shortly to gain the congressional bid for the World's Fair—much to the dismay of the wealthy and prominent cities in the East. The city boasted of vast financial resources, a swirl of rapidly advancing business activity, an envious architectural achievement in the magnificent Auditorium, and miles upon miles of Hereford beef in their famous stockyards. There was no question about it—Chicago had become one of the leading cities of the United States.

On the darker side Chicago, sometimes known as the "city of fallen souls," was rampant with immorality, drunkenness, crime, and political corruption. The rough western city drew some of the vilest elements in society. The cancer in politics was so great that at the beginning of the decade, an enraged citizenry began to exert severe pressures of their own against prominent civic leaders. Many of the "fallen souls," however, had been reclaimed by Moody who arrived in 1856. He had cast a lengthy evangelistic shadow over the city for over thirty years through the work of his Sunday school, the YMCA, and the Illinois Street Church, which he founded in 1864.

Moody, a native of Northfield, Massachusetts, had been converted to Christ shortly before his arrival in Chicago. It was not long before he began his Sunday school work, which grew to such proportions that he gave up his business as a shoe salesman to enter full-time Christian work. His evangelistic campaigns in the British Isles from 1873-75 had catapulted him to international recognition. From that time on he was the recognized leader in evangelism, and carried on great campaigns in the leading cities of the United States and abroad.

Known as the Great Commoner, he was never ordained and preferred the simple title, "Mr. Moody." He had little formal education, but was dominated by a contagious faith and zeal for the Lord's work. His broad shoulders on a stocky, heavy-set frame gave him a commanding appearance, but it was his rare spiritual power which attracted the audiences. In his personal contacts he generated warmth and kindness, and was especially known for his gentle, affable manner. Ever mindful of winning men to Christ, he spoke to at least one person a day about his soul.

It was this yearning desire to reach the unreached of Chicago which had prompted Moody's most recent venture—the organization of the Chicago Evangelization Society on February 12, 1887. The vision and purpose of the CES is stated in the words of the incorporation charter. "To educate, direct and maintain Christian workers as Bible readers, Teachers and Evangelists who shall teach the Gospel in Chicago and its suburbs especially in neglected fields."[4]

Lecture classes were begun to achieve these aims, but it became increasingly apparent that a building, organization, and regular staff were needed for the Society. In the spring of 1889 a conference was held with a view to establishing the Institute, and in less than a month property was purchased and construction begun on a building. The formal opening of the school, however, was on September 26—the day Torrey arrived from Minneapolis.

The financial burden at the beginning was staggering, and the lack of facilities created severe drawbacks. Some very generous gifts alleviated the financial problems, however; and the men's dormitory, which also housed the offices of the Institute, was completed after the first year. It became the familiar 153 Institute Place. Torrey penned in his diary, nine months after his arrival, "I have had many difficulties since I came, some of which seemed insuperable, but the Lord in answer to prayer has overcome them all."[5]

Moody could have chosen few men of such stature who would be as loyal. The relationship of Moody and Torrey was akin to that of David and Jonathan: "the soul of Jonathan was knit with the soul of David, and Jonathan loved him as his own soul" (I Sam. 18:1). Moody was brusque, impulsive, and uneducated; Torrey, polished, logical and scholarly. But despite this sharp contrast and the greater intellectual stature of Torrey, he loved and obeyed Moody—even to the performing of such menial tasks as caring for his soiled shirts and shining his shoes. Torrey was aristocratic and independent by nature, but he recognized a spiritual insight and wisdom in Moody that was often superior to his own.

In turn, Torrey became Moody's right arm and chief confidant. Moody knew well his failings and came to lean on Torrey a great deal. There was no one he trusted more implicitly. He placed great faith in Torrey's opinion of speakers at the Institute and gave him a free hand in the Chicago ministry. As Evangelist J. Wilbur Chapman has noted, "No man, really, had Mr. Moody's confidence more completely, and justly so, for no one could ever be more loyal to another than R. A. Torrey to D. L. Moody."[6]

Moody was greatly pleased with the work of his superintendent when he cast his eyes on the report of the first full year's work. There was a total of 253 men and women enrolled representing thirty-one states and nine foreign countries; 3,380 meetings of various types were conducted, and 22,766 personal visits were made. Of the almost 12,000 inquirers dealt with, 2,729 made professions of faith.[7] It was evident that God's hand of blessing was upon the work of the Institute and Moody's choice of this modern Bazaleel whom God had filled with His Spirit and wisdom.

Few men could have carried out Moody's plan so well and have established the Institute on so sound a foundation. Chapman believed that Torrey was "without question the most capable man that Mr. Moody could have found for this very important position. He has preeminent endowments which qualify him in a very special manner to conduct this work. . . .He is a man of most delightful spirit, and has a profound knowledge of the word of God, which he has wrought up in a most thorough form, and which is with intense earnestness taught the students." [8]

Moody had found his man of God.

[1]F. G. Beardsley, *Heralds of Salvation* (New York: American Tract Society, 1939), p. 179.

[2]Torrey, *Moodyanna,* p. 5.

[3]Ibid., p. 6.

[4]Charter of the Chicago Evangelization Society, February 12, 1887.

[5]Torrey, *How God,* p. 12.

[6]William Culbertson, "An Appreciation of R. A. Torrey," *Great Pulpit Masters* III, (New York: Revell, 1950), p. 7.

[7]Bernard R. De Remer, *Moody Bible Institute: A Pictorial History* (Chicago: The Moody Press, 1960), p. 32.

[8]J. Wilbur Chapman, *The Life and Work of Dwight L. Moody* (Philadelphia: John C. Winston and Company, 1900), p. 236.

10. Moody's New Bible Institute

"Eleven o'clock, Bible Doctrine," read the Institute schedule. As the new students filed into the lecture room, they got the first glimpse of their instructor. With rapid stride and with Bible and doctrine book under his arm, he mounted the platform just before eleven. Students were soon to learn that the time to begin was not "eleven o'one."

His presence was striking. With head set solidly on broad square shoulders and massive frame, he stood about five feet, ten inches, but his long trunk and arms made him appear taller. He was heavy, weighing about two hundred and twenty, muscled but not fat. His high forehead, Roman nose, and strong chin were distinctive; his neatly-trimmed Van Dyke mustache and beard, prematurely white (he had many a chuckle over older men offering him their seat on the trolley car!) gave him an appearance of dignity.

He wore a finely tailored Prince Albert coat with white shirt, starched collar and cuffs, and white bow tie. His shoes were polished. There was hardly a wrinkle in his clothing. He gave the impression of immaculate cleanness and neatness, and had a stunning look of culture and dignity. His penetrating grey eyes with blue tint had a searching quality about them. There was no bluffing when he fixed his gaze upon the students.[1]

Presently Torrey spoke, "Let us pray." After the brief prayer for guidance and power—so terse that to some it seemed sacrilegious—he promptly asked the students to take Scripture passages for recitation. His procedure was rigidly inductive. Once the passage was read, Torrey endeavored to draw out from the student its meaning by asking him a series of pointed questions. He felt it was vital that the student see it for himself.

His apparent sternness often caused new students to forget everything they knew in their recitation. But Torrey would sympathetically help the trembling neophytes to recall the vanished knowledge and upon succeeding would then lend them encouragement, "There! You see, you knew it all the time." Torrey expected students to study their lessons. "Not prepared" was seldom said in his classes. He always asked the reason why. If the answer was acceptable, he was kind, but if not, he could be quite severe. He was cool in his disciplinary measures with erring or lazy students. [2]

His students liked to watch him as he taught. It was never necessary to call the class to attention. His commanding presence and the business-like atmosphere of the classroom forbad inattention. At times the classroom seemed to be charged with a spiritual presence—particularly when he spoke on such subjects as the Inspiration of Scripture, the Holy Spirit and the Second Coming of Christ.

Yet at times the classroom had its lighter moments when on rare occasions Torrey's sense of humor emerged. One day William Evans, a young cockney from London, delivered a sermon in homiletics class. At the close Torrey arose in his usual dignified manner to give his criticisms. But before so doing he asked a student to go across the hall and bring back a broom and dustpan. Teacher and students silently waited his return. Then Torrey remarked, "Sweep up all those 'h's' Evans just dropped!" The class roared with delight, and Evans dropped fewer "h's" after that. [3]

Torrey's sense of humor was more pronounced in an informal atmosphere. At parties he often acted as the genial master of ceremonies and regaled students with his witticisms and masterful storytelling. A student, E. W. Wadsworth, later president of the Great Commission Prayer League, once remarked, "In private life and with students he would enter heartily into games, and was the 'life of the party'—full of laughter and pleasantry." [4] This was often a startling revelation to students who knew him only as a serious administrator and instructor.

His seemingly distant manner was misleading to those who did not know him. He had a keen and sympathetic interest in his students, and was especially a friend to those in need. The London student, Evans, recalled a great sorrow which came into his life while at the Institute. "Dr. Torrey came to my room, counseled and comforted me; and there we stood with head on each other's shoulders—the great teacher weeping with his poor student; then we knelt and prayed." [5]

In setting up the curriculum of the Institute Torrey was guided by two simple principles—"Will it please God?" and "Will it help the student?" He intended for every course of study—whether in English, Bible doctrine, or music—to be both painstakingly thorough and intensely practical. To achieve this end, the mornings were devoted to instruction, the afternoons to study, and the evenings to Christian work. Students were given soul-winning assignments in churches, missions, jails, home visitation, or on the streets. These afforded an opportunity to put into practice what they had learned during the day.

Torrey's aims for the students are revealed in an early issue of the *Institute Tie*:

(1) Thorough consecration
(2) Intense love for souls
(3) A good knowledge of God's Word and especially how to use it in leading men to Christ
(4) Willingness to "endure hardness as a good soldier of Jesus Christ"
(5) Untiring energy
(6) The Baptism with the Holy Spirit [6]

These qualities, which were reflected in his own character and experience, he consistently brought before his pupils and expected them to be followed.

Torrey did not charm or fascinate the students, as some visiting lecturers did, but he instilled divine truths in them

and placed granite in their character. There was perhaps
no greater area in which character was stressed as in the
value of time.

An incident took place during a Bible conference at the
Institute which indelibly impressed the value of time upon
the students' minds. A missionary attending the
conference was graciously given ten minutes by Torrey to
speak on an already well-filled program. Throughout his
talk the missionary complained about his ten-minute time
limit. Suddenly he heard Torrey's voice behind him, "Your
ten minutes are up. Let us sing number ___ after which
Dr._____ will deliver the closing address."

At the dinner table afterwards the unfortunate man
wished to talk further about his treatment but was silenced
by Torrey's crisp remark, "You were given ten minutes to
tell of the work. If you chose, rather, to talk about yourself,
and the treatment you had received, you are to blame, not
I. Ask the Lord to forgive you for wasting time." [7]

Torrey governed his own life by a meticulous schedule.
Rising promptly at five each morning bright as a light, he
took fifteen to twenty minutes for dumbbell exercises
(except on Sunday) and a cold bath. After a short season
spent in Bible reading and prayer, he came to the breakfast
table with a keen and radiant optimism. After breakfast
and devotions with his family, he was off to a full day's
work.

His first and most perplexing duty was the daily
correspondence. He received a staggering number of
inquiries in addition to strictly religious matters, on such
diverse subjects as home relationships, financial problems,
and even lawsuits. By chance he once helped to convict two
men of forgery because of his adeptness at handwriting
analysis. Afterwards letters began to pour in asking him to
serve as a witness in such cases. In addition to the large
correspondence about Institute matters, he wrote many
personal letters. Usually his letters were not brief. Rather,
they were painstakingly thorough.

He usually took a brisk walk after the morning's

correspondence and arrived fresh for his doctrine class. The afternoons were devoted to study, writing, and occasionally to the teaching of other classes. In the evenings he was busily engaged in preaching and personal evangelism. He ministered in the lowest quarters of the city where even the police were afraid to go, as well as in the most fashionable congregations. Torrey also taught the International Sunday School Lesson on Saturday (sometimes to as many as 2,000) and a Bible class on Sunday afternoon. His Sundays were always full, whether he was in Chicago or in some distant city.

Upon returning to his home in the evening, he regularly spent an hour in prayer before retiring. Thus family members who were up after ten o'clock were given a gracious but not to be ignored suggestion that they retire to their rooms. He averaged only five hours of sleep a night, but he boasted of restful sleep with few dreams. An afternoon nap of about fifteen to thirty minutes' duration right after lunch helped him to meet the demands of such a rigorous schedule.[8]

Torrey's greatest stress to the students, however, was the necessity of love for individual souls and the knowledge of how to lead them to Christ. Dr. James M. Gray, who eventually became president of the Institute, said later concerning Torrey's evangelistic stress, "Torrey was. . .a personal soul winner, and to him almost more than to D. L. Moody, does the Institute still owe its reputation for turning out men and women stimulated and equipped to deal face to face and heart to heart with human souls about salvation. Mr. Moody furnished enthusiasm for that work, but Dr. Torrey taught us how to do it."[9] He stressed absolute reliance upon the Holy Spirit to carry home the message of the Scripture.

There was the case of a student who came to the Institute in great spiritual darkness. Such students were not ordinarily admitted, but an exception was made for him because of repeated entreaties on the part of his minister father and friends. His case was so desperate that he was sent to the Institute under armed guard. Soon after his arrival Torrey confronted him with his need of conversion.

The young man began by saying, "I have committed the unpardonable sin." Torrey immediately replied, referring to John 6:37, "Jesus does not say, 'Him that hath not committed the unpardonable sin that cometh to me I will in no wise cast out.' He says, 'Him that cometh to me I will in no wise cast out.' " The student repeatedly asserted his hopelessness by saying he had sinned willfully after receiving the knowledge of the truth, that he was possessed of the Devil just like Judas Iscariot, that his heart was as hard as a millstone, and that he did not care to come to Christ. Torrey countered each objection precisely as he had the first, using the same Scripture.

The student's objections finally exhausted, Torrey instructed him to get on his knees and follow in prayer. He was told to repeat after him, sentence by sentence, "Lord Jesus, my heart is as hard as a millstone. . . I have no desire to come to Thee. . . But Thou hast said in Thy word. . . 'Him that cometh unto Me I will in no wise cast out'. . . Now the best I know I come. . . Therefore though I don't feel it. . . I believe Thou hast received me."

The young man began to melt, and though he had some severe struggles, he clung tenaciously to the promise of John 6:37. In a short time he became a very dedicated and useful Christian—in fact one of the most widely used laymen Torrey had ever known.[10]

The most significant feature of Torrey's personal evangelism, however, was his dealing with skeptics, infidels, and agnostics of all classes. His unalterable conviction of the reality of God, combined with his own severe struggles with skepticism, gained him the confidence of this class of people.

One day a graduate of a British university came to his Institute office and explained his difficulties. He stated that his case was "very peculiar"—as indeed it was. He had a remarkably varied background, having dabbled in

Unitarianism, Spiritualism, Buddhism, Theosophy and most other "isms." He was in an absolute state of agnosticism, neither affirming nor denying the existence of God, and felt his case was hopeless.

Torrey, as was his usual custom, determined first of all just what the man *did* believe. In his case he did believe there was an absolute difference between right and wrong, so Torrey got him to take his stand on the right wherever it might lead him. Then drawing the man's attention to John 7:17, "If any man is willing to do his will, he shall know of the teaching, whether it is of God, or whether I speak from myself," he explained. "Now Jesus makes you a fair proposition. He does not ask you to believe without evidence, but He asks you to do a thing your own conscience approves, and promises you that if you do it, you will come out of skepticism into knowledge."

Then Torrey asked him, "Will you follow out this clue? Will you pray this prayer? 'O God, if there is any God, show me whether Jesus Christ is Thy Son or not, and if You show me that He is, I promise to accept Him as my Saviour and confess Him as such before the world.''

"Yes, I am willing to do that, but there is nothing in it; my case is very peculiar."

Taking the Gospel of John and pointing out its stated purpose in 20:30,31, Torrey further said, "Will you take this Gospel and read it, not trying to believe it, but simply reading it with a fair mind, willing to believe it if it approves itself to you as true?"

"I have read it time and time again, and could quote a good deal of it."

Torrey replied, "I want you to read it in a new way; read a few verses at a time, ask God for light each time you read, and promise to act upon as much as you see to be true."

The man promised to do so, but closed by saying, "There is nothing in it, my case is very peculiar." A short time later, however, when Torrey met him again, the man rushed up to him and said, "There *is* something in that."

"I knew that before," Torrey replied.

"Why, ever since I have done what I promised you to do, it is just as if I had been taken up to the Niagara River and was being carried along." In a short time all of his doubts had vanished.[11]

Torrey believed there was no more interesting or easier class of people to deal with than honest skeptics and infidels.

The soul-winning, evangelistic emphasis of the Institute was never reflected in any greater way than in its endeavors with the World's Fair of 1893. It was held in Chicago May 1 to October 30 and was called the Columbian Exposition in honor of the four-hundredth anniversary of the discovery of America (it was actually to have been held in 1892 but had to be postponed a year).

The mainspring of the campaign was Moody himself. Spurred by the vision of reaching the multiplied thousands coming into the city with the Gospel, he made the most elaborate plans of his entire ministry. He brought preachers from near and far—D. W. Whittle, A. J. Gordon, A. T. Pierson, Charles Inglis, W. G. Morehead, A. C. Dixon, and John McNeill, to name a few. McNeill, the noted Scotch preacher, was there for the entire six months. In preparation for the event, two additional stories were added to the Institute building, which became the headquarters for the campaign.

Torrey superintended the campaign and carried out Moody's specifications. Meetings were scheduled in over eighty different churches, tents, theaters, missions, and halls all over the city. The students of the Institute were busily engaged in personal work, passing out tracts and assisting in the services. Among the key ministries of the Institute were the Gospel wagons, which held services all over the city in different locations. There were many meetings in a single day, and Torrey not only supervised these but made multitudinous appearances himself.

Torrey had severe reservations about one of his appearances, however. Near the close of the Fair, Chicago Day was observed in memory of the great fire twenty-two years previous, and the city made extensive plans to attract people on a large scale. Learning of this, Moody instructed Torrey to engage the Central Music Hall for that day from nine to six. Torrey was aghast.

"Why, Mr. Moody, nobody will be at this end of Chicago on that day."

Moody brusquely replied, "You do as you are told!"

When the day came for the meetings, an anxious and heavy-hearted Torrey, thinking few would be there, proceeded to the hall. He was to be the speaker for the noon hour. Much to his amazement there was such a press of people in the building and in the vestibule that he could not get in. Had he not been able to slip in the back window, the audience would have lost their speaker for the hour.[12]

The results of the Fair ministry exceeded all expectations. One of Moody's greatest evangelistic achievements, the attendance at the meeting was phenomenal, and on one day over 130,000 people attended the various services held around the city. Not only did a vast multitude profess faith in Christ during the campaign, but the unique ministry of the Institute gained considerable renown. Moody was greatly pleased with the work of his chief lieutenant in directing the campaign.

There were also other important events in the year 1893. The Torreys became the proud parents of a baby girl, Margaret, on February 16. Then there were also two other important additions, this time to the Institute family. Dr. James M. Gray, noted Biblical scholar, first became associated with the Institute during this year. Torrey especially admired Gray's valuable synthetic Bible studies, which proved to be most helpful to the students. The music department added the fine musician, Dr. D. B. Towner, who subsequently trained some of the greatest Gospel songleaders in America. He did the most to build up that department in the Institute. The first graduate of the Institute, William Evans, and William R. Newell, a noted Bible teacher, were also subsequently added.

In the same year Torrey wrote concerning the Institute,

"I believe that there are few organizations on earth that will accomplish for the Church of Christ in the coming generation what this Institute will, in the way of winning souls, promoting Bible study, and increasing the spirituality of the Church."[13]

The fulfilment of that prophecy was already much in the making.

[1]Torrey, Jr., interview 1965.

[2]R. A. Torrey, "Prayer and the Ministry of the Word," February 1, 1917, *Moodyanna* collection, (unpublished sermon).

[3]Torrey, Jr., personal letter, April 7, 1965.

[4]Interview with Dr. Ernest Wadsworth, November 22, 1958, *Moodyanna* collection.

[5]William Evans, "Dr. Torrey As I Knew Him," *King's Business,* XXVII (January, 1936), p. 15.

[6]R. A. Torrey, *The Institute Tie,* I (October 30, 1892), p. 177.

[7]John Hunter, "Dr. Torrey As a Teacher," *King's Business,* XXVII (January, 1936), pp. 8,9.

[8]Torrey, Jr., interview.

[9]William Culbertson, "An Appreciation of R. A. Torrey," *Great Pulpit Masters* III, (New York: Revell, 1950), p. 9.

[10]R. A. Torrey, *Real Salvation and Wholehearted Service* (London: James Nisbet, Ltd, 1905), pp. 132-137.

[11]R. A. Torrey, *How to Work for Christ* (Chicago: Revell, 1901), pp. 118-121.

[12]R. A. Torrey, *Why God Used D. L. Moody* (Chicago: The Moody Press, 1923), pp. 24, 25.

[13]R. A. Torrey, "Historical Sketch of the Moody Bible Institute," Moody Bible Institute catalog, 1924-25, (Chicago: The Moody Bible Institute of Chicago, n.d.), p. 4.

11. Blameless Bishop

There were squeals of delight as first Blanche, then Reuben, then Elizabeth came zooming down the long balustrade in the men students' building. Then followed a jolly race down the halls and a game of hide and seek in the dark nooks and crannies. Presently a group of students came into the hall, and a first-class frolic was on. In the middle of the excitement one of the students, thinking of Torrey's sternness in the classroom and puzzling over the youngsters' merriment, asked, "Aren't you afraid of your father?" The children looked at each other knowingly and broke out in fresh peals of giggles. To them, this question, so frequently asked by students, was the greatest joke on record.[1]

Torrey's relationship with each member of his family was one of warmth, love, and enjoyment. They were a very closely knit household and were as happy as any family could be. Each member of the family, although widely differing in personality, was very devoted to both his or her father and mother.

Edith Clare, the eldest, very serious and studious, and, even now in her early teens, was governed by a strong sense of spiritual responsibility. She was less robust than the other children, however—not at all inclined to slide down balustrades—and was often afflicted with poor health. Blanche was entirely different. Because she was pretty and vivacious, full of life and fun, some did not realize the depth of her devotion to the Lord. She had an outgoing personality—the "sunbeam" of the family—and made friends much more easily than Edith.

Reuben was an active young man who idolized his

father. The two were very close and spent many happy
times together on hikes and outings. It was a familiar sight
to see him standing with his father in the foyer at the close
of a church service. Sweet, winsome Elizabeth instantly
attracted others and was very close to Reuben. Baby
Margaret was a pretty child with warm, loving ways, but
more like Edith in her quiet disposition.

Torrey ruled his household with a firm but tender hand.
He took to heart the injunction that "a bishop must then
be blameless. . . one that ruleth well his own house, having
his children in subjection with all gravity" (I Tim. 3:2,4).
In family prayers he often called these verses or Ephesians
6:1—"Children, obey your parents in the Lord, for this is
right"—to their remembrance. In later years Reuben
recalled, "I seem to hear his voice still as we knelt in family
prayers, and he prayed for each one of us by name and
pleaded that we might grow up 'in the nurture and
admonition of the Lord.' "[2]

Family devotions were always held immediately after
breakfast. Torrey, unless absent, always led in the quoting
of a familiar chapter of the Scripture in unison. Sometimes
the chapters varied, but John 14 and Psalm 23 were always
quoted on Saturday and Sunday respectively. These
devotional times, especially their father's prayers for each
one, meant much to the children. He endeavored to instill
within them a true love for the Lord Jesus Christ and the
Word of God.

He also kept a careful watch over the friendships the
children formed, realizing the tremendous influence of bad
companions. It was an unfailing source of merriment to the
children, when they mentioned a new acquaintance among
themselves. One of them always gleefully piped up with the
three questions their father invariably shot at them: "What
is his father's name?" "What is his father's business?"
"What church does he go to?"[3]

Torrey's approach to the government of his children was
simple. He laid down a few *principles* of action but not a lot
of *laws* as to what they should or should not do. He did not

always explain the "why" of these, as he wanted them to learn the principle of authority. He and his wife expected the children to get thoroughly acquainted with them so they would know instinctively what would please them without waiting to be told. There was hardly ever an instance of disobedience, and Reuben recalled only one time that his father ever laid a hand on any of the children. It wasn't necessary. For Torrey to say in sharp tones "Reuben!"—that was enough.

The devoted attitude of the children toward their parents is reflected in an incident involving Blanche. President William McKinley and Commodore Dewey (just after his great victory in Manila) visited Chicago. There was such a surge of people in the city to see them that a religious gathering was planned for the illustrious gentlemen to be present. Any Sunday meeting in those days, even in Chicago, had to be religious, but it was obviously for the real purpose of allowing the people to see the visitors.

Since it was impossible for everyone to attend, the admission was by ticket. Some of these were given to the public school for selected students, and Blanche was offered two but refused them. Her astonished teacher asked, "Did your father forbid you to go?"

"No," she replied, "but I don't think it would please him if I did, so I am not going." [4]

The children gladly accepted the principles which their parents laid down for them. As Reuben in later years recalled,

> We did not resent the fact that theaters, dancing, and the like were denied us, for two reasons. First, the reasons why these were not countenanced were fully explained. . . Second, we realized how continually our parents were endeavoring to meet the youthful craving for pleasurable activity and excitement by making possible good times that were wholesome and normal. What dance could compare with the thrill of meeting Father in Lincoln Park for an afternoon's skate and the jolly tramp home as the old gas lamps began to twinkle?

> Who cared to sit in stuffy theaters when there were art
> galleries and museums to visit with one who appreciated
> them so keenly and knew so much of history and
> science? [5]

Torrey scheduled certain times to be with his children as
their time. On Saturday afternoon it was either hunting,
fishing, swimming, hiking, canoeing, golfing, horseback
riding (remember his expert horsemanship), picnicking, or
tennis in the summer. Ice skating was the favorite in the
winter. Torrey, the life of outings, always swam or skated
the longest, played the hardest, and caught the biggest fish.
The family also enjoyed frequent visits to zoos, museums,
art galleries, and other places of interest.

Whatever his schedule, he scrupulously observed
Monday night as a family time. How delighted the children
were to hear their father tell them stories and play such
then-popular games as Upjenks, Rook, Crockenole, and
Pillow Dex. Picture the exuberant father bounding into the
house, swinging his leg over a chair, saying, "I feel like
jumping over the house!" (and with a little persuasion he
might have tried it). Then with boyish enthusiasm he
struck a boxing pose, and chased a wary, back-peddling
Reuben all around the living room.

At times his exuberance seemed to go too far. Torrey had
an exceptionally strong physique, and now and then the
children playfully chided him about it. In one such
repartee, he said, "Well, I can carry the whole family
upstairs!" This provoked expressions of unbelief, but they
knew he would try it. So amid squeals of delight, Torrey
placed his wife and baby Margaret on one arm and Edith
holding Elizabeth on the other. Then with Blanche and
Reuben clinging to his back and neck, he carried them up
the stairs, which had a crook in it, without a hitch and
deposited them safely. [6]

The children also tried to trap him in another of his
remarkable characteristics—a marvelously retentive
memory. With his "flypaper" mind he had an almost
uncanny ability, with the rarest of exceptions, to remember

what chapter of the Bible any verse appeared. Usually he could tell the exact verse number of the quotation. During his evenings at home the children made a real game of it and tried time and again to catch him in the hardest and most obscure passages. Each time they failed.

Another of the special times for the family was Christmas. Torrey had the self-appointed task of buying the nuts, candy, and fruit for the stockings, as well as trimming the Christmas tree. Imagine the dignified Torrey tip-toeing down the stairs in the dark of early Christmas morning to light the candles on the tree while eager eyes peered from the staircase. When the children opened their presents, Torrey stood smiling at the gleeful company—but with wet sponge in hand to prevent a possible fire. [7]

Torrey planned the summer vacations, usually in the month of August, with a complete change of scenery in view. He sought also to provide important new Christian friendships for the children. The summers at the Northfield Bible Conference especially provided a wholesome Christian atmosphere which greatly affected the children. During these summers with his family, as Edith later recalled,

> My father made it a point to enjoy the things we enjoyed. We used to have a number of picnics. Father went on these picnics with us, and always appeared to enjoy them to the full. It wasn't until I grew up that I learned how he really detested picnics. [8]

Torrey's devotedness to his children was great, but it did not compare to the deep attachment which he had for his wife Clara. Although some thought Torrey to be not particularly affectionate, his intimates could not help but notice the tender love and consideration which he showed to her. Whenever possible, she always went with him on his journeys. When he was away from her, the daily letter was a must no matter how pressing the duties. A birthday or wedding anniversary was never forgotten. Word came no matter how far he was away from home. Torrey delighted to catch trains from an engagement at unseasonable hours, or to otherwise change his schedule, so as to arrive earlier than expected and surprise his beloved. Many a time he minutely studied train schedules just before a trip so as to have some reason to be with his wife a little longer.

Clara was deeply devoted to her husband, but was modest, self-effacing, and kept out of sight most of the time. She was active in Christian work, however, participating in the ladies' group of the Chicago Avenue Church, teaching a Sunday school class, and helping the poor. Ordinarily she was in the best of health, but did develop hearing trouble while in Chicago. This was some distress to her husband, but her eventual use of a hearing aid greatly alleviated the problem. She was an excellent household manager and a firm but kindly disciplinarian with the children, who gave her their complete love and confidence.

Perhaps the strongest impression Torrey made on his family was his unfailing spiritual optimism even under the most trying circumstances. Whenever troubles or problems arose, Torrey smiled and said, "Well, that's one of the 'all things' "—referring to Romans 8:28. That reaction became a never-to-be-forgotten family tradition. Speaking of his father's greatest personal characteristic, in later years his son, Reuben, said without hesitation, "It was that radiance. . . a radiant optimism." [9]

The radiant testimony of his family was in part responsible for one of Torrey's most victorious soul-winning experiences, that of his eldest brother Albert. He had tried to reach him ever since his conversion at Yale. In fact, he had spent a whole night in prayer for him and wrote him urging an acceptance of Christ. A letter came almost by return mail ridiculing Torrey for his efforts. Though disheartened, he had continued to pray for Albert for over fifteen years—even though every effort to reach him gained only even more antagonistic rebuffs. The first winter Torrey was in Chicago, however, the Lord seemed to say, "You need not pray any longer; I have heard your prayer. Now just wait and watch." So Torrey watched.

A number of years later Albert, who was now living in

Chicago, accepted an invitation to dinner at the Torrey home. While there he came down with a severe case of rheumatism and was compelled to stay for two whole weeks. Torrey did not speak to him directly about his soul, but the Christian atmosphere greatly impressed him. The children spoke so fluently and naturally of spiritual things and of their love for Christ. The day Albert left, Torrey walked with him to the Institute office, his guest intending to go on to his own home. But soon after leaving the house, his brother said, "Archie, I am thinking of going into temperance work [he had had grave problems with drink]. How do you begin?"

"The only way that I know to begin temperance work is by first of all becoming a Christian."

"Why," he replied, "I always supposed I was a Christian."

"You have the strangest way of showing it of any person I've ever known in my life."

"Well, how *do* you become a Christian?"

Taking him to one of the Institute offices, Torrey explained the way of life, and the man gladly received it. He became a very earnest Christian, attended the Institute for a short time, and within a year was preaching as a layman in a Presbyterian church some forty miles from Chicago. It was only a short time later, however, that Torrey received a telegram with the terse message, "Your brother, Albert, passed away at two o'clock this morning." [10]

How glad Torrey was that he had continued to pray for his brother for over fifteen years.

[1]Torrey, Jr., "Home," p. 68.

[2]Ibid., p. 67.

[3]Ibid., p. 68.

[4]Torrey, *Power*, pp. 108-110.

[5]Torrey, Jr., p. 68.

[6]Torrey, Jr., interview, 1965.

[7]Ibid.

[8]Harold Paul, "Student Gets Glimpse Into Life of R. A. Torrey," *Wheaton Record* (November 4, 1948). Based on an interview with Edith Clare Torrey.

[9]Torrey, Jr., interview. Edith noted in later years, "If I were not a Christian, the very consistency of my father's life would force me to become a believer. The testimony of friends of ours who were not spiritually in sympathy with father's work was that they could not observe one inconsistency in his life." Paul, "Student."

[10]Torrey, *Power*, pp. 38-41.

12. Chicago Avenue Church

"But, Mr. Moody, I have more work than I can do now."

But Moody was adamant. He was elated at the church's desire to call him and determined that he should be the pastor. "That is what I have been wanting all the time. If you will only accept the call, I will give you all the help that you ask for, and provide men to help you in the Institute." Upon these conditions Torrey relented and became the pastor of the Chicago Avenue Church.[1]

The circumstances of his call, however, were peculiar. The church had been founded by Moody in 1864, but his many ministries and frequent absences gave few opportunities for preaching and doing pastoral work. In the past the church had outstanding pastors—Dr. W. J. Eerdman, Rev. George C. Needham, and Rev. Charles A. Blanchard (later President of Wheaton College), to name a few. Upon the most recent resignation of Rev. W. F. Goss, the church voted, at the advice of both Moody and Torrey, to call the celebrated Rev. George H. C. MacGregor, a very gifted man from Aberdeen, Scotland. Moody had first met MacGregor in England and was delighted with his ministry later at Northfield.

In the interim, Torrey supplied the pulpit, and such great blessing attended his preaching that quite a number of people began to pray that the Scottish preacher would not accept the call! As it turned out, MacGregor did not accept, and the church issued an immediate call to Torrey.

Torrey embarked upon his new charge with enthusiasm and diligence. Within six months, however, the strain of the twin responsibilities of church and Institute began to show. Moody wrote to his valued lieutenant, "Fitt thinks you are overworked. I hope not and if you feel worn, why not hand over all the work you can to others. We do not want you to break down just now. . . .You should keep strong so you can lead the hosts on to victory." [2]

When he accepted the pastorate, the church building would seat 2,200 people—1,200 on the main floor and 1,000 in the gallery. In the preceding years the gallery had been opened only on special occasions or when Mr. Moody was there. Almost immediately it became necessary to open the gallery; and in the evening service, with every inch of standing room taken, as many as 2,700 packed into the building. Overflow meetings in the rooms below the auditorium became necessary, and occasionally additional services were held in the Institute lecture rooms. [3]

Even more important, there were large numbers of conversions. The great majority of the converts did not unite with the church because they were visitors or frequent attenders at other churches. Some churches sent their people over to Chicago Avenue to be converted, then subsequently added them to their own church! He was leading "the hosts on to victory."

What was the reason for the phenomenal success of his ministry there? Torrey's simple answer was 'Prayer.' In his first message as pastor of the church he remarked, "How glad your new pastor would be if he knew that some of you men and women of God sat up late Saturday night, or rose early Sunday morning, to pray for your new pastor."[4] Many took the challenge and began to pray earnestly for their new leader.

There was another reason for the success of the work—his systematic and thorough training of the people in personal soul winning, just as he had done previously in Garrettsville and Minneapolis. Not only did he believe that a trained membership in personal work would bring revival to any church, he felt that "one of the most dangerous heresies is the one-man ministry—when the preacher does it all."[5] He often stated, "I do not depend on my preaching to save the lost." Systematically, Torrey put these principles into action.

He partitioned his church into sections with a superintendent and several workers in each section. The arrangement was such that any visitor who came into the church—and there were many—was only a short distance from a personal worker. If a visitor left, a personal worker followed him and spoke to him either in the foyer or outside the church. Every visitor was spoken to about his soul, and if not a Christian, invited to the inquiry meeting after the regular service. Torrey was also fond of his "fishing deacons," who combed the streets and public places on Sunday afternoons for likely prospects. Many an unlikely person was converted to Christ through this channel.

One should not conclude, however, that Torrey's Spirit-anointed preaching was not responsible for many a conversion. One of the most striking instances of this was the night a flashily-dressed man with a diamond on his shirt visited the services. As Torrey preached, the man listened with intense earnestness, edging forward to the front of his seat and fastening his eyes on the preacher. In the midst of the sermon, Torrey, intending to forcefully drive a point home, said in rhetorical fashion, "Who will take Jesus Christ right now?" The words had scarcely left his lips when the man sprang to his feet, and his voice echoed like a pistol shot through the church, "I will." Torrey stopped then and there and gave the invitation. He remarked later, "I was not there to save sermons but to save souls." [6]

One of the most remarkable sermons Torrey ever preached at the church came about as he was indelibly impressed with the text, "He shall baptize you with the Holy Ghost and with fire." For days the text haunted him. He took the matter to prayer. "Father, I am not to preach on Sunday morning; and that is a morning text"—he preached to Christians in the morning and to the unconverted in the evening. "I want an evening text."

But he could see nothing but "He shall baptize you with

the Holy Ghost and with fire." Finally he said, "Well, Father, if that is the text You want me to preach on, morning or evening, I will preach on it, but I want to know." Just then there came looming up out of the Bible two other texts, and both of them had the word "fire" in them. While he was on his knees, he had the three texts for his sermon. When he preached Sunday night and gave the invitation, the inquiry rooms were jammed. Many responded to his invitation to receive the fullness of the Spirit; others were unsaved seeking Christ.[7]

The church sought to reach all classes, as the sign above the door indicated, "Ever welcome to this house of God are strangers and the poor." The membership was a curious blend of the rich and the poor, the ignorant and the intelligent. It was one of the most cosmopolitan churches imaginable. On the board were a number of former drunkards and outcasts who were now living exemplary lives.

Partially because of the large number of poor, the church had not been entirely self-supporting. Also, in the past, the people had depended largely upon Moody's generous gifts from his evangelistic campaigns. There were no pledges of any kind, and a number of people seemed to think they were doing the church a service by coming. Now Torrey was never one to exert pressure about giving, but he felt for the people's sake they should learn to give. So he taught the people in systematic giving. He confessed that it was a long and trying process, but soon afterwards the church was paying all of its expenses and also helping considerably in both foreign and home mission enterprises.[8]

Amid the successes of the church there was also occasional criticism. But Torrey was unmoved by personal criticism. One of his parishioners, Edith Norton, has recalled his reading from the desk of the church one Sunday morning, with a singular lack of vanity, a request that he refrain from repreaching so often his old sermons. The note was caustically put, but Dr. Torrey read it all placidly and unconcernedly, and went right on with his repetitions.[9]

Torrey had an excellent relationship with the people and also the church board, which was composed of a number of men "once drunkards, outcasts, and thoroughly reprobate," who are now living "most exemplary lives." Speaking of the regular Friday night meetings of the church board, he related, "I have told some of the brethren what I thought of their opinions," but they have been "perfect love feasts." He regarded the church as the most united he had ever known.[10]

Not long after accepting the pastorate of the church Torrey selected William S. Jacoby, an Institute student in his forties, as his assistant. Jacoby, who had just entered the Institute in late spring, replied, "Oh, I can't do that. I am a poor stick."

Torrey retorted, "Yes, you can. Caleb was a poor stick, but God used him. You come and try." At Torrey's further urging, Jacoby accepted the position.[11]

Now it was certainly true that Jacoby had been a "poor stick." He had left home at ten and started drinking. He lived the rough life of a sailor for three years and then joined the army to fight wild Indians. Subsequently he was dishonorably discharged from the army and because of his violent acts was outlawed by the Iowa town of his birth. He became a gambler and boxing promoter and was exceptionally desperate when drinking. Eventually, however, Jacoby was converted and came to the Institute for training. He became one of the best loved men in Chicago and an invaluable help to Torrey.

He even filled in for Torrey in entertaining his children when the latter could not spend Saturday afternoon with them. Many pleasant hours were spent with this jolly and genial "uncle," who was very devoted to the children. They knew his ring when he arrived at the Torrey home with a handful of oranges. He rolled them across the floor, and this provoked a gleeful free-for-all.

In fact, it was one of these afternoon visits which changed the course of his life. He had begun his Saturday visits before he became Torrey's associate. One day he

became very discouraged and had decided to leave the
Institute when he paid what was to be his last visit to the
Torrey home. But as soon as he entered the door, Baby
Margaret climbed up into his arms, clung to his neck, and
said, "Coby, I luv oo." It melted his heart. He finished the
Institute course and became Torrey's assistant.[12]

   Torrey also had other capable helpers in the church.
Towner was his choirmaster, and for a time a talented
young Institute student, Charles M. Alexander, directed
the children's music. A. F. Gaylord, business manager of
the Institute, was his capable and energetic Sunday school
superintendent. Dr. James Gray frequently spoke in
Torrey's absences. Both Torrey and Gray were signally
successful in their talks with the children, who loved to
hear them speak.

   Meanwhile there was still the responsibility of the
Institute work, and Moody continually prodded Torrey
into new endeavors. He wrote in late 1894, concerning the
start of further classes, "It does seem as if we should push
ahead and advance all along the line. If we stand still, we
will go under. We must push on to new fields in 1895."[13]
And so Torrey continued to push.

---

[1] Torrey, *Power*, p. 47. The church had its beginning in the Sunday
School work of Moody, but in 1864 was organized as the Illinois Street
Independent Church. This structure was destroyed in the Chicago fire of
1871, and the North Side Tabernacle was erected in its place—the first
public structure erected for religious and educational purposes after the
tragedy. The Chicago Avenue Church was erected in 1876, and was the
forerunner of what is now the Moody Memorial Church.

[2] Letter from D. L. Moody to R. A. Torrey, October 8, 1894.

[3] Torrey, *Power*, pp. 48, 49.

[4] Ibid., pp. 47, 48.

[5] *Nashville Banner*, October 29, 1906.

[6] Torrey, *Holy Spirit*, p. 48.

[7] *The Southern Cross*, (September 10, 1902), pp. 74, 75.

[8] Letter to Lyman Stewart, March 29, 1915.

[9] Edith Norton, "Reminiscences of Dr. Torrey," *King's Business*,
XXVII (January, 1936), p. 12.

[10] A. P. Fitt (ed), *Moody Church Herald*, I (January, 1902), p. 5.

[11]Torrey, Jr., interview 1965.
[12]Ibid.
[13]Letter from D. L. Moody to R. A. Torrey, December 22, 1894.

13. Northfield

Torrey had received an invitation to preach at the large, influential Fifth Avenue Presbyterian Church in New York City. But just before he started for New York, Moody drove up to Torrey's home in his carriage and said, "Torrey, I just want to ask one thing of you. I want to tell you what to preach about. You will preach that sermon of yours on 'Ten Reasons Why I Believe the Bible to Be the Word of God' and your sermon on 'The Baptism With the Holy Ghost.' "

Time and again Moody would tell him, when about to be off on a preaching engagement, "Now, Torrey, be sure and preach on the baptism with the Holy Ghost." Once Torrey asked him, "Mr. Moody, don't you think I have any sermons but those two?"

"Never mind that, you give them those two sermons." And as usual, at the word of Moody, Torrey did as he was told! Moody was the only person who ever dared tell Torrey what to preach. [1]

It was Moody who kept "pushing" Torrey into new ministries,[2] and one of the most significant of these was the Northfield Bible Conference, Northfield, Massachusetts. Northfield, the birthplace of Moody, was a quaint little New England town with stately elms forming beautiful overhanging boughs over the long main street. The countryside, with the Connecticut River winding like a silver band through the green meadows and rolling hills, was one of the most scenic and restful spots to Moody.

Moody felt it was a splendid place for a Bible and spiritual-life conference, so in 1879 he had established the Northfield Conference Grounds. It had become by this time

the most outstanding in the world. He brought some of the
finest spiritual leaders there—A. J. Gordon, George H. C.
MacGregor, Major D. W. Whittle, A. T. Pierson, Andrew
Bonar, Andrew Murray, F. B. Meyer and G. Campbell
Morgan, to name a few.

Torrey instantly became one of the most popular
lecturers. His messages centered upon the Word of God, the
second coming of Christ, prayer and the Holy Spirit. This
latter topic, especially his stress on the importance and
necessity of the baptism with the Spirit, became a hallmark
of his preaching. It was in this area that he had perhaps his
greatest impact in his Bible conference and church
ministries.

Torrey taught that it was the right and privilege of every
believer to be baptized with the Holy Spirit. He often said
in this connection,

> "I aim to be just as dogmatic as this Book. I do not
> think that I have attained to that as yet, but that is my
> aim, and if this Book says in the most positive and
> dogmatic terms that if you do certain things you shall be
> baptized with the Holy Spirit, I do not hesitate to affirm
> without the slightest fear that my affirmation will prove
> untrue, that anyone who does these certain things, who
> takes these certain steps, will be immediately 'baptized
> with the Holy Spirit.' "[3]

The "certain steps" he outlined were seven—acceptance
of Christ as personal Saviour, repentance of sin, open
confession of faith in Christ, full surrender to Christ, an
earnest desire for the baptism, prayer for it, and acceptance
of it by faith. These steps he based squarely on Acts 2:38,
Acts 5:32, John 7:37-39, Luke 11:13, and Mark 11:24.[4] As a
result of his preaching and counseling on this subject, the
lives and ministries of a multitude of ministers, students,
and laymen were completely transformed.

There were those, however, who winced at Torrey's
terminology, believing that the baptism with the Spirit was
either confined to the apostolic age or that it referred to an
incorporation of the believer into the body of Christ. A
number of Moody's close associates and teachers at

Northfield held to this latter position. Moody called them
together at his home after one of the conference sessions
one night and asked Torrey "to talk this thing out with
them." The talk lasted for hours and the discussion was
amicable, but there was no appreciable change of viewpoint
on their part.

Moody requested Torrey to linger for awhile, and after
some serious reflective thought, said,

> "Oh, why will they split hairs? Why don't they see that
> this is just the one thing that they themselves need? They
> are good teachers, they are wonderful teachers, and I am
> so glad to have them here; but why will they not see that
> the baptism with the Holy Ghost is just the one touch
> that they themselves need?" [5]

The crux of the matter was not simply a question of
terminology. It involved the important question as to
whether a believer had the right to pray for and expect a
special enduement of power of the Holy Spirit. While firm
in his conviction about proper Bible terminology, Torrey
said subsequently, "I do not care how you phrase it. You
may call it 'the filling with the Spirit,' the baptism with the
Spirit, the enduement of power or what you please. I would
rather have the right thing with the wrong name than the
wrong thing with the right name any day." [6] He was
adamant, however, about a personal appropriation of the
Holy Spirit for power.

Another strong emphasis in Torrey's preaching was the
second coming of Christ. Although he had settled the broad
view of the Scripture teaching on this topic, still when he
first arrived in Chicago he sometimes wished that the Book
of Revelation were not in the Bible! But over the years his
convictions deepened, and his lectures on the Second
Coming were very eagerly received.

One day at Northfield, as he was speaking on this topic, a
most startling incident took place. The audience was
spellbound as Torrey pictured the glorious return of the
Lord. Then just as he was speaking of the sound of the
trumpet and the heavenly angelic shout, one of those
sudden, violent thunderstorms, unnoticed by the audience,

swept down the Connecticut Valley over Northfield. With a terrific crash and blinding flash, lightning struck one of the towers of the building and streaked down the lightning rod.

The effect was electrifying. People sprang to their feet and some shrieked. But Torrey said sternly, "Oh, sit down. There is nothing to be afraid of. This is nothing to what it will be when the Lord Jesus actually comes again." One of Moody's daughters came up and said afterwards, "Oh, Mr. Torrey, I thought the Lord had really come and I was so disappointed that it was not so."[7]

Encouraged by Moody, Torrey built a summer home at Northfield on a very scenic spot overlooking the grounds. Thus Northfield became to Torrey what it was to Moody—a pleasant and restful change. The summers there were especially enjoyed by the family. One of the highlights of the journey to Northfield each year was the ride by carriage with Moody the last lap of the way. Moody was just like an uncle to the Torrey children, and it was a real event to be with him during the summers there.[8]

Moody took this occasion to counsel and pray with Torrey concerning important matters in Christian work and at the Institute. It was a frequent sight to see the two touring the beautiful Massachusetts countryside in a carriage early in the morning, talking over important spiritual matters. Torrey also permitted himself more time for socializing at the conference—particularly since Moody *insisted* that he and the other speakers come to his house after the evening services for watermelons or ice cream.

Of course, as Torrey's stature increased in the eyes of the Christian public, he began to be in frequent demand as a speaker in YMCA rallies, Christian Worker's conventions, student and missionary conventions, Bible and missionary conferences, evangelistic meetings and as a pulpit supply in prominent churches. It was simply not possible to accept all of the engagements offered to him, yet he maintained a staggering schedule of outside engagements—this despite his rigorous church and Institute responsibilities.

An incident took place at a state YMCA convention in

Pennsylvania which is revealing. Although he was the featured speaker for the occasion, he was accidentally given a small, poorly ventilated room with only a washstand, chair, and bed. When George Mahy, a leader of the convention, visited the room, he was indignant and planned to protest to the management. But Torrey wanted no protest. "If you can get me a small table at which to study, I should be perfectly comfortable."[9] Had he not told his students to endure hardness as a good soldier of Christ?

A much more trying experience took place when he served as a chaplain for several months in the Spanish-American War. He held special services and did personal work among the American troops as they were trained at Chattanooga and Chickamauga. The dry and dusty marches during a prolonged drought, the awful camp conditions and particularly the demoralizing effect of the war made an indelible impression on Torrey.

Torrey's ministry was also widened as his ability as an author emerged in the publication of several important volumes. Most of the material in the volumes had first been given to the students in the lecture room, and all of it had been tested in the crucible of his own spiritual experience. *How to Study the Bible for the Greatest Profit, How to Obtain Fullness of Power,* and *The Baptism With the Holy Spirit* were smaller practical studies for the Christian life.

The most important of all of his works during this period, however, was *What the Bible Teaches*—a rigidly inductive and unique approach to the study of the Bible and its doctrines. It is akin to a systematic theology; however, it is intensely Biblical and deals only with doctrines clearly revealed in the Scripture. Its simplicity and absence of theological jargon is striking. The procedure for each topic is the stating of a category, listing the relevant Scriptures, drawing propositions from them and often commenting on the significance of the propositions.

The following is an example, dealing with the topic of Christ's death.

I. The Importance of Christ's Death

FIRST PROPOSITION: The death of Jesus Christ is mentioned directly more than one hundred and seventy-five times in the New Testament. Besides this there are very many prophetic and typical references to the death of Jesus Christ in the Old Testament.

(2) Heb. 2:14—"Forasmuch then as the children are partakers of flesh and blood, he also himself likewise took part of the same; *that through death* he might destroy him that had the power of death, that is, the devil."

SECOND PROPOSITION: Jesus Christ became a partaker of flesh and blood in order that He might die.

The incarnation was for the purpose of the death. Jesus Christ's death was not a mere incident of His human life, it was the supreme purpose of it. He became man in order that He might die as man and for man. [10]

Ever sensing the need for students to dig out Biblical truth for themselves, he often said to his students that his volume was "What the Bible Teaches *Torrey.*"

The students of the Institute also profited from the ministries of outstanding guest lecturers. Many of the men on the Northfield Conference program also came to the Institute. When G. Campbell Morgan came to deliver a series of messages on Malachi, the students were elated. But in this case Morgan was just as elated with the ministry of the Institute, feeling that it was doing "a splendid work" and giving the students "a capital Bible training." [11]

This rich ministry of Bible training soon began to expand beyond the environs of the school itself. In 1897 an Extension Department was launched in different parts of the city. By 1900 extension Bible classes were held in both St. Louis and Detroit. Moody and Torrey continued to "push on. "

It was during this period in the late '90s that two incidents—one tragic and the other unfortunate—took place. The loss of little nine-year-old Elizabeth on March 16, 1898, was one of the greatest trials the Torrey family was ever to undergo. [12]

One Saturday afternoon when the children returned

from a visit to Lincoln Park, Elizabeth was not feeling well and went directly to bed. Although it did not seem serious, her sick feeling persisted until Tuesday, when it was discovered that she had diphtheria. The family physician was sent for at once, but he did not deem it a serious case and did not administer any antitoxin. Her progress was so rapid that Torrey had written letters to Moody and other concerned friends that the crisis was past.

But just as the Torreys were talking together about her remarkable progress, the nurse who was caring for her rushed to the top of the stairs and called, "Come up quick!" Rushing upstairs, they found Elizabeth with eyes closed and breathing very rapidly. It was obvious the little heart was giving out. Torrey quickly dropped to his knees to pray, but before he had time to begin, the little soul had taken its flight Homeward. It was so sudden and unexpected that it was almost crushing.

The funeral was sad. The nature of the disease prevented her brothers and sisters from attending the funeral or even seeing the body again. No one attended except the parents and Jacoby, who insisted on coming. It was very stormy, and the rain pitilessly poured on the little casket. It was almost unbearable. A tearful Clara turned to her husband, "Archie, I am so glad that Elizabeth is not in that box."

The Torreys were obliged to spend the night in a strange motel while the house was fumigated. It was so lonely, and the night was an unceasing flash of lightning and crash of thunder. Exhausted from sorrow and lack of sleep, Torrey left for the Institute the next morning. But before reaching there, he broke down on the street under the burden of grief and cried, "Oh, Elizabeth! Elizabeth!" Just then he had a remarkable experience. The Holy Spirit which he had within "broke forth with such power as I think I had never experienced before, and it was the most joyful moment that I had ever known in my life."[13]

Torrey's grief over Elizabeth's death was exceptionally painful. This was due not only to his great love for her, but also to the fact that he partly blamed himself for her death.

Despite the unusual circumstances in her case and her apparent recovery, he later felt that he should have insisted on the doctor's administering an antitoxin. His experience with the Holy Spirit's comfort, however, seemed to be God's way of telling him that it was one of the "all things."

Some of the greatest words of comfort came in a telegram from Moody, who said only, "Elizabeth's prayer is answered." The brief comment referred to a remark by one of the Northfield conference speakers the previous summer. The speaker had mentioned something to the effect that a beautiful character made a beautiful face. The thought had captivated Elizabeth and when she returned home, she prayed, "O God, send Margaret as a foreign missionary, and make me very beautiful."[14]

The other incident mentioned earlier took place shortly before Moody died, and was to have an important bearing on Torrey's future ministry at Northfield. Partly at the suggestion of Torrey, who had read one of his Yale addresses on "Secret Prayer," Moody invited Dr. George Adam Smith of Scotland to Northfield. In the meantime, however, some other things came to the surface about the Yale lectures which caused Moody apprehension. Nevertheless, he did not feel he should withdraw the invitation. But Moody did ask Torrey to meet with him and Smith privately to discuss the matter. Dr. S. Parkes Cadman, a prominent Congregational clergyman, was also present.

The point at issue was Smith's espousal of certain higher critical views. Moody broached the subject generally with Smith, but Torrey questioned him pointedly.

"Professor Smith, you teach that the 110th Psalm is not Messianic, and that it was not written by David; that it refers to a brother of Jonathan Maccabeus, and is not by David at all, but by some unknown man of that period. If that be true, one of two things must also be true—it is certain, either that Jesus Christ knew it was not by David, and did not refer to Himself, in which case, in building an argument for His divinity upon it, He deliberately pulled the wool over the eyes of those to whom He spoke, or else He did not know it, in which case He built an argument for His Divinity upon a mistake. In either case what are you going to do with the Divinity of Christ?"

Smith replied, "I do not build my faith in His Divinity on the 110th Psalm."

"Neither do I," answered Torrey, "but having found out that He is Divine, I must maintain that He knows what He is talking about when He built an argument for His Divinity on the 110th Psalm."[15]

To this Smith gave no reply.

Commenting on the incident later, Torrey said, "Mr. Moody backed me in every statement I made and every position that I took, and he told me afterwards that he had told Professor Smith that he was doing the Devil's work. He also told me that he regretted that he had ever invited either of these men (Smith and Cadman) to Northfield."[16]

The conversation was carried on in a dignified, courteous manner with no display of anger. Smith and Torrey both acted like gentlemen and had no feelings of animosity toward each other. Unfortunately, Will Moody took a different view of the situation. He sympathized more with Smith and regarded Torrey's questioning as discourteous and belligerent. The incident was to have repercussions for years afterward.[17]

Another event, however, was just looming on the horizon which was to have profound affect upon the entire Christian world.

[1]Torrey, *Moody*, pp. 57-59.

[2]Gene Getz, *MBI, The Story of Moody Bible Institute* (Chicago: Moody Press, 1969), p. 122. The program did not begin, however, until some years later. The first lessons were Torrey's "Bible Doctrines" and "Practical Christian Work."

[3]Torrey, *Holy Spirit*, p. 156.

[4]Ibid., p. 156 ff.

[5]Torrey, *Moody*, pp. 59,60.

[6]*The Southern Cross*, (September, 1902), p. 75.

[7]R. A. Torrey, *Christ of the Bible*, (New York: George H. Doran, 1925), pp. 228,229.

[8]Torrey, Jr., interview.

[9]"Testimonials to Dr. R. A. Torrey," *Moody Monthly*, XXIX (December, 1928), p. 172.

[10]R. A. Torrey, *What the Bible Teaches* (New York: Revell, 1898), p. 144.

[11]Jill Morgan, *Man of the Word* (New York: Revell, 1951), p. 98.

[12]Even though in his seventies tears came to the eyes of Reuben A. Torrey, Jr., as he related this tragedy. He was very close to Elizabeth, and the two were sometimes mistaken for twins. Torrey, Jr., interview.

[13]Torrey, *Holy Spirit,* pp. 93-95. Torrey felt especially grieved about Elizabeth's death because he thought perhaps he had placed too much confidence in a physician as King Asa had done. Torrey, Jr., interview.

[14]MacClean, p. 36.

[15]*The Southern Cross*, (September 10, 1902), p. 77.

[16]R. A. Torrey, "Mr. Paul D. Moody's Gross Calumny of His Honored Father, D. L. Moody," *Moody Monthly*, XXIV (October, 1923), p. 51.

[17]Unfortunately Will Moody took a dim view of Torrey's questioning of Smith and related in his father's biography: "Awful! Awful! They often put us to shame by their more Christian attitude." Will Moody, *D. L. Moody* (New York: MacMillan, 1930), pp. 447,448. Fleming Revell, son-in-law to Moody, has reflected an entirely different conception of the interview: "Moody and Mr. Torrey spent an entire evening as well as into the wee small hours of the night, in a very clear and positive discussion, in which there was anything but an endorsement of Mr. Smith's views." Torrey, "Paul Moody," p. 174. The incident was to affect Torrey's future connection with Northfield after D. L. Moody's death. Further, Cadman became one of the most strenuous opponents of the later Torrey campaigns in America.

PART IV

Opening of a Great Door and Effectual
(1902-1905)

14. Moody's Monument

"Moody is Dead!"

In newspapers all across America this headline shocked the Christian world. On December 22, 1899, the commoner of Northfield passed on to his eternal reward.

The evangelist had begun a series of meetings in Kansas City, Missouri, on November 12. They had been planned on a vast scale, and the opening crowds were overwhelming. Within just a few days, however, the evangelist had shown signs of exhaustion and apparent illness. Relunctantly Moody was persuaded to return to Northfield—the first time in forty years of ministry that he had to withdraw from a meeting. He summoned Torrey to finish the campaign.

Moody lingered for over a month, then just before Christmas he breathed his last. His two main regrets in departing were the leaving of his family and the glorious ministry to which God had called him. He felt that a great revival was coming soon, and he wanted to have a hand in it. Funeral services were held the day after Christmas, and memorial services observed in many parts of the country.

Several well-known Christian leaders spoke at the funeral; however, Torrey's remarks seemed to be the most fitting. He took two texts. The first was I Corinthians 15:10, "By the grace of God I am what I am." He developed the thought of God's grace exhibited in Moody's birth, conversion, character and death. His second text was Joshua 1:2, "Moses my servant is dead; now therefore arise, go over this Jordan, thou, and all this people, unto the land which I do give to them, even to the children of Israel."

A prophetic ring characterized his words.

> The death of Mr. Moody is a call to go forward—a call
> to his children, to his associates, to ministers of the Word
> everywhere, to the whole church. "Our leader has fallen;
> let us give up the work," some would say. Not for a
> minute! Listen to what God says, "Your leader is fallen;
> move forward. 'Moses my servant is dead; therefore arise,
> go in, and possess the land. Be strong and of a good
> courage, be not afraid.' As I was with Moody, so I will be
> with thee. I will not fail thee nor forsake thee!" . . .His
> death, with the triumphal scenes that surround it, are
> part of God's way of answering the prayers that have
> been going on for so long in our land for a revival.[1]

Torrey had no intention of slackening the pace; he was
planning to "move forward." There was a good deal of
gloom at the Institute, but Torrey made it clear that
"though Mr. Moody was the president and leading spirit of
the Bible Institute, our work will go on just the same."
There was only one significant change. At the next meeting
of the trustees they voted to change the name of the school
to "The Moody Bible Institute of Chicago." Unofficially it
was already so known, but Moody would not permit a
change of name "as long as I am alive."[2]

Moody had often said, "The only monument I want after
I am dead and gone is a monument with two legs going
about the world—a saved sinner telling about the salvation
of Jesus Christ."[3] There were many at the funeral who
sadly thought, "Who shall take his place?" And the only
answer which came to their minds was "no one." Yet
standing in their very midst was one who was to become
Moody's monument in evangelism.

Within two years of Moody's death two events of
significance transpired on the evangelistic scene. The first
was the publication of one of the most monumental and
comprehensive works ever done on evangelistic
methods—Torrey's *How to Work for Christ*. The material
had first been given in lecture form to the students and had
appeared in earlier issues of the *Institute Tie*. Its special
stress was on personal witnessing although it had extensive
material covering all types of Christian work. It also
included valuable helps on preaching and teaching.

In the preface Torrey announced, "The Church of Christ is full of people who wish to work for their Master but do not know how. This book is intended to tell them how. It contains no untried theories, but describes many methods of work that have been put to the test of actual experiment and have succeeded."[4] The book had a wide impact and led many into their first experience of winning others to Christ. One of the most notable was A. P. Fitt, the son-in-law of Moody, to whom he had entrusted the Institute upon his death.

The second occurrence took place within a month of Moody's death. It was at the close of the January week of prayer that Miss Strong, superintendent of women at the Institute, asked Torrey, "Why not keep up these prayer meetings at least once a week and pray for a world-wide revival?" The suggestion commended itself to Torrey and the Institute faculty, and a time for prayer was appointed for each Saturday night from 9:00-10:00, just after Torrey's popular Bible class.

The attendance at the prayer meetings soon grew to as many as four hundred. After the regular meeting was over, Torrey and a few close associates retired to his study to pray until early morning for a world-wide revival. Seldom did these smaller meetings conclude before 2:00 Sunday morning.

Many came to Torrey after the prayer meetings had been in progress for some time and asked, "Has the revival come?"

"No, not as far as we know."

"When is it coming?"

"I do not know."

"How long are you going to keep praying?"

"Until it comes."[5]

There had been some signs of revival stirring in several lands, particularly Japan, but the moving was not as extensive as the prayer band expected it to be. In November, however, signs of a significant revival began to appear in Torrey's own Chicago Avenue Church, and a concerted evangelistic effort to reach the North side of Chicago got underway. Said Torrey, "I have been expecting a great revival to break out throughout the country, but had no thought it was to have its beginnings in the church of which I am pastor."[6] Still, a greater movement was expected.

The prayer meetings had continued for about a year when at one of the smaller gatherings after the regular meeting Torrey was led to utter spontaneously the strangest and most remarkable prayer of his life. "I was led to ask God that He would send me around the world preaching the Gospel, and give me to see thousands saved in China, Japan, Australia, New Zealand, Tasmania, India, England, Scotland, Ireland, Germany, France and Switzerland."[7]

The prayer was stunning in its effect. Both Torrey and his associates thought, "How could he leave such a large church with its growing membership and large responsibilities? How could he leave the Institute, particularly with the added burdens he had assumed upon the death of Moody?" The "how?" was in question, but from that day forward Torrey knew that he was to be an instrument of a mighty world-wide revival.

Shortly afterward two strangers, a Mr. Warren and Mr. Barber, who were from Australia, visited Torrey's services at the church and his lecture sessions at the Institute. After a few days the gentlemen asked for an appointment. They explained that they had been sent to Great Britain, Canada and the United States to find a suitable evangelist for a campaign in Melbourne, Australia. They had decided that he was the man and asked, "Will you come to Australia?"

Torrey, although sensing the Lord's leading much as Peter must have to the messengers of Cornelius, said, "I do not see how I can possibly get away from Chicago." But he added, "I shall pray about the matter and leave it to God to decide."

"Well," the undaunted gentlemen replied, "you're

coming. We're going to pray you over!'' In fact, Mr. Barber insisted on meeting Mrs. Torrey, as he fully expected to be entertaining them both in Australia.[8]

A few months later in October, while Torrey was attending a Bible conference in St. Louis, a cable came from Melbourne asking him to reply at once whether he could begin meetings in the spring of the following year. Torrey withdrew from the conference for a time of prayer and, having received clear guidance in the matter, cabled the one-word reply, "Yes." How quickly the mantle fell from Elijah to Elisha!

It also became clear to the Church and Institute that as the Spirit spoke to the church at Antioch, "Separate me. . .Saul," that He was also thus speaking to them. The problems which seemed so large were speedily solved. As to the Institute, some of the adjustments which had been made upon the death of Moody fit in nicely with a leave of absence. Fitt was the capable executive secretary of the board. A. F. Gaylord was a splendid business manager, and Henry P. Crowell, the wealthy Quaker Oats magnate, now a member of the Board of Trustees, lent valuable spiritual and financial assistance to the Institute. Even more significant was the increasing prominence of Dr. Gray, who already shared some of Torrey's large administrative responsibilities.

Torrey challenged the Chicago Avenue Church, which had welcomed over 2,000 into its membership in his eight-year ministry,

> God's unlimited power is at our disposal. We can each of us make the year one of great growth and usefulness or we can make it a year of failure. Which shall it be? . . .The success of our church does not depend so much upon whom God may send to us to preach the Word, as it does upon the fidelity of each individual member of the church.[9]

Fortunately, however, the Church was able to engage the services of the very gifted and dedicated Baptist minister, Dr. A. C. Dixon, to supply for their pastor in his absence. This selection had the hearty endorsement of Torrey, as he regarded Dixon "a bright preacher, a good Bible scholar, thoroughly orthodox and. . .a pusher!"[10]

One of the very first things Torrey did after his decision to go was to send letters—approximately 5,000 of them—to those of his friends whom he knew could effectively pray.

> God has opened the way for me to go around the world, preaching the Gospel and teaching the great fundamental truths of the Bible. . . .I write you in order to ask your prayers for God's blessings upon this missionary journey. Its success, on man's side, depends more upon prayer than anything else. . . .Will you not pray very earnestly each day for God's blessings upon us and the preaching of His Word? Pray that God may get the very largest possible glory to His name from our testimony and teaching.[11]

One of the hardest jobs he ever tackled was the personal signing of all those letters.

On December 23—almost exactly two years after Moody's death—Torrey and his wife left for the evangelistic tour. Blanche, Reuben and Margaret stayed with Torrey's sisters in Brooklyn. Edith, who had enrolled previously in Holyoke College in Massachusetts, resided at the school. How the Torrey's missed the children on Christmas Day! Someone else would have to fill the stockings this year.

But their sense of loneliness was somewhat mitigated when Torrey was asked to conduct a Christmas service for those on the steamer. He was even asked to sing a solo! Writing to Gaylord, he said, "Tell Towner that I do not know what I should have done if I had not taken the music course at the Institute." He further related that many were seasick on the voyage but "I did not have *that* pleasure."[12]

En route Torrey spoke twice in hurried meetings at Honolulu, Hawaii, and then began a twenty-nine-day itinerary in Japan. He visited the cities of Sendai, Yokohama, Tokyo, Nangeya, Kioto, Osaka, Kobi, Yamaguchi, Saga, and Nagasaki. In all, seventy-two meetings were conducted. They were attended with "remarkable results, scores of natives professing conversion in a single meeting." During the two days in Kioto 119 were converted including two Buddhist priests. In Kobi there were eighty-two converts, and at Yamaguchi, ten miles from a railroad, over sixty professed Christ. In Tokyo he preached to over a thousand men who had never attended a Christian meeting, and many professed conversion.

One of the most memorable of the meetings was before a state university gathering. Torrey was advised not to preach but rather to lecture on the necessity of morality in education. Torrey replied, "I have no lecture on that subject and would not deliver it if I had." Rather, he preached on the text, "What Shall I Do Then With Jesus Which Is Called Christ?"

He first stressed the deity of Christ and then presented His atonement for sins. At the conclusion he asked those who were convinced and willing to take Christ to stand. There was a short silence; then one Japanese sprang to his feet and stood like a soldier. Then others arose, and the chaplains were busy after that. The next day a list of 131 names were given as the number who had received Christ. His "advisor" confided to Torrey, "I am going back to preaching the Gospel."[13]

From Japan Torrey traveled to China for thirty-one days. He usually had four services a day—two for English-speaking audiences and two for Chinese. The meetings were held in Shanghai, Hangchow, Soochow, Foochow and Canton. Members of some of the leading families, political and commercial, were converted. This included the daughter of one of the richest men in China. The young lady feared her father would disinherit her; however, he was pleased with her commitment to Christianity—much to the joy of Torrey.

In late March Torrey left China for Australia where he was to meet Charles Alexander, his songleader for the mission.

Alexander, a former student of Torrey at the Institute, was born in a log cabin in the hills of Tennessee. His parents were very poor but God-fearing and strongly

MR. CHARLES M. ALEXANDER

endowed with musical talents. Young Charles gave early signs of his fine singing ability and attended Maryville College to study music. Upon his graduation he was appointed Director of Music in the College.

When his father died, however, Charles gave up his secular work in music and decided to attend the Bible Institute in Chicago. He had an intense yearning to receive special Christian training, particularly in the field of sacred music. He received an excellent Biblical foundation and was given many opportunities for service in singing. These included such diverse activities as leading singing for a summer in the notorious "Hell's Kitchen" in Chicago, directing the singing in the 1800-member Sunday school of the Chicago Avenue Church, and assisting Dr. Francis E. Smiley in evangelistic meetings.

In the autumn of 1894 Alexander had joined Evangelist Milan B. Williams and continued as his songleader for eight years. In this capacity he demonstrated a ready facility for directing revival choirs and leading singing in large campaigns. As an evangelistic team the two were remarkably successful, although both were little known at the start. In 1901 Williams decided to take a trip to Europe and the Holy Land, however, and this left Alexander some time free to make his own arrangements in evangelistic work. Torrey, learning of this, had invited him to go to Australia. He arrived shortly before Torrey in April.[14]

[1]Chapman, pp. 425-429.

[2]De Remer, p. 36.

[3]James M. Gray, Editor's notes, *Moody Monthly,* XXXI, (October, 1930), p. 51.

[4]Torrey, p. 3.

[5]Torrey, *Power,* p. 175.

[6]Chicago Daily News, November 24, 1900.

[7]Torrey, *Power,* p. 94.

[8]Margaret McNaughton, "Giant Among Men," *Moody Monthly,* XLVIII, September, 1947, p. 11.

[9]Letter to Chicago Avenue Church, December, 1901.

[10]Letter to A. P. Fitt, Glasgow, March 4, 1903.

[11]Letter to Miss Della McNeil, Chicago, November 25, 1901.

[12]A. P. Fitt (ed), "News From Mr. and Mrs. Torrey," *Moody Church Herald,* I, (January, 1902), p. 23.

[13]R. A. Torrey, "The Missionary Message," *King's Business,* IX (July, 1918), p. 559.

[14]Mrs. Charles Alexander, *Charles M. Alexander* (London: Marshall Brothers, LTD, 1920), p. 48.

15. "The Man With God A'Back of Him"

I bring you a message from the Book of Books—"My soul, wait thou only upon God, for my expectation is from him." I rejoice in the organization; I rejoice in the amount of prayer that has been ascending for the past seven weeks—but I am not looking to the organization, nor to the fifty missioners, nor to the singers, nor to the four secretaries, nor even to the heroic chairman: I am looking to God. And, friends, God is going to hear. . . . I say it from no confidence of my own, but because I believe I have heard the voice of God, that you and I are to see one of the mightiest movements in the history of the church of Jesus Christ on earth. [1]

Torrey's words were prophetic as he addressed the vast throng of over 2,500 Christians in the Melbourne Town Hall as an introduction to the mission. The meeting was the most significant and memorable of any religious gathering up to that time in the capital city of Victoria. Torrey set the keynote of the mission by encouraging the people to look to God for success. He confessed that one of his hardest tasks was to get the eyes of the people off himself and Alexander.

Melbourne had made extensive preparations for the mission. As early as 1889 the saintly Rev. John McNeill, who died shortly before Torrey arrived, and four other ministers had begun to pray for revival for two hours every Saturday afternoon. Out of these weekly meetings grew the home circle prayer groups started by Mrs. Warren, wife of one of the men who had originally invited Torrey to Australia. She was greatly inspired by the words "pray through" in Torrey's little book, *How to Pray*. Largely through her efforts there were 2,100 home prayer meetings in progress when Torrey arrived in Australia. Over 40,000 attended these meetings two weeks prior to the beginning of the campaign. In addition, every house in the city was visited twice in preparation for the meetings.

The suburbs of the city were divided into fifty mission centers with local pastors and evangelists from every evangelical denomination ministering in these districts. The largest halls available, in addition to thirty tents, were secured for the meetings. The first two weeks of the mission were concentrated in the fifty mission centers, but the last two weeks were held in the Melbourne Town Hall, seating about 3,000 people. It was filled to overflowing each evening and many times in the afternoon sessions for men. Torrey conducted all of the Town Hall meetings.[2]

Torrey was an impressive figure on the platform in both manner and appearance. An observer noted:

> "His erect figure, his broad shoulders, the manly face with its massive brows give an impression of great strength. . . and his face, when seen close at hand, with its bright complexion and clear eyes and a certain radiancy of smile, has still the freshness of youth."[3]

Although Torrey was only forty-six, his prematurely white hair lent him an air of dignity. English audiences, much as those in Australia, were especially struck with his "look of royalty," and many compared him to King Edward VII, son of Victoria.

The most remarkable thing about Torrey, however, was his rare power. This was a puzzle to most. He spoke primarily to the conscience and reason rather than to the emotions, and rarely raised his voice beyond a conversational tone. His sermons were so direct and sharp that many expected the audience to get up and walk out *en masse*, but they stayed—and many were converted. It could only be, as one mission leader commented, "that divine gift—undefinable, but unmistakable—'the power of the Holy Ghost.' A gleam from the fire of Pentecost is in his sermons."[4]

Torrey's appeal to the conscience and reason is typified by some of his remarks in the message, "The Drama of Life in Three Acts." Speaking of the prodigal son, he observed:

> He began to think. That is one of the best things any
> lost man can do. I have heard people say that they were
> not Christians because they thought for themselves. I
> venture to say, for every person who is not a Christian
> because he thinks, I can show you ten who are not
> Christians because they do not think. Ah, how many
> there are in this audience tonight who are not Christians
> because you don't think, because you won't think,
> because you are bound not to think. . . . If I could only
> get some of you here tonight to thinking, I could get you
> saved. [5]

A rather startling feature was Torrey's method of giving
an invitation at the close of his sermon. Some had prepared
themselves for the religion-made-easy methods of a certain
school of evangelism then in vogue. But there was no card-
signing or simple hand-raising for Torrey. His procedure
was simple, definite and businesslike.

He said to an audience of men one night in Hawthorne
Town Hall,

> I would like to ask every man here tonight who is not a
> Christian, and who has no longer any reason that he
> thinks he can give to God at the Judgment for staying
> away from Christ, and who will therefore take Christ
> tonight as his Saviour, to stand up. I have no confidence
> in the conversion that will only allow a man to get his
> hand up as far as his shoulder. If you are really in earnest
> about that soul of yours, for which Christ died, stand up
> before these people tonight. [6]

He was interested only in genuine, clearcut, public
decisions for Christ.

Some of the most popular and effective sermons of
Torrey were: "What Are You Waiting For?" "Heaven:
What Is It Like?" "The Judgment," "Hell, and Who Is
Going There," "Three Fires," "The Greatest Sentence
Ever Written," "Infidelity: Its Causes, Consequences and
Cure," "The Need of a Hiding Place," and "Heroes and
Cowards."

One of the most significant aspects of the entire mission
was the midday address which Torrey gave each weekday
afternoon. His topics included the Bible, prayer, the Holy

Spirit, and infidelity. His message on "Ten Reasons Why I
Believe the Bible to Be the Word of God" was especially
needed, as destructive criticism had begun to wend its way
into Australia.

Moody had said previously,

> Thirty years ago people did not question the gospel.
> They believed that the Lord Jesus Christ, by dying on the
> cross, had done something for them. . . . And my work
> was to bring them to a decision to do what they already
> knew they ought to do. But all is different now. The
> question mark is raised everywhere. There is need for
> teachers who shall begin at the beginning and show the
> people what the gospel is.[7]

Torrey was well aware of the new climate—he had been a
destructive critic himself. Thus his aim was not only
evangelization but also "teaching the great fundamental
truths of the Bible."

But in addition to Torrey's powerful preaching ministry,
there was also the "sunshine brightness" of his associate in
song, Charles Alexander. The vital part Alexander was to
have in the Melbourne meetings was almost missed. Only
through the strong hand of Providence was Alexander
prevented from returning to the States soon after his
arrival. Through a misunderstanding, the committee did
not know that Alexander was coming, so they had engaged
the talented J. J. Virgo for the music. Virgo, in a gesture of
utter selflessness, however, insisted on Alexander's taking
charge. Thus a serious setback was only narrowly averted.

The American songleader's first meeting with the
Melbourne committee was somewhat of a disappointment.
They were very apprehensive of the spectacular in
musicians and plainly told him "no fooling." In fact, the
committee had already instructed the cooperating
churches in the different mission centers that "no choir
should contain more than fifty voices, that nothing should
be sung outside of Sankey's volume, that no choirmaster
armed with the baton should be visible, and that the choirs
should be accommodated, not on the platform, but on the
ground floor."[8]

Alexander made no reply to the cautions of the committee but merely flashed a bright smile and extended his hand across the table to the committee members. His genial manner seemed to conquer their apprehensions.

But the tall, thin Tennessean with flashing black eyes and radiant smile conquered more than that. From the first meeting in the Melbourne Town Hall he instantly won the hearts of the people. In a matter of moments he had the crowd singing hearty peals of praise—even those who couldn't sing. His sway over both the choir and the congregation was phenomenal.

Alexander turned the audience into a vast choir—something no other songleader had ever done. He taught them to sing, and they loved every minute of the scolding, rallying, praising, censuring and encouraging. His personable "Shine up your face," "Folks, wake up there," "Can't you sing. . . then whistle" never failed to elicit a ready response. His songleading and solos prepared the audiences for the message and were responsible for the conversion of not a few.

One interesting feature of the music was the response of the people to "The Glory Song," written by Charles H. Gabriel. It rapidly spread all over Melbourne and proved to be an instrument of conversion to many. The familiar strains could be heard almost everywhere—

> When all my labors and trials are o'er,
> And I am safe on that beautiful shore,
> Just to be near the dear Lord I adore,
> Will through the ages be glory for me.
>
> O that will be glory for me,
> Glory for me, glory for me,
> When by His grace I shall look on His face,
> That will be glory, be glory for me.

The Australian audiences also especially liked "No Not One," "Count Your Blessings," "Trust and Obey," "I Am Happy in Him," "I Surrender All" and "There's Power in the Blood." Alexander's tender singing of "Where Is My

Wandering Boy Tonight?" and "Tell Mother I'll Be There" moved many to decision for Christ.

At the mission's end, everyone was acclaiming the worth of Alexander in the four weeks' campaign. This was true even of the mission committee—despite the fact that he led with a baton on high red dias, directed huge choirs on the platform, and circulated his own little red-backed hymnbook with many non-Sankey hymns! Torrey considered Alexander the best Gospel songleader of the day—in fact, would have brought no one to Australia had he not been available. And everyone was thrilled with the "happy combination of strong speech and sweet song personalized" at the meeting's end.

There was a total of 8,642 converts recorded in the Melbourne mission. A gigantic rally of those converts—no one else was admitted—was held in the Town Hall at the close of the mission. Torrey spoke to them on seven essential steps to the living of a successful Christian life—a message which became the pattern for the close of all his campaigns:

> 1. Be sure that you build all of your life and service on Jesus Christ.
> 2. Maintain open and constant confession of Christ before the world.
> 3. Put away every sin out of your life.
> 4. Surrender absolutely to God.
> 5. Read the Word of God and study it every day of your life.
> 6. Pray often.
> 7. Go to work for Christ. [9]

The meetings also had a tremendous effect on the community. Many an unscrupulous businessman mended his ways, and a local law-enforcement officer said that if the meetings continued, the jails would have to close their doors. There was very little to do during the meetings except govern the huge crowds attending.

When Torrey was questioned, "Has the Melbourne Simultaneous Mission been on as large a scale and as fruitful in results as you anticipated?" he replied, "Yes, it has, so far as it has gone. . . . Though I like to see immediate conversions in an evangelistic mission—and we have seen them in this movement—I look, rather, for a great arousing of the Churches, so that the revival may not be stopped as soon as the evangelists have departed." [10]

The marvelous results in Melbourne brought numerous invitations to visit other Australian cities. Thus an itinerary was set up to include the Victorian towns of Warrnambool, Geelong, Ballarat, Bendigo, Maryborough and Terand; Launceston and Hobart in Tasmania; and Sydney, New South Wales. These meetings were scheduled to continue through the next fall. Most of the cities made similar preparations, though far less extensive, as Melbourne.

The opening service at Warrnambool, which was the very next city on the evangelist's itinerary, was a "hard meeting" and in sharp contrast to the ready response of the people in Melbourne. Torrey preached a powerful sermon on "Thou art weighed in the balances and found wanting," but there were few visible results. Torrey remarked, "I have never known such a poor response as this to a similar message, but I am not discouraged, for I know where our strength is." [11]

There were many who said that it just couldn't be expected that there would be as ready a response in the smaller country districts. And besides Warrnambool was a hard place. A large percentage of the people were Roman Catholic, and it was a town known both for fast horses and fast living. Some also said that Torrey had made a great mistake in asking the people who were on the Lord's side to stand. "Why," they said, "you can't do that in Warrnambool, for if you stood it would be known all over the town!"

But the discouraging did not deter Torrey. For as he said later to a group of ministers at Sydney,

If we believe in God, if we believe in the Bible, if we believe in the Holy Ghost, if we are willing to set our faces like a flint, believing that nothing is too hard for the

> Lord, and then hammer away, under the most
> discouraging circumstances, we will get revival in any
> place in the earth. [12]

And hammer away he did!

The closing meeting was so impressive that the
Warrnambool *Standard*—which at the first hardly noticed
the mission or missioners—had this to say:

> The scene outside the Town Hall last night was
> without precedent in the history of Warrnambool, and
> was sufficiently impressive to have convinced the most
> hardened skeptic that Dr. Torrey and Mr. Alexander had
> succeeded in "moving" the people to a degree they had
> never experienced before. . . and when, at the conclusion
> of an impressive address delivered by Dr. Torrey, the
> missioner appealed to the audience to make a public
> avowal of their decision for Christ, the great gathering
> appeared to rise *en masse*, and an indescribable thrill
> seemed to pulsate through the building. Now the people
> willingly *stood* to declare themselves for Christ. [13]

After a week's successful mission in Geelong, where the
evangelists received an enthusiastic response from the very
beginning, they began a meeting of similar duration in
Ballarat. While at Ballarat, Torrey made some very telling
remarks against dancing which greatly irked one of the
local dancing clubs. Thus a challenge was issued to Torrey
asking him to come and visit the club so that he could see
for himself that there was nothing indecent or improper in
their activities. Much to their surprise Torrey accepted,
and after one of the services, proceeded to the ballroom.

He was ushered in and given a place on the platform to
observe the dancers. Unknown to those present, their
observer had been an excellent dancer in his college days
and knew well the different types of dances. He noticed
that a number of the scheduled dances had been omitted
and that the waltzes were rehearsed. The dancers
endeavored to waltz by holding or crossing their hands
instead of the usual way and repeatedly missed their
timing. One by one the confused and embarrassed dancers
retreated for the cloakroom. Before they could disband,
however, Torrey called them back. Then and there he

preached a brief sermon on "Where Shall I Spend Eternity?"—to which the dancers gave an attentive hearing. [14]

Speaking on topics such as smoking, dancing, gambling, and drinking earlier met with considerable resistance, because a large share even of Christians engaged in at least some of these activities. The people regarded these as "conscience questions." Torrey agreed. And when questioners asked him, "Are not these things wholly a matter of the individual conscience?" Torrey replied, "Yes, and that is where I am trying to put it—on your conscience!"

It should be noted, however, that while Torrey was plain and uncompromising in speech, he did not deliberately set out to offend his hearers. His constant prayer before his messages was, "Prevent Thy servant from saying anything he ought not to say, and give him grace to leave out nothing he ought to say."

Take, for example, an incident which took place in the same city of Ballarat. While he was speaking one evening, a number of educated Chinese came into the service. In the course of Torrey's sermon, "Where Art Thou?" he asked the question, "Are you a child of God or a child of the Devil?" He had thought to leave it out since it might unnecessarily offend the visitors, but he felt impressed to mention it. The next evening the Chinese visitors were present again, and each one came forward at the close of the service. When Torrey asked the leader of the group why they had decided for Christ, he replied that it was the question he had asked the previous night. They knew they were not children of God, so concluded they must be children of the Devil. Thus they decided to become children of God. [15]

During the week's mission at Bendigo, a conversion took place which had a decided bearing on the future ministry of both Torrey and Alexander. A young man, son of the mayor, who was not a Christian, was engaged to play the piano for the meetings. Robert Harkness was really unsympathetic with anything evangelistic, but agreed to do so in order to please his godly parents.

He soon felt this was a mistake, however, as the meetings were *much* warmer than he expected. Torrey, sensing his antagonism, approached Harkness about becoming a Christian—only to receive a rather discourteous reply. Alexander, appreciating his musical talent, took a special interest in him. He at first resisted Alexander's appeals, but the warmth of the smiling Tennessean finally won him over. After his conversion at the end of the week, Harkness became the regular pianist for all the Torrey meetings and was intimately associated with the evangelist during his later years. [16]

There was one service at Bendigo which almost proved to be a tragedy. Torrey had been preaching on the subject of Hell, and the air was charged with an atmosphere of judgment. Just as he began the invitation, there was a loud crash. A part of the choir seats fell, tumbling some of the members some distance to the platform. It seemed for a moment the crowd would panic. But the unperturbed Torrey said in loud, authoritarian tones, "Sit down!" At his word the crowd hardly moved, thus avoiding a possible panic. Presently the choir members got up unhurt and in perfect order, and the invitation continued. Over fifty came forward to make their profession of faith in Christ. Torrey later asked Harkness, "What did you think the outcome would be?" His associate's reply amused him, "They won't collapse again in a hurry."

There were few situations that Torrey was not in complete command. But there were exceptions. In one of the Australian cities while Torrey was speaking, he heard the annoying bray of the kooka, or Australian jackass. It caused some disturbance in his delivery, and with a little exasperation he finally stopped and asked, "Where is that jackass?"

Actually the noise had been occasioned by some mischievous boys on the roof, and a ready answer came through the transom at the top of the building, "On the platform." Torrey apparently felt the less said the better and went on with his sermon.

The evangelist's next engagement was in Maryborough for a meeting of eight days. One incident is worth noting. An unusually fine-looking man with a splendid physique came to see Torrey after one of the services, asking, "I want to know what you have against me."

"What I have against you?" Torrey exclaimed, "I don't even know you."

"I mean this. I am not a Christian. I don't pretend to be a Christian, but I am a moral, upright man, and no one can deny it. Now, tell me what you have against me."

"You have not taken Christ as your personal Saviour and surrendered your life to Him as your Lord and Master and confessed Him as such before the world?"

"No, sir."

"Then," Torrey said, looking him straight in the eye, "I charge you with high treason against your divinely appointed King."

A dark cloud came over the man's face. He abruptly left the room never even looking back.

Months passed as Torrey preached in other parts of Australia and Tasmania. Then he returned to Ballarat some forty miles from Maryborough, for a short second mission. After one of the services this same man approached Torrey again, saying, "I have come all the way to Ballarat to tell you that you will never charge me with high treason again." And there both dropped to their knees as the man prayed, "Lord, Jesus, I hand in my allegiance; I give up my treason; I take Thee as my King." [17]

After a short three-day mission in the country town of Terang, the evangelists proceeded to the beautiful isle of Tasmania for campaigns in the cities of Launceston and Hobart.

The eighteen-hour voyage across the straits was one of the roughest Torrey was ever to experience. His companions were all below, but a more robust Torrey decided to weather out the storm on the deck with the captain of the ship. Abruptly the captain blurted out in a loud, pompous voice, "The golden rule is good enough for me."

Torrey, ever alert to witnessing opportunities, shot back, "Have you kept it?"

The captain dropped his head.

Torrey continued, "Your morality is no passport to Heaven. The Bible says that all your righteousnesses are as filthy rags." It was not long before the captain wilted under such powerful argument and yielded to Christ. [18]

The two-week meeting in Launceston stirred the city to its depths. Large numbers of conversions were recorded, but many thought the deepening of the religious life of the Christians and the strong impact on the communities were even greater results of the mission.

One of the pastors and committee members wrote concerning the powerful sermons of Torrey,

> It seemed as though one could hear the impact, the thud of some truth, as it got home. . . . People actually came to believe, before he finished, that he thought a quotation from Isaiah or John or Paul, or any of the inspired writers was sufficient warrant for deciding the gravest questions of life, and for doing so at once, without one moment's delay. . . . He just pinned us down to the Bible we had been reading all our lives, as though the Bible settled it, and there was an end of it. This making of Scripture the ultimate and final authority of all matters of conduct, without any appeal from Scripture to the scholars, or to recent thought, or to the modifications which modern exegetes had introduced, was done with such cool nerve and overmastering conviction that it was simply staggering. [19]

One of the leading converts who heard the "thud" of Scripture truth and decided "at once" in the very first service he attended was Jim Burke, heavyweight champion boxer and member of the Tasmanian Parliament.

His initial contact with Torrey was curious. Torrey was often referred to as "Doctor," and thinking he was a physician, Burke requested him to visit his invalid wife. Imagine Torrey's surprise when he realized he had been

taken for a physician! Yet he was a spiritual physician, and
he persuaded Burke to attend the evening service. Torrey's
"Heroes and Cowards" touched Burke, and he made the
great decision. His conversion caused quite a stir in
Launceston.

The Launceston reports had already stirred the city of
Hobart, and the evangelists looked forward to similar
blessings there. Some of the most notable services were
those held for children. Torrey usually conducted services
for children in every place where, as in Hobart, they heard
him gladly. He preached as he often did on the little maid
in the story of Naaman. Those who responded to the
invitation were dealt with carefully and thoroughly. Some
of the most solid conversions of his ministry, as attested to
in later years, were children in his meetings.

By the time the Hobart mission was completed, the
Tasmanians had a new designation for the American
evangelist. "When he said that he knew God better than he
knew his dearest friends or family, and that 'I've got God
a'back of me,' his audiences were inclined to believe him."
He ever after became known as "the man with God a'back
of him." [20]

After a short second meeting in Ballarat, the missioners
proceeded to Sydney, New South Wales, for what proved to
be a most remarkable campaign of two-and-a-half weeks'
duration. Many felt that perhaps the greatest permanent
impress of the Torrey meetings here was the midday
services for men. Large numbers of business and
professional men flocked into the place of meeting along
with the many common laborers. Torrey spoke on the
Bible, the resurrection of Christ, and infidelity.

One of the most popular features of these sessions was
the period allotted to questions by the listeners. He
requested they be turned in to him on the day previous so
that he might give some consideration to them; however, he
often took questions from the floor. Torrey especially
relished the answering of questions, and his answers
revealed common sense, wisdom, and sometimes humor.

His readiness of retort gladdened his audiences. The questions dealt with all sorts of subjects, and often reflected the influence of the new theology and destructive criticism. The following are illustrative of the questions and answers in these sessions.

"Can a person who accepts the scientific doctrine of evolution believe the Bible is inspired?"

A man can be an evolutionist and believe the Bible to be inspired. I used to be an evolutionist and believed the Bible inspired. I have given up the doctrine of evolution, but not for theological reasons. I have given it up for scientific reasons—it is an absolutely unproved hypothesis. . . . The doctrine of evolution is not science, but metaphysics and speculation from beginning to end.

"Do you think ministers should preach sermons on purity or ignore the subject, as so many ministers do?"

Most assuredly. I do not believe in too many purity meetings, and I do not believe in putting too many books into a boy's hand on the subject of his conduct. Because if a boy reads too many books of that kind, he gets to thinking over it. Get him to read one very carefully chosen book. Talk with him personally, and get him to take his stand upon it, and then tell him to dismiss the subject from his mind.

"Is it not a fact that Christianity has always been on the side of ignorance as against enlightenment?"

If it has, how come all the great universities were founded by Christians? Where is there a great university founded by infidels?"

"How can prayer be reconciled with the universality of cause and effect?"

Prayer is itself one of the most potent of causes. God knows from eternity what prayers will be offered to Him, and in the arrangement of His plans takes these prayers into account.

"Can a Christian play ping-pong?"

"Well," replied Torrey, with the air of one wrestling with a metaphysical problem, "if he devoted a good deal of time to it and practiced assiduously, I daresay he could!" [21]

There was an interesting incident which occurred in

Sydney. Torrey ordinarily did not mention false systems by name in his sermons, but in the course of one of his messages he stated that a liberal minister of Chicago had said that Christ was crucified by the orthodox people of the day. Commenting on this Torrey stated rather that Christ was crucified by the Unitarians of His day on the specific charge that He claimed to be the Son of God. The local Unitarian pastor and his offical board were enraged and published a statement in the local press challenging Torrey either to withdraw or prove his statement. Torrey announced that he would answer the challenge on the following day.

There was tension in the atmosphere as the crowd gathered for the service. The Unitarian pastor and board had been invited to occupy the front row of seats in the auditorium. Torrey was very courteous to the visitors but did not allow any rebuttal on the part of the Unitarian pastor. Torrey had before him a rather sordid account of a person bearing the same name as the pastor, and he stated that he could not allow a man to share the platform with him if this record were true. Torrey was very careful to state that he was not making an accusation against the pastor, but until he knew they were not one and the same, he could not allow him to speak. This caused a burst of applause from the audience and some uneasy squirming among the visitors. No denial of the statements was forthcoming.

Then Torrey proved his statement in a masterly way using John 10:27-33; Mark 14:60-65 and John 19:6,7, showing clearly that the reason the Jews crucified Christ was that He claimed to be the Son of God.[22] Within a month of that date the Unitarian pastor was convicted of fraud and sentenced to seven years in the penitentiary.

Seven years later Evangelist J. Wilbur Chapman visited the penitentiary and met this man, who had now completely renounced his old life and had been converted to Christ. When Chapman asked what brought about his change of opinion, he replied, "It was the unanswerable

conviction of Dr. Torrey's statement regarding the deity of
Christ uttered seven years ago." Upon his release he
returned to his native America and became the pastor of an
evangelical church. [23]

The Sydney Mission concluded the Torrey-Alexander
evangelistic meetings in Australia. The five months of
meetings had exceeded all expectations. There were almost
20,000 recorded conversions, a deepening of the Christian
life, a great and continuing impulse to Christian service, a
marvelous unity among evangelical Christians, and a
significant change in entire communities. Such remarkable
happenings did not go unnoticed. Christians around the
world had been watching. . . and waiting.

[1]*The Southern Cross*, (September 10, 1902), pp. 8,9.

[2]William Warren, "The Genesis of the Australian Revival," XXVI
Missionary Review of the World (March, 1903), pp. 201-203.

[3]*The Southern Cross*, p. 5.

[4]Ibid., p. 6.

[5]Ibid., p. 19.

[6]Ibid., p. 18.

[7]Richard E. Day, *Bush Aglow* (Philadelphia: The Judson Press, 1936),
p. 210.

[8]*The Southern Cross*, p. 33.

[9]Ibid., pp. 28-30.

[10]Ibid., p. 87.

[11]Ibid., p. 34.

[12]Ibid., p. 76.

[13]Ibid., p. 39.

[14]Letter to A. F. Gaylord, June 13, 1902.

[15]Torrey, *God Hath Spoken*, p. 147.

[16]George T. B. Davis, *Twice Around the World With Alexander* (New
York: The Christian Herald, 1907), pp. 46-49.

[17]Robert Harkness, *Reuben Archer Torrey* (Chicago: The Bible
Institute Corporation, 1929), pp. 55,56.

[18]Beardsley, p. 188.

[19]*The Southern Cross*, p. 55.

[20]Ibid., pp. 58-60.

[21]Ibid., pp. 73, 78, 85.

[22]*The Southern Cross*, pp. 73, 78, 85.

[23]Harkness, p. 39.

16. The Macedonian Call

"We should like these men to come to us."

This twentieth-century version of the Macedonian call, "Come over and help us," was echoed in many parts of the Christian world. Torrey and Alexander's first invitation was to visit the principal cities of New Zealand—Wellington, Christchurch and Dunedin. The thirty-day mission (ten days with each city) met with remarkable success. Their most significant mission was in Christchurch where they had the largest religious gathering ever to assemble under one roof.

A new and unusual feature of the New Zealand mission was the brief service conducted at train stations, while traveling the scenic journey from Christchurch to Dunedin. Requests had come from many quarters for these meetings, and at one place as many as 2,000 people assembled for the fifteen-minute service. The procedure was simple but hurried. As the train approached the station, the evangelistic party went into action. Harkness and Alexander quickly leaped onto the hastily-made platform, passed out hymn sheets and led the people in a few minutes of song. Then Torrey followed with a few telling points from the Scripture.[1]

The New Zealand campaign had a great impact. One observer noted:

> The year 1902 will ever be memorable in the history of New Zealand; those three missions have proved to be unique in at least three respects—firstly, in the universal prayer offered for the success of the mission; secondly, in the unparalleled unanimity of the cooperating churches; and thirdly, in the marvelous awakening amongst Christians of almost every creed. The entire movement

Dr. Torrey Preaching at the Last Meeting, Melbourne, Australia

has thus been stamped with the hallmark of God's Holy Spirit. [2]

Departing from the shores of "the Great Britain of the South," Torrey reminded the Christians, "A fire has been kindled. Let every child of God do his very best to cause it to spread. Now is the day of visitation. Let everyone recognize it and make the most of it." [3] From New Zealand the evangelists traveled back to Melbourne for a great farewell service and from thence sailed to India.

The entourage, which now included Robert Harkness as pianist, and Rupert Lowe as secretary to Alexander, especially enjoyed the trip to India. It gave them some time to relax and recuperate from the heavy strain of the previous weeks and months. There had not been many leisure hours for Torrey, but when he had them they were spent with Mrs. Torrey. They might be found sight-seeing, visiting a gold mine or just picking wildflowers on the countryside.

It was while Torrey was on the steamer to India that he met a leader of the Hindu faith who was living in open sin. When the leader endeavored to defend his religious belief, Torrey simply replied, "By their fruits ye shall know them." The Hindu was so struck by the unexpected answer that he later sought out Torrey, asking him how to become a Christian. The Hindu leader was the first fruits of the Indian harvest. [4]

The party landed first at Madura, where they spent a few days ministering to a large congregation of Hindu people. It was while visiting one of the spectacular Hindu shrines that a Brahmin priest approached him. He assured Torrey that the worshipers bowing before the shrine would gain eternal reward. "Do not the Vedas proclaim it?"

Torrey instantly replied, "But as many as received him, to them gave he power to become the sons of God." He spoke directly to the puzzled priest of the claims of Christ and His power to redeem. Although the priest made no commitment to Christ, it is not likely that he forgot Torrey's words and the deep conviction with which they were uttered! He was simply illustrating one of his firmest

convictions: "It doesn't matter whether a person believes
the Bible. It is the Sword of the Spirit, so just stick them
with it!"

The evangelists had planned to stay only a short time in
India, going on to Calcutta for a few days and then quickly
to Bombay. But, Torrey noted, "God had other plans, and
we fell in with them." Colombe, Madras and Benares were
added to the itinerary and extended their stay to a full six
weeks.

Two of the most memorable of the meetings were those
held in Calcutta and Madras. In the latter city the non-
Christian student population especially relished hearing
Torrey, coming in large numbers despite a terrific monsoon
all week. Torrey noted concerning his audiences:

> The attention of these meetings on the part of men who
> were professed heathen was quite remarkable. Indeed,
> they openly applauded some of my strongest statements
> of truth. I did not hesitate to speak right out about the
> utter inadequacy of Hinduism to bring pardon and peace
> and deliverance from sin's power. I spoke equally strong
> upon the deity of Christ, the atonement, and the other
> doctrines that the Hindu is suppose to hate. I did not
> know at times that there would be a storm when I looked
> squarely into their eyes and said, "You know that Jesus
> Christ is the Son of God if you only had the courage to
> confess it; you know that Hinduism never gave any man
> peace"; but the storm did not come. It was pathetic to
> look into those earnest, thoughtful faces and to think
> what a crisis it was in their lives. [5]

About a hundred of them from various walks of life,
including a number of soldiers and seven medical students,
made an open profession of faith in Christ.

Many felt that Torrey's greatest impact upon India was
his addressing four hundred missionaries at the Decennial
Missionary Convention at Madras for four days. He gave
them "new faith in God, and a new vision of the power of a
fully-surrendered and Spirit-filled life. Only eternity will
reveal the far-reaching effects of Torrey's addresses at that
memorable convention." [6] (It was the beginning of a great
Christian work in India.)

He was also invited to address the students of one of the most well-known missionary colleges in the country. It was under Christian auspices, but the leaders of the school did not teach or preach the Gospel, fearing that it might offend the students. This approach caused many students to develop an ardent hatred for Christianity. Torrey's fearless "address" not only succeeded in reaching a number of the students for Christ; it transformed the direction of the school.[7]

The marvelous reports of the meetings in Australia, New Zealand and India had stirred the hearts of Christians in the British Isles. While the evangelists were in India, they decided "if God opens the way, to spend a few months in England and Scotland." Originally they had intended to be drawing near New York—they had been away a full year—but there were urgent invitations from the English brethren. Their hearts had been stirred by the marvelous successes of the evangelists, and they longed for similar fruits in the British Isles. God opened the way, and the evangelistic party sailed for England.

Among the many noted Christian leaders on hand for a welcome meeting in Exeter Hall, London, on January 9, were Lord Kinnaird, who had directed the great campaign with Moody; Rev. Thomas Spurgeon, son of the famous Charles Haddon Spurgeon; Dr. W. H. Griffith Thomas; and Dr. A. T. Pierson.

There were many words of welcome but not more significant than those of the saintly F. B. Meyer, leading Baptist pastor in London and close friend of the late D. L. Moody.

> I would not for a great deal have missed the opportunity to welcome Dr. Torrey and Mr. Alexander in London. First, Dr. Torrey is holding and has been holding for many years a foremost place in Chicago, and Chicago is one of the most go-ahead cities of all American cities. . . .For a man to be able to keep in front place in Chicago means that he has got grit and brains, muscle and sinew.
>
> Secondly, Dr. Torrey does not come to us because he has nothing to do in his own country. I notice that some

men start evangelizing when everybody is tired of them at home. He has got a fine church and a congregation that any man might like to speak to.

Thirdly, I happen to know, from my own intimate friendship with dear Mr. Moody, that there were few friends, if any, in whom he had a more absolute confidence than in Dr. Torrey.

Fourthly, I think we ought to be thankful to have in Dr. Torrey a man who knows what he believes. He has reasons for his belief, and is not afraid to state them in most unmistakable terms. One cannot listen to him for half-an-hour without knowing that he is a man of conviction, and he brings his hearers round to his opinions. If all the clocks in London said it was half past six and Dr. Torrey said it was seven, I would stand by Dr. Torrey.

Fifthly, Dr. Torrey deserves confidence, because he does not preach a half-and-half gospel. Salvation is something more than getting into Heaven somehow by a back door, and getting whitewashed in the hour of death. We need to have the Gospel brought into contact with our daily lives. [8]

As was his custom at the welcoming meetings, Torrey spoke on Psalm 62:5. With the prophetic eye of faith he remarked,

A revival in earlier days meant something more or less circumscribed. A revival in this age of post, telegraph, newspaper, all the ease of modern communication, a revival in Australia means a revival all round the globe, and you and I are across the threshold of one of the greatest epochs in the history of the Church of Christ upon earth. [9]

The first three weeks were spent conducting meetings in Mildmay Park Conference Hall, North London. The hall at the beginning was only half-filled, and its chilly, gloomy atmosphere seemed to affect the people. But before long Alexander's enthusiastic songleading, combined with Torrey's straightforward preaching, stirred the people to response and action. The primary purpose of these meetings was to awaken the people to their soul-winning responsibilities and prepare them for the later London meetings.

Their first actual mission in the British Isles was in Edinburgh. To some it seemed a most unlikely place to begin an evangelistic campaign. The Scottish capital city was rich in ecclesiastical tradition, and there were few places where it was regarded as more fashionable and respectable to be identified with a church. Further, influenced by its historic University, it was both scholarly and cultural in its outlook. Then there was the natural hesitancy of the conservative Scotsmen to respond in a public service.

But despite all of these features and the bitterly cold and rainy February weather there was a remarkable response from the very first. Torrey's logical, reasonable approach met with great success in the midday services for businessmen and also with the University students in the evening. Torrey mentioned that one evening in the gallery reserved for University students "more men stood up to accept Christ than in all the other parts of the house together." In fact, Torrey regarded the work with the students of the Edinburgh Union as one of the most rewarding aspects of the four-week mission.[10] Not only did the meeting result in a number of conversions, but it also helped to stem the tide of higher critical thinking.

Torrey's convictions about higher criticism of the Scriptures and its advocates only deepened as a result of his observations in Edinburgh. When Fitt wrote to him just after the close of the mission, suggesting using a lecturer at Moody Institute who was "something of a higher critic," Torrey gave an unhesitating reply. He observed:

> That is enough to settle it. Let us keep at least one Institution clean in these days. You have little conception of the havoc that has been wrought by the destructive criticism here and of the uprising that is now against it. . . .It would greatly weaken the hands of men who are trying to fight God's battles over here, if we should invite to the Institute any man who is in the least degree tainted. This is no time to join hands with the enemy. Do not think of it for a moment. As a matter of policy, it would be the most fatal thing we could do. I know of many men, friends of the Institute, who would

draw out of it altogether if it was done, among them is the
writer.[11]

The invitations to hold missions in various parts of the
British Isles continued to pour in. This prompted Torrey to
remark to Fitt, "I presume I shall be away a good deal for
two or three years." Their next engagement was in Glasgow
where, because of the successful Edinburgh meeting, they
had an even warmer reception. The accommodations were
so taxed from the very beginning that it became necessary
to hold separate meetings for men and women. In the four-
week campaign nearly 3,000 decisions were registered. Mr.
William Oates, campaign secretary and worker in the
earlier Moody-Sankey meetings, observed that the work
was in many respects "more remarkable than the work of
grace in 1874." His only complaint was the "brevity of the
mission"—both Edinburgh and Glasgow desired extended
time.[12]

After another campaign in Aberdeen, Scotland, the
evangelists traveled to Belfast, prosperous Protestant city
of the Green Isle. There was an overwhelming response.
The greatest drawback was the finding of a place large
enough to hold the meetings. Finally Torrey suggested to
the committee, "Why not try the Market Place? It will seat
7,000 people." It was somewhat of a strain on Torrey's
voice, but at least would accommodate the crowds. But at
the first meeting in St. George's Market Place there were
7,000 on the inside and 6,000 on the outside. The number of
conversions abounded. Of the approximately 4,000
decisions of the mission, there were 1,220 in the last few
nights. There was never a city Torrey more regretted
leaving than Belfast.[13]

The evangelists witnessed a glorious farewell as
thousands in Belfast gathered on the shore to see them off
to America. There was a brief service, and as the ship left
the docks, Alexander led the people with his handkerchief
in "God Be With You Till We Meet Again."

On the journey home many of the passengers were aloof
toward the evangelistic party at first. But Alexander's

The Great Meeting in St. George's Market, Belfast, Ireland

genial smile and Torrey's heartily entering into the deck games, in which he was unusually adept, soon warmed their attitude. By the end of the voyage they were the most popular passengers on the ship.

As the liner steamed into the harbor at New York, the Torreys became very restless and excited in anticipation of seeing their family waiting for them on the dock. Torrey was not at all excited, however, about the prospect of meeting New York reporters. He dreaded their indiscreet remarks and would gladly have forfeited that task.

In Chicago a great welcome meeting, which drew one of the largest crowds in the history of the windy city, was planned. Luther Mills, a leading Christian lawyer of Chicago, presided and said to the packed auditorium,

> Dr. Torrey has returned to us a conquering hero, home from the holiest of wars, the battle for the redemption and uplifting of men's souls. He has been recognized in every civilized land, and in China, Japan, India and Hawaii for his work and worth as the real successor of Moody, and as such we give him welcome. With him comes Charles Alexander, the sweet singer, whose music has set half the world to singing. [14]

Presently Torrey was introduced and addressed the great throng telling of outstanding incidents of blessing during the missions. His most telling words were in the form of a challenge.

> You, who think we need a new Bible, something better than the Bible, the old Bible, an expurgated Bible, take heed to our experiences. Eighteen months of preaching its Gospel, thirty thousand men and women won to Christ, proves that the Bible, the old Bible, is what the world needs, what the twentieth century needs. [15]

The short two months of "rest" were spent in a whirlwind schedule of Bible conference sessions in which both Torrey and Alexander shared the Pentecostal blessings of the evangelistic tour. The time passed quickly, and soon preparations were made for the return voyage. They had engagements in the British Isles through the spring of 1905.

One thing the Torreys had definitely decided—their

family would accompany them this time. Edith[16] and Blanche were twenty-one and nineteen respectively and were without school responsibilities. Reuben was almost sixteen; Margaret, ten. Tutoring was arranged for them. In addition to the family, the evangelistic party had added Miss Grace Saxe, who did a most valuable work in setting up Bible classes to follow up the missions. Jacoby, his former assistant at Moody Church, and Towner, of the Institute music faculty, joined them later.

There was an air of excitement as the party prepared to leave for Liverpool. Torrey regarded the earlier victories as only the threshold of revival. "God did great things for us in answer to your prayers during our recent tour around the world. But He has greater things in store. The God of the future is greater than the God of the past." [17]

[1]Davis, *Twice Around,* pp. 56, 57.

[2]*Outlook Illustrated Memento of the Torrey-Alexander Mission* (August-September, 1902) p. 2.

[3]Ibid., p. 4.

[4]Robert Harkness, *Reuben Archer Torrey* (Chicago: The Bible Institute Corporation, 1929), pp. 58, 59.

[5]*Moody Church Herald,* II (January 15, 1903), p. 19.

[6]*The Indian Witness,* XXXII (November 13, 1902), p. 90, 91.

[7]Torrey, "Missionary Message," pp. 558, 559.

[8]J. Kennedy MacClean, *Triumphant Evangelism* (London: Marshall Brothers, n.d.), pp. 12, 13.

[9]Ibid., pp. 14, 15.

[10]Ibid., pp. 17-19.

[11]Letter to A. P. Fitt, March, 1903.

[12]MacClean, *Triumphant,* p. 29.

[13]Ibid., pp. 33, 34.

[14]Davis, *Twice Around,* pp. 67, 68.

[15]Davis, *Torrey,* pp. 99, 100.

[16]Edith had withdrawn from Holyoke College the previous March because of a nervous condition. She continued her education at a subsequent date.

[17]R. A. Torrey, *A Parting Message and Appeal From Mr. Torrey and Mr. Alexander,* (August 21, 1903). A pamphlet distributed at the time of their departing again for England.

17. Two Hearty Fishermen

"Pray for great things, expect great things, work for great things, but above all pray."

So read the brief message by Torrey on the thousands of postcards which were distributed on the second phase of the revival tour in the British Isles. Torrey was expectant as he arrived for the meeting in Liverpool. And his expectation, which was always from God, was well justified. The Liverpool meeting exceeded the evangelists' previous successes in the British Isles and set the pace for their missions for the next two and a half years. Accommodations were severely taxed from the very beginning, and it was soon necessary to hold separate meetings for men and women. The final services for men and women witnessed the greatest number of conversions the evangelists were to experience on the entire tour. Two hundred ten women and 450 men made public professions on that final day.[1]

Throughout the month of October Torrey and Alexander labored in Dundee, Scotland, the home of the sainted Robert Murray McCheyne, William Burns and John McPherson. Torrey noted in his initial address that McPherson's volume, *Revival and Revival Work*, "had not a little to do with the prayer that ascended from my heart one night that God would send me around the world preaching the Gospel."[2]

Considerable opposition was aroused by the meetings, and the newspapers gave much space to the discussion of Torrey's theology—particularly his view on Hell. This only succeeded in arousing further interest in the meetings, however. Torrey was also cautioned by his brethren not to give a public invitation, or at least a less open one. Staid and conservative Scottsmen simply would not respond. But Torrey was adamant. A public confession of faith was God's method, and he considered no other. In no case was there any marked reaction toward a public invitation, and usually large numbers responded. In fact, two men who had committed adultery and murder were converted by reading Torrey's sermon, "The Judgment," in the newspaper and said they were willing to make a public confession even though it meant hanging.[3]

One of the most remarkable answers to prayer in Torrey's entire ministry occurred in Dundee. The city was known for its "grey days" of gloomy, rainy weather, and the visit of the evangelists was no exception. It rained almost every day of the entire campaign. Imagine the mission committee's surprise when Torrey suggested an open-air meeting to reach the nonchurch-going people. Despite their objections Torrey decided on the meeting. The time was set for 2:00 in the afternoon. Torrents of rain descended all through the morning, and much prayer was made for the rain to cease. At ten minutes until two the rain suddenly stopped. A forty-five-minute service was held, and within five minutes of the benediction, the rain came down in torrents once again.[4]

Before the arrival of the evangelists in Manchester, England, for their November mission, there had also arrived some malicious and false allegations about their financial arrangements. The charges that the evangelists set a high price on their services and received enormous amounts in their missions were so widespread that it was necessary to publish a pamphlet to answer them.

Torrey made his position on finances crystal clear. He pointed out that he remained on salary from the Institute so that he would eliminate the financial element as much as possible. All of his contributions, minus actual expenses, were sent to the Institute. In every place both he and Alexander placed themselves entirely in the hands of the local committee. They received "sometimes a great deal,

sometimes a little, sometimes nothing at all." He refused to
set any figure on his services, and often paid expenses out of
his own pocket—such as the time he had to request forty
pounds from Revell on his book royalties.[5]

With this issue satisfactorily settled Torrey went on to
have a great mission in Manchester. There were
remarkable conversions from all classes of people. Rev. E.
Abbey Tindall, a leader in the mission, observed,

> Take some instances, twenty-eight boys in one church
> choir, a large number of abandoned men and women,
> more drunkards than I have been able to count, ministers
> of religion dragged to the gutter through drink. . .
> prodigal sons of ministers, infidels, church wardens,
> people whose minds have been unsettled by the great
> questions of modern thought, and ladies of good society
> position.[6]

An outstanding convert was one of Manchester's
foremost infidel lecturers who soon afterward went as a
missionary to India.

After a three-weeks' tour of some of the smaller towns of
Scotland in bitterly cold weather, the evangelists welcomed
the Christmas vacation, as a much-anticipated occasion for
rest and relaxation. Unfortunately Alexander became ill at
Christmas and spent one of the loneliest days of his life in a
London hotel. Torrey rejoined his family at Southport, a
pleasant little seaside resort town, where they were
residing.

Much prayer and planning went into the Birmingham
meeting which greeted the evangelists for the next six
weeks in January and February. The large Bingley Hall
was engaged for the meetings, but it soon proved to be
inadequate. Thousands were turned away nightly during
the second half of the campaign. The Birmingham mission
did more than any previous meeting to draw attention to
the marvelous way in which God was using Torrey and
Alexander. A total of 7,700 conversions were recorded—the
largest number of any of their missions in the British Isles.

The godly Dr. J. H. Jowett, chairman of the mission,
commented,

The mission has fertilized the Christian life of the town. Few will be the churches which are not enriched by its labors. A wave of spiritual expectancy has swept over the city. I have heard of prayer meetings in churches which were fast dying, but which have been recreated and vitalized. Ministers have once again had their eyes fixed upon the primary work. Disciples have been won to the Lord in thousands! "It is the Lord's doing, and it is marvellous in our eyes."[7]

Torrey attributed the great success to "the people working on the apostolic pattern—upon the plan of God's Model Revival laid down in Acts 2—everyone filled with the Holy Ghost, and everyone going to work!" Scarcely had he given out the invitation the first night in Birmingham when the great hall became a beehive of activity. Christians spoke to others near them and went out on the streets to reach others. Jowett further observed,

When Dr. Torrey has finished his address, you feel instinctively that the real business is to begin. Both missioners then engage in the task. It suggests nothing so much to my mind as two hearty cooperative fishermen dragging in the nets for their Lord.[8]

One of the significant ventures of the Birmingham campaign was the Saturday Midnight Sweep. Christian workers combed the streets for drunkards and outcasts and brought them—3,000 of them—to a midnight meeting at Bingley Hall. Imagine the motley group which greeted the evangelists! They were in all stages of drunkenness, using obscene language and mimicking those on the platform. But Alexander's singing soon soothed the audience so that comparative quiet prevailed. Torrey, who had been waiting his time with folded arms, then rose to speak. Of the poor unfortunates, 135 stood to receive Christ. [9]

While the evangelists were in Birmingham, a serious and unusual crisis arose. Torrey had been suffering from a severe cold and cough. After one Saturday afternoon in which it was feared Torrey might not finish his sermon, Alexander rushed a cable to the Institute, "Pray for Torrey's voice and health." Much earnest prayer was offered for him, and the next morning he was completely well. He reported, "Last night was the first night I have been able to sleep in three weeks."

It was also while the evangelists were here that an event of great personal significance took place—the engagement of Alexander to Miss Helen Cadbury. Miss Cadbury, the daughter of the late well-known businessman, philanthropist and earnest Christian, Richard Cadbury, had been an enthusiastic and untiring worker in the meetings. Her dedication caught Alexander's attention. Miss Cadbury was also strangely drawn to Alexander and his bright Christian spirit. It was not long before their relationship ripened into love, and right after the Birmingham Mission they became engaged.

Their engagement took the rest of the evangelistic party by surprise. The entire group, which had now grown to twelve including the secretaries, had been invited to the Cadbury's beautiful home in Malvern Hills for a brief rest. Alexander, however, had strangely absented himself. Two days later, one of the secretaries, J. Kennedy MacClean, rode by carriage to the place of retreat and handed Torrey a letter from Alexander announcing the engagement. After reading a few lines the startled Torrey looked up, "Is this serious, are you sure it's no joke?" Assured that it was not, Torrey made the glad announcement to the remainder of the group at dinner that evening.[10]

Torrey told Alexander,

> I am glad of the news. I am sure you can do better work married, but I have never before met anyone whom I would have been glad to see you marry. Miss Cadbury will become more to you every year. You think you are in love now, but you won't know what love means until you have been married for years, as Mrs. Torrey and I have. [11]

Torrey's gladness was not exactly shared by Blanche and Reuben, who were very close to Alexander. Reuben urged him to "reserve a little corner for your old 'Pal,' " and Blanche queried, "You will still be my 'Uncle Charles,' won't you?" The happy couple made plans to be married in Birmingham in July at the conclusion of the missions in the spring.

The evangelists' next engagement took them to Dublin, capital of the Green Isle. Considerable difficulties of many varieties faced them in Dublin, but none more disconcerting than the sectarian jealousy among the cooperating churches. It was an even greater hindrance than the intransigent Roman Catholic clergy, who had warned their parishoners not to attend the meetings. Torrey reported a conversation of two of those Catholic parishioners, who were discussing the meeting. The first said, "The people of Dublin do not like Mr. Torrey's preaching." The other said, "That is strange. Why is that?"

"Because he tries to bring them up too close to the Bible."[12]

But despite the initial difficulties the complexion of the mission began to change. By the meeting's end there had been a greater union of churches than ever before in the history of Dublin. A large number of the 3,000 recorded decisions came from the heavy Catholic population, which out-numbered the Protestants three to one.

April through mid-July was spent in the English towns of Bristol, Bradford, Brighton and Blackpool. The greatest of the meetings was in Bristol, the field of labor of George Muller. The most disappointing of all their major missions was Bradford. Little enthusiasm and lack of preparation on the part of the sponsoring churches and concerted opposition from unsympathetic ministers were the chief factors.

On July 14 in Birmingham Alexander and the gifted, sweet-spirited Helen Cadbury were united in marriage in a simple Quaker ceremony. The Torreys stood in the place of Alexander's mother, and Blanche served her "Uncle Charlie's" bride as a maid of honor. Shortly afterward the happy couple took a honeymoon voyage to America and the Alexander home in Tennessee.

The Torreys, as was their usual custom, retreated to the Continent, vacationing mainly in France, Germany and Switzerland. They visited art galleries, museums, scenic and historical sites—something Torrey especially relished. Often Torrey's pace in visiting places of interest was a little too much for the rest of the family. On one such occasion in Paris the rest of the family retired to the hotel, but Torrey and a very weary Reuben continued their sight-seeing. Reuben became so exhausted trying to keep up with his father that he literally went to sleep while crossing a street. It was only a strong jerk by his father which kept him from serious injury by a passing carriage. [13]

Torrey also enjoyed hiking and mountain climbing. Reuben always went along with him on these ventures, and many times the Torrey penchant for daring got them into some tight spots in scaling mountains. These were treasured moments for Reuben, however, as he and his father conversed on all sorts of subjects ranging from the Bible to culture to science. Torrey was especially fond of pointing out and explaining geological formations—an interest which had remained since his college days under Dr. James Dana.

Mrs. Torrey wrote from Switzerland, "Mr. Torrey is just in his element now; he delights in walking and climbing, and this outdoor exercise is the rest he needs." [14] That included getting up at 3:30 in the morning and climbing 630 feet! He was always ready for a good hike and would often be seen taking a walk with Margaret, Blanche or Reuben. Reuben didn't fully share his enthusiasm for hiking the day the two walked thirty miles!

The summer seemed to be frightfully short. It was not long before September had arrived, and the family was departing to England for the Bolton mission. Jacoby, who now joined the evangelistic party, assisted in the personal work. His testimony, given on a number of occasions, proved to be very effective. He was at his peak when he spoke to a sea of human derelicts in a memorable midnight sweep in Bolton, where 160 of them received Christ.

An American editor, puzzled at the success of an evangelist with "no emotional power" or "eloquence," visited Bolton to see for himself. Amazed at the great throngs of people and the response to Torrey's message, he could only conclude, "It is nothing but the power of God."[15]

In October the evangelists made their first and only visit to Wales, holding meetings in the city of Cardiff. Great crowds came, and the Welshmen reponded enthusiastically to the singing of Alexander, but there was little response to the invitations. Torrey attributed this to the fact that Cardiff is. . .

> . . . a place where a very large proportion of the people make a profession of religion, where, in fact, church membership is quite the fashion, and there are many in the churches with whom religion is merely a matter of form, but who do not know the real regenerating grace of God. [16]

Further, there were few places where Torrey had so much difficulty getting the Christians to do personal work. The first half of the campaign, according to Torrey, "dragged." But he kept hammering away on the Christian's responsibility in witnessing and then appointed a special day of fasting and prayer. From that day forward the tone of the mission changed. The meeting ended on a triumphant note, even exceeding the results of the successful Bolton meeting.

But it was only the beginning. The hard-sought revival did not stop. The meetings went right on after the evangelists departed—a goal Torrey always set out to achieve. Meetings were held every night for a year, and multitudes were converted. The revival fire spread throughout Wales and was the beginning of the famous Welsh Revival.

During the next two months the evangelists held their second Liverpool mission—the only time they twice visited a city in the British Isles. The success of the first campaign prompted the invitation to return, and preparations were made on a much larger scale. The great tournament building, which would accommodate close to 13,000 and was considered to be the second largest in Great Britain, was brought from Manchester and re-erected.

The bigness of the endeavor seemed to hinder at the beginning. Torrey wrote Fitt,

> In the early part of the mission and before the mission began there was a tendency to exalt men, to boast of our big hall, our enormous choir and things of that sort, and I believe this grieved the Spirit; but everyone is coming to see that man must be put out of sight, and God exalted.[17]

Despite the disadvantages of the location, which was three miles from town with no electric cars running to it, the accommodations for some of the meetings were still not enough. The hall was filled night after night, and on the closing day of the meeting there were *two* services with a standing-room-only crowd of 15,000 with others on the outside who could not gain admission.

It was the custom of Torrey in all of his meetings to issue a challenge to honest skeptics, agnostics and atheists. He promised, if they were honest, to show them how to be convinced beyond the shadow of a doubt that the Bible was the Word of God and that Christ was the Son of God.

There was a man in Liverpool who doubted everything, but nonetheless, responded to Torrey's challenge. Soon after their conversation, the man wrote a letter to Torrey describing his conversion. Torrey read it in one of the services. Suddenly a man, with face all aglow, sprang to his feet and said, "I am here." Torrey immediately told him, "Well, then, stand up on that chair and give your testimony." The incident made quite an impact on the crowd.[18]

A notable feature of the mission was Torrey's midday studies on Bible themes. Because of the length of the mission he concentrated on a more systematic instruction dealing with the atonement, justification by faith, regeneration, sanctification, the Holy Spirit and the Scriptures. A unique honor was bestowed on Torrey. He was invited to speak in the Corn Exchange and delivered eleven addresses.

An unusual feature of the Liverpool meeting was the Wedding Feast in honor of Alexander's recent marriage.

The choir decided to give a feast to all the poor of the city of Liverpool in honor of the couple. Two thousand three hundred invitations were sent out, and on the specified night the hall was crowded with the unusual company of guests. After the dinner a regular service was conducted, and 217 persons made a public profession of Christ.

During the Liverpool mission the evangelists encountered serious opposition from the *British Weekly*. Although the Torrey meetings were not without previous criticism, they were generally characterized with great praise by both press and public. Remembering the words of Christ, "If they have persecuted me, they will persecute you also," Torrey manifested some concern.

> I often thought, Oh, if I could only suffer a little for my Lord! I felt I was having too easy a time altogether. I wanted them to say unkind things about me occasionally. They got to doing it finally, praise God, but it was nothing. I often thought it would be a comfort if they would only stone me once in a while.[19]

The *Weekly*, which had been sharply critical of the earlier Moody campaign, now cast the largest stone. It took a plebiscite of the ministers in the cities where the missions were conducted and published their replies in a series of articles. The majority were far from complimentary. It appeared to many observers that the campaigns were a failure and generally detrimental to the religious life of the nation.

Torrey replied to the *Weekly* in the *Sunday School Chronicle* and brought into sharp focus the reason why the letters did not reflect a true estimate of the permanent value of the campaigns. One had only to examine the names of the ministers whose replies were published. In the midst of the controversy he had written to Fitt that "they seem to have been careful to select largely from the ministers who were known from the outset as being in opposition to the work, or as having held aloof from it."[20]

He outlined three classes of opposing letters:

(1) Letters by men known to be bitterly opposed to both evangelical truth as well as evangelistic work. For example,

there was one reply from a Unitarian Congregational minister and another from a minister who made a practice of going to every city to attack the evangelist before he arrived.

(2) Letters from ministers who never came near the mission either because of their remoteness or their indifference.

(3) Letters from men at the head of very small churches or chapels that were not well known. [21]

It would be most unnatural to see many converts unite with these churches. Speaking of the nonevangelical and indifferent churches, who received mainly children into their memberships, Torrey said to Fitt, "People old enough to decide for themselves would naturally hold aloof from such churches if our work were any good." [22]

On the other hand, Torrey noted that there were no opposing letters from Church of England ministers. He received some of his most solid backing from these ministers, and their churches naturally showed the most in the way of results. Further the letters showed that many churches and their nominal members experienced awakened consciences in their spiritual lives. In addition, they also became sensitive to ethical and moral issues in community life. Another significant feature of the letters was the large number of children who had experienced conversion.

Torrey did not disparage the criticism. He strongly felt that an evangelistice meeting should be able to undergo careful scrutiny, and he sincerely endeavored to learn from the criticism. Speaking to a friend he once stated that,

> I have always found more help from criticism than I have ever found from praise. I think a good many brethren need praise. . . . I am of such a temperament that criticism, even though it is unfriendly criticism. . . does me far more good than praise ever does. [23]

His only disturbance over the *Weekly* criticism was their unfortunate policy of unfair representation. Nevertheless, he did not feel the articles would do any real harm.

Endeavoring to learn from the criticism, however, he outlined three improvements—not innovations—for his future evangelistic campaigns.

(1) More diligent care in the selection and training of personal workers so as to instruct the inquirers more thoroughly.

(2) Insistence upon uniting with a local church at once for purposes of fellowship, instruction and service.

(3) Stress on the type of church converts should join. [24]

This last principle illustrated a deepening conviction which Torrey expressed in a letter to Fitt in Chicago.

It is folly to send the names of inquirers to ministers who are known to be antagonistic to evangelical truth, or who do not believe in conversion. To send the name of a young convert to such a minister is to send a lamb out to be harried by a wolf. Hereafter I intend to advise the inquirers to seek fellowship in churches where the minister believes and preaches the Bible, to avoid churches where the Bible is pulled to pieces; to seek fellowship in churches where they will be welcome, and not seek fellowship in churches where they will receive the cold shoulder.[25]

Torrey called attention to Pentecost, the first and greatest revival.

Jerusalem as a whole was far from unanimous in favor of the apostles. They were opposed bitterly by many of the most eminent religious leaders of the time, and if the "Jerusalem Weekly" had sent around a year afterwards to the rulers of the various synagogues, to find out what the permanent effect of the mission upon the religious life of Jerusalem, it is not likely that many of the rulers of the synagogues would have reported favorably on the work, or told of the many accessions to their membership.[26]

Torrey experienced, as did Paul, "A great door and effectual is opened unto me, and there are many adversaries."

There was one minister in Liverpool who, although he did not share Torrey's theology in every particular, decided to attend a meeting and observe for himself. He wrote his observations to the *Post and Mercury* "partly because many have been testifying both for and against the evangelist, and partly because a minister must have a keen professional interest in any preacher who has obtained so large a hold on the public." He spoke of him as a "gentleman of Christ" who "neither said nor did anything to offend the most fastidious critic." Observing the intellectual sanity and graciousness of the evangelist's address, he left the meeting "convinced that the preacher was a single-hearted lover of the Lord Jesus and a faithful servant of the Evangel."[27] The minister was the famous Ian McLaren (Dr. John Watson).

Christmas vacation saw the Torreys once again scurry away to Germany. It was necessary to travel Christmas Day, and the family had planned to stop and eat a sumptuous Christmas dinner. Much to their dismay, however, they found restaurants in every city closed and had to be satisfied with buns and sausages on the train instead. The family visited Cologne, Dresden, Berlin, Heidelburg, Munich, Erlangen and Leipzig. Torrey had the opportunity to speak at Leipzig University and gave them his own testimony as a student. He had tried to satisfy his own heart with philosophy but "had found that it would not work." Torrey especially delighted showing his family around the two universities and discussing with them his college days.

The brief vacation was a welcome rest, for the next five months were to be one of Torrey's greatest challenges. In February he and Alexander were to begin in the leading metropolis of the world, London.

[1] MacClean, *Triumphant*, p. 38.
[2] Ibid., p. 39.
[3] Ibid.
[4] Harkness, pp. 21,22.
[5] E. Abbey Tindall, *et al*, *Information About Dr. Torrey and Mr. Alexander* (Manchester: Religious Institute, 1903). Letter to A. P. Fitt, November 29.
[6] MacClean, *Triumphant*, p. 44.
[7] Ibid., p. 62.

[8] Ibid., p. 61.

[9] McNaughton, XLVII, p. 68.

[10] Mrs. Charles Alexander, p. 83.

[11] Ibid.

[12] A. P. Fitt (ed.), *The Institute Tie*, V, (May, 1904), p. 300.

[13] Torrey, Jr., interview, 1965.

[14] Letter to A. F. Gaylord, August 10, 1905.

[15] *An English Mission, Impressions of an American Editor,* (n.d.) pp. 4-13.

[16] MacClean, *Triumphant,* pp. 82,83.

[17] Letter to A. P. Fitt, December 16, 1904.

[18] Ibid.

[19] R. A. Torrey, "Our Lord's Second Coming a Motive for Personal Holiness," *King's Business*, V (May, 1914), p. 257.

[20] Letter to A. P. Fitt, November 14, 1904.

[21] MacClean, pp. 274,275.

[22] Fitt, November 14, 1904.

[23] Letter to Lyman Stewart, April 17, 1914.

[24] MacClean, pp. 286,287.

[25] Fitt, November. 14, 1904.

[26] MacClean, pp. 289, 290.

[27] *Post and Mercury* (Liverpool), January, 1905.

DR. R. A. TORREY AND HIS FAMILY IN ENGLAND

Left to right: Edith, Blanche, Mrs. Torrey, Margaret, Reuben, R. A. Torrey, William S. Jacoby

18. Wind of Pentecost

It is seven o'clock on a wet Saturday night, yet thousands of men are pouring into the score of entrances to Royal Albert Hall, which seats 11,000 people. Members of Parliament, bankers, lawyers, doctors, soldiers, merchants, common laborers and derelicts soon fill the vast circular arena, the tiers of private boxes, the gallery and the balcony. Despite the fact that it is a "for men only" meeting, a throng of women, who have been waiting patiently outside, fill the final seats in the balcony at 7:30.

Then there is a hush among the vast crowd as if prearranged. A radiant and smiling figure mounts the high red dias on the platform. The audience spontaneously bursts out in applause. Alexander quiets the applause, "Let us begin by having a word of prayer. I find we get on better if we have a talk with the Lord first. Our Father, bless us in our singing tonight. May many touch the hem of His garment and find peace."

He announces the hymn and turns the vast ocean of faces before him into a gigantic choir. He scolds, "Watch my hand"; admonishes, "Sing it as if you meant it!" and jokes, "You've been practicing it!" As if hypnotized, the crowd watches the flowing gestures of the tall, slim figure, responding to every word. They not only sing—they sing as he wants them to.

Presently he reads a letter telling of a conversion in the men's meeting the previous Saturday, then calls for testimonies from a group of visiting Cambridge students who came to help in personal work. One after another they arise to tell their experiences.

Then he announces the "Glory Song." "I want you to sing

it all the rest of your life," the leader cries. After the first stanza, he calls on those who have loved ones for whom they are praying to sing it. There is intense feeling as they sing. The remainder of the stanzas the audience sings with a crescendo that is overwhelming. At its conclusion Alexander sings the tender and fetching melody,

> **Tell mother I'll be there, in answer to her prayer,**
> **This message, blessed Saviour, to her bear!**
> **Tell mother I'll be there,**
> **Heav'n's joys with her to share,**
> **Yes, tell my darling mother I'll be there.**

The crowd hushes with emotion.[1]

Torrey quickly mounts the red rostrum, pauses briefly for prayer and immediately plunges into his message. He relates an interview with a London reporter, "Do you expect to convert men by the kind of preaching you do?"

"What is the matter with it?"

"You don't appeal to the emotions; you just reason with men."

He then says to his audience of men,

> Gentlemen, I have had experience with men extending over a great many years. My church is largely a men's church, and I have found this out about men—and it is one of my firmest convictions—that the way to get a man truly converted is to talk to his conscience through his common sense. I think the average speaker along religious lines underestimates the thinking power of the average man, and especially the average working man. . . .Now, I am addressing you men tonight as intelligent human beings. I am presenting to you reasons that you cannot escape to show that you ought to be for Christ, and in a few moments I am going to show my confidence in you by asking you to stand up and take your stand for Christ. And I believe you are going to do it.[2]

For forty-five minutes Torrey presents the claims of Christ to his listeners. With no effort at oratory and with little emotion, he speaks logically, simply and straightforwardly. He rarely moves or gestures or raises his voice, but the audience rivets their attention upon the striking, dignified figure so much in appearance like King Edward VII. His piercing grey eyes gaze into the very soul; he seems to be speaking to each one individually.

Then abruptly the speaker stops, offers a brief prayer and says,

> Now without a song, without any further persuasion, I want to ask every person in the building, old or young, who will here and now yield to the love of God, who will accept Jesus Christ as your personal Saviour, surrender to Him as your Lord and Master, begin to confess Him as such publicly before the world, and live from this time on to please Him in everything day by day—every one who will thus accept Jesus Christ tonight, stand up, all over the building.

There is silence. Then one, and another, and another rises to his feet until there are people standing in every part of the building. Torrey responds, "God bless you. . .and you. . .and you. . . I can't keep track of you all; as you rise just say, 'I will,' and we can hear even if I do not see you."

As the men continue to arise, Alexander sings touchingly, "When I Survey the Wondrous Cross." Others stand to their feet. A good sprinkling of "Amens!" and "Hallelujahs!" come from the lips of rejoicing hearts.

Presently Torrey invites the standing company, in commanding tones, "Step to the front." Long lines of men, young and old, rich and poor, stream toward the platform. Torrey then asks the converts to face the audience and repeat after him, "I have taken Jesus as my Saviour, my Lord and my King." Then the many personal workers take a seat with each convert to pray and give further counsel concerning the Way of Life. Other workers speak to those in the audience. Approximately five to ten minutes lapse, then Torrey addresses the converts gathered together at the front, outlining to them the essentials of living a strong and useful Christian life.

Alexander strikes up, "Praise God From Whom All Blessings Flow," and the crowd, enthusiastic with the great victory, makes the huge hall ring with melody. Alexander dismisses the crowd, but they still linger. He then continues to lead them in revival melodies for another thirty minutes before closing with prayer.[3]

Thus concludes a typical Albert Hall service for men on Saturday nights. These were some of the most successful and influential meetings of the entire Saturday meetings. The two children's meetings, held on Saturday afternoon during the campaign, were also highlights of all their children's work. On both occasions approximately 12,000 boys and girls with their guardians were present.

The London campaign began on February 4. The earlier meetings at Mildmay were primarily an introduction of the evangelistic party to the British Isles. There was no concerted or organized effort to reach the metropolis. But this time it was different. Arrangements were made well in advance to secure approximately 7,000 workers—4,000 choir members, 1,000 ushers, 600 personal workers, 800 house-to-house visitors and 600 committee workers. An unexpected aid was the blaze of publicity given to the meetings by the usually religiously-indisposed press.

The press, however, was not without its skepticism. On the opening night of the campaign a leading London reporter interviewed Torrey just before the service.

"You have taken this building for two consecutive months?"

"Yes," replied Torrey.

"And you expect to fill it every day?"

"Yes."

A little flabbergasted the reporter replied, "Why, no one has ever attempted to hold two weeks' consecutive meetings here of any kind. Gladstone himself could not fill it for two weeks, and you really expect to fill it?"

Torrey answered, "Come and see."[4]

What the reporter saw that night should have been enough. The great hall was filled to capacity with an estimated 10,000 on the outside.

There were apprehensions, however, in the first service. Many wondered whether Alexander could conquer the vast new audience, but very shortly he completely captivated the hearts and voices of the people. Before long the entire metropolis was singing the revival melodies of "Alexander the Great," as he came to be known.

Torrey spoke with great conviction that first evening on "What It Costs Not to Be a Christian." At the invitation the first person to stand and publicly confess Christ was an officer in the British army, Colonel Horace G. P. Beauchamp, who was seated on the platform. The man immediately became an earnest worker, and his conversion was one of the most influential of the mission.

Possibly the most remarkable conversion, however, judging from the impact it made on metropolitan London, was that of Quentin Ashlyn, a concert hall singer and entertainer. His life was a complete transformation, and soon he was conducting services and giving his testimony in the concert hall where he had previously performed.

Popular noonday meetings for businessmen were also scheduled in the large chamber of the Cannon Street Hotel. Torrey delivered during these sessions his usual lectures on the Bible, the Holy Spirit, the resurrection, prayer, and infidelity, and also devoted some time to questions.

One day as he was speaking on "Why I Believe the Bible to Be the Word of God," two men promptly stood up, evidently at a given signal, to question the preacher. One was in the center of the auditorium; the other, in the gallery behind the speaker. Both began speaking at once. Torrey hesitated but a moment before the wondering congregation and pointed his finger at the man before him, "What is your name?" The man tried to evade the query, but Torrey repeated his statement. The sharp, stentorian tones of the preacher caused the man to waver a little. Then Torrey said, "Gentlemen, this man is ashamed of his name, and I am ashamed of him." The objector sank into his chair. In the meantime the man in the gallery had become quiet. But Torrey turned sharply upon him, "Are you ashamed of your name also?"[5]

The incident was closed. Torrey had little patience with an insincere or interrupting critic. For instance, there was the time when one of his questioners asked, "Seeing you claim to be so much like Christ, will you kindly tell us if you can walk on water?" The crowd laughed, but as the merriment ceased, the speaker said, "Yes, I can walk on water. . .(long pause) much better than I can on whiskey!"[6]

Few were the times when Torrey was not in full command of the situation. Sometimes he turned a perturbing situation into one of merriment. One night in Albert Hall as he had come to the final and critical division of his message, a colossal man in the third row arose and made his way to the exit. His heavy step made an awful thud, and his boots creaked unmercifully. Torrey stopped as the man, unmindful of the disturbance he was causing, continued down the long aisle. When he was almost to the exit, Torrey thundered out, "In our country creaky shoes indicate they are not paid for." The crowd roared, but the incident was soon forgotten as Torrey continued his message.

Torrey made a striking impression upon the people of London. He was of English stock, dignified and had the look of royalty about him. Then there was that rare power, puzzling to most, that never failed to move men and women to decision for Christ. He did not shout but always made himself heard—one of the few ever to achieve this in Royal Albert Hall. He was remarkably free from mannerisms and was just himself as he stood before the people. He seemed to be so different from the usual evangelist; yet marvelous results attended his preaching.

An associate, George T. B. Davis, noted,

> One of the most beautiful features in his work is the short prayer which he invariably offers just before delivering his sermon. For two or three minutes he seems to forget the things of this world and to stand in the very presence of God; and it is wonderful to see how his prayer for the salvation of men is often answered ere the service is concluded.[7]

Londoners also noticed the closeness that existed

Torrey-Alexander mission Albert Hall

Cook Photo 819 Fulham Rd

between Mrs. Torrey and her husband, a reminder of the relationship of the famous Gladstone and his wife. She accompanied him to all of his meetings, and many observed their tender affection for each other, displaying itself in some little word or act. They were inseparable even in public life. Mrs. Torrey, in her quiet, unassuming way, was a constant source of strength and inspiration to her husband. Further, she actively engaged herself in personal work in the meetings.

The two months' campaign closed on Wednesday, March 29. The great hall was filled, and thousands outside were clamoring for admission. And who was Torrey to see but the same reporter he had talked to on the opening night. Torrey stepped up to him and said, "Has it been filled?" The reporter smiled and answered, "It has."

Torrey regarded the meetings as some of the most remarkable he had ever witnessed, "There was no loud excitement, but the awful hush of God's own presence. People seemed to sit spellbound, held by the power of God's Spirit. The interest throughout the sermon was intense, at times painfully intense, and then when the invitation was given out the response was prompt and large." [8]

Lord Kinnaird, the president of the London Evangelistic Council, said:

> It has exceeded our most sanguine expectation. There never has been a continuous series of meetings with so large an attendance. The meetings of Moody and Sankey did not attract larger numbers, and in no instance did these missioners stay so long in one place. . . .We have reached the people we intended to reach, and to a most astonishing extent. [9]

A. C. Dixon, who was abroad participating in the Baptist World Congress, was the special guest of Kinnaird toward the end of the campaign. He came away from the closing service with the burning conviction that "the wind of Pentecost is blowing upon the church of God."

The evangelists spent the months of April, May and June in Brixton, South London, and on the Strand. The accommodations in both places would allow no more than a 5,000-seating capacity, but it gave the people in different sections of London an opportunity to share in the mission. The meetings, which were similar though not as spectacular as those in Royal Albert Hall, continued to stir the city of London.

The combined recorded decisions for the full five months in London were 17,000. It climaxed one of the greatest evangelistic efforts of all time. Londoners were inclined to believe him when he said one night in Brixton,

> I would rather win souls than be the greatest king or emperor on earth; I would rather win souls than be the greatest general that ever commanded an army; I would rather win souls than be the greatest poet, or novelist, or literary man who ever walked the earth. My one ambition in life is to win as many as possible. Oh, it is the only thing worth doing, to save souls, and men and women, we can all do it.[10]

But such extended efforts begin to tell on a person, particularly when he is speaking as many as eight times a day, and more frequently at least five times. At the conclusion of the mission Torrey began to show signs of physical strain. During the mission the committee, enthusiastic about the marvelous results, wanted Torrey to preach also on his rest evenings—usually Monday. This suggestion did not sway Torrey, however, for he believed in one day of complete rest and always took it. Without it he might not have been able to conclude the London mission.

It was indeed a refreshing thought to spend his vacation once again in Germany for the summer. There was only the Christian Endeavor Convention in Berlin, then he would be on his own. But, unfortunately, the London Committee had made further arrangements for him to speak in Berlin.

Mrs. Torrey was a bit perturbed when she wrote to Gaylord from Germany,

> They arranged for him to conduct evangelistic meetings for the rest of the week, which meant two meetings a day for four days longer. I did not like it at all, and do not think it was right. But as they had it all arranged and there is a religious awakening in Berlin and on account of the great interest at this time, Mr. Torrey

consented to finish the week in that way. . .(There were) forty professed conversions at one of the afternoon meetings. He has spoken through an interpreter and been so happy that he could preach the Gospel to the Germans.[11]

Mrs. Torrey also reported that her husband had fainted in the elevator coming up for breakfast that morning—something most unusual for the ordinarily robust Torrey. Many conversions, however, were witnessed in the evening meetings, especially when he ministered in the large tent, seating about 5,000.[12]

The remainder of the summer was a splendid time for Torrey and the family. They engaged in the usual recreations and enjoyed them immensely. During the summer Torrey held a brief conference in Liebenselle, Germany. A revealing incident took place when he came before the custom's officials. With an air of credulity, they asked him for his marriage license. Torrey was indignant. "I am a minister of the Gospel, and I have been preaching across the whole continent of Europe, and you ask for my marriage license. The very idea."

The officials were cowed and Reuben was greatly surprised at his father. He had never heard him talk like that before. But later his father laughed unroariously, and he saw that it was an act. Explaining the situation to him he said, "Reuben, sometimes you have to answer a fool according to his folly."[13]

Soon the summer was over, and preparations were made for the final three missions in Sheffield, Plymouth and Oxford, England. The places were interesting because of the different classes of people. Sheffield was a manufacturing center with many cutlery workers; Plymouth, a military and naval center with approximately 25,000 personnel; and Oxford, a great university center with a large student body. Many conversions resulted from the Sheffield and Plymouth meetings, but Oxford was a little harder to convince.

At first there was considerable opposition in Oxford, even among the professedly Christian students. But the personal contact of both Torrey and Alexander with the students in their dormitory rooms and at dinner aided greatly in breaking down the barrier. They had more personal contact with the Oxford students than with any other group in their entire world tour.

Torrey recognized some of the peculiar obstacles of the cultural, intellectual class of people, but it in no way altered his message. Speaking to both "town and gown," he pointedly remarked in one of his sermons:

> The road to pride has two sides; the genteel side and the vicious side, but it is the same road and it leads to the same place. A great many of you people want to be saved in the literary and aesthetic way. You want to be saved by going to church and listening to pulpit orations and have the light stealing in through beautiful stained-glass windows, to the exquisite beauty of a matchless organ wonderfully played so that the music thrills you and steals through your whole heart, and where there is incense and everything that is delightful to the senses, where you get to feel very aesthetic and very much soothed and very delightful, and you think this is art religion. It won't save you. . . .There is just one door into the Kingdom, and everybody has to stoop to enter it. Everyone has to enter that door as a sinner.[14]

An incident of note occurred during the meetings, but it was not known until after their conclusion. One of the most prominent men in the colleges composing the university had openly denied in his classes the infallibility of Christ either in doctrine or in conduct. After the meetings, however, the same scholar presided at an Evangelical Missionary meeting and announced his acceptance of the truth he formerly denied. He said, "Under God I owe all this to Dr. Torrey."[15]

By the end of the Oxford meeting the complexion had changed so considerably that Torrey felt that the time was "among the most profitable spent in this country." It was a fitting climax to the four-year stay abroad. Despite a multitude of invitations to key cities in the British Isles—"the English people would like to keep us for years"—as well as to Sweden and South Africa, Torrey was ready to return to America. It had been a very profitable but strenuous four years and Torrey had not missed a single service in all of that time.

In an interview at the close of the missions in the British Isles, he was asked to comment on its chief characteristics. He replied:

> Dependence upon God; prayer to God of thousands of people all over the world; large expectations from God; a belief in the entire Bible as a divine revelation; a persistent preaching of the old doctrines that have ever proved effective in winning men to Christ; and the emphasis laid upon the personality and work of the Holy Spirit.[16]

In the statistical realm the approximate number of available registered decisions in Great Britain were as follows:

Glasgow	3,000	Bristol	4,500
Aberdeen	2,000	Bolton	3,600
Belfast	4,000	Cardiff	3,750
Liverpool (first)	4,000	Liverpool (second)	6,000
Manchester	4,000	London	17,000
Birmingham	7,700	Plymouth	3,500
Dublin	3,000	Sheffield	3,300
		Oxford	800

The aggregate total is over 70,000 although the number does not include all of the British cities visited. It is noteworthy that "in most British cities the results of Torrey's meetings surpassed those of Moody's."[17]

Torrey's main concern, however, was not with the decisions of the present. He often told Christians that if the revival has been real "it will not terminate in yourselves." Reuben observed later,

> Even of recent years I have met persons from England and Scotland who were converted in my father's meetings and frequently I have been told that the results of his meetings have stood and made a more permanent effect on the religious life of these countries than other such meetings. This they have ascribed to his logic, avoidance of emotionalism and insistence on joining a church and studying the Bible.[18]

On November 28 a great farewell service was held for the evangelists in Liverpool. An album containing an illuminated address was given to them, bearing the signatures from members of the committees in every city they had visited in the British Isles.

The text read,

> We thank God upon every remembrance of you. We thank Him for your winning personality; for your clearness of judgment, and for the graciousness of your address. We thank Him for the way you have opened to us the Scriptures; for new light from the old lamp; for instruction in what the Bible teaches; for the marvelous effect with which you have wielded "the Sword of the Spirit," and for the help given to many to a clearer realization of the love of the Father, the grace of the Son, and the communion of the Spirit.[19]

Torrey then gave a brief address on Philippians 4:4 and Ephesians 6:10, which was aimed principally at the converts. Then during the closing song, as was his custom, he quietly slipped away.

[1]Davis, *Twice Around,* pp. 177-181.

[2]MacClean, *Triumphant,* p. 162.

[3]Davis, pp. 177-182; Torrey, Jr., interview.

[4]Torrey, *Uplifted Christ,* p. 18.

[5]Harkness, pp. 64, 65.

[6]Ibid. p. 68.

[7]Davis, *Torrey,* pp. 244, 245.

[8]MacClean, *Triumphant,* pp. 188, 189.

[9]Davis, *Twice Around,* p. 161.

[10]Davis, *Torrey,* pp. 209, 210.

[11]Letter to A. F. Gaylord, July 17, 1905.

[12]Rev. Fred Brose, personal letter, October 27, 1964. Mr. Brose was a student in Germany at the time.

[13]Torrey, Jr., interview

[14]MacClean, *Triumphant,* pp. 264, 265.

[15]R. A. Torrey, *The Divine Origin of the Bible* (Chicago: Revell, 1899), p. 31.

[16]MacClean, *Triumphant,* pp. 227,228.

[17]William McLoughlin, Jr., *Modern Revivalism* (New York: The Ronald Press, 1959), p. 367. Torrey was both conservative and conscientious in his estimate of numbers. He felt that in most cases the statistics were placed too high.

[18]Torrey, Jr., personal letter, April 7, 1965. As recently as 1972, on a ship crossing the English Channel, this author met a minister of the Free Church of Scotland who joyfully recounted how his mother had been converted in Torrey's campaign in Dundee.

[19]MacClean, *Triumphant,* p. 269.

PART V

"Holding Forth the Word of Life"
(1906-1928)

19. Prophet With Honor

"A prophet is not without honour, but in his own country," Jesus said of His own recognition in Galilee. For Torrey it was similar. As one of his closest friends said, "Torrey was never appreciated at his full value, until the rest of the world communicated its estimate of him to his homeland."[1] It took the honor of Japan, China, Australia, New Zealand, India and the British Isles to convince Americans that they had a prophet *with* honor in their own country.

Despite the great impact of the campaigns abroad, which exceeded the dreams of even the most faithful, there was a lingering doubt as to a similar Torrey-Alexander success in their native land. No small part of this hesitancy stemmed from a new climate toward evangelism which had developed among a large share of America's religious leaders. Considerable opposition greeted the evangelists even before they touched American shores.

One group of Congregationalist ministers, after a visit to Great Britain to observe the work of the evangelists, voiced considerable opposition. One of them, Dr. Samuel Parkes Cadman, of Brooklyn, observed:

> I am in active sympathy with all genuine evangelical work, but I am opposed to its being used for the advancing of any peculiar theological views which create division in the church and excite just opposition among thinking men everywhere. We are not going to win the great fight which is upon us by clinging to obsolete traditions which have been discarded by the sane, reverent and constructive scholarship of Christianity; and when these traditions, which are matters of private opinion, are insisted upon as dogmas necessary to salvation, I for one

refuse to be allied with any such human perversion of the
Divine truth. [2]

His objections were primarily directed toward three focal
doctrines—the plenary inspiration and inerrancy of
Scripture, the substitutionary atonement of Christ and the
eternal punishment of the wicked. To Torrey it seemed a
little strange to label these historic church doctrines as
"peculiar theological views," "obsolete traditions,"
"private opinions" and "perversions of the Divine truth."
He viewed Cadman's remarks as simply reflecting the
growing liberal sentiment of the time.

Other criticism centered in the validity of conversion.
One prominent critic objected to any revival "which treats
redemption as getting out of Hell into Heaven—that is, out
of horrible pain into celestial pleasure; which teaches any
man to think himself 'saved' unless his character is
transformed." He stated further that a genuine revival
should "lead to higher and holier living. . .leave behind
them the churches strengthened, the sources and springs of
vice weakened, higher standards of honesty in business,
public spirit in politics, purity in society and love in the
home." [3]

Such objections seemed quaint since the Torrey
meetings were especially marked in their radical impact on
the life of the individual, the church and the community.
Rev. A. T. Pierson, noted evangelical, replied that
"wherever Torrey has labored, not only have marked
conversions followed, but all evangelical work has been
stimulated. . . .The closer the work has been watched, the
more satisfactory have the results been found." [4] But as the
same critic said, referring to the lasting nature of the
Finney and Moody meetings, "It may be too soon to look
for similar fruits of Mr. Torrey's ministry."

Still others criticized the tendency to commercialism and
the large machinery of the meetings—the staff of workers,
the large choir, the big auditoriums, in short, everything on
the scale of bigness. But Torrey probably felt more keenly
about this than his critics. He had said earlier in a letter to
Fitt, "A good deal of commercialism has been creeping into

our work, and more and more machinery and I fear less dependence upon God." [5]

The commercialist tendency was unintentional, but rather easily became an issue in the minds of many through the sale of Alexander's popular little red-backed hymnbooks. Although the objection seemed more apparent than real—Alexander didn't make a penny of personal profit—Torrey took definite measures to curb this tendency and did not allow their sale in America.

As to the "bigness" of the meetings, originally Torrey had planned his campaigns along simple, old-fashioned lines with only preacher and singer. But the campaigns vastly exceeded the expectations of everyone, and it became necessary to add workers and do things on a grander scale. Torrey did not object in principle to bigness; however, he was disturbed when others seemed to depend upon it for success. He felt the great need was "dependence upon the Holy Spirit, a work that from start to finish is carried on in an atmosphere of prayer 'in the Holy Ghost.' " [6]

Then there was the usual critique about emotionalism. This attack was less frequent in the Torrey campaigns, however, as few would dare to label him as an emotional preacher! In fact there were some who criticized the meetings because of the lack of emotion. Torrey's attitude is reflected in an interview with a reporter. "I cannot say that I fully advocate the old-time style of revival where emotion was the chief instrument. . . .I always think of myself as a lawyer when I get up to speak and of the audience as a jury." [7] As Torrey frequently said, "I am one of those persons who has to get along without an overabundance of emotion."

Those who objected on this count usually leveled it at Alexander, and particularly in his use of such songs as "Tell Mother I'll Be There." Alexander originally hesitated using this song because of the same reason. But once he saw the genuine spiritual effect it had upon others in his earlier meetings with Milan Williams he made standard use of it.

Whatever criticisms and reservations others had concerning revival in America, Torrey was unmoved by them. After a short welcome meeting and conference in Chicago, he proceeded to Toronto, Canada, in January for his first meeting in North America. This figure of "radiant activity," as one Toronto newspaper called him, preached to crowds which could not be handled in the 4,000-seat Massey Hall. It was one of his most successful four-week meetings, and approximately 4,500 decisions were recorded. [8]

On the final day of the campaign two brothers traveled almost one hundred miles to hear the evangelists. One of the brothers described the service.

> We arrived early and the Hall was crowded. What Dr. Torrey said I do not remember. But I will never forget the way he repeated his text, Isaiah 53—"But He was wounded for *my* transgressions; He was bruised for *my* iniquities; the chastisement of *my* peace was upon Him, and with His stripes *I* am healed."

This sixteen-year-old lad, along with his brother, stepped out to make the great decision. He was Oswald Smith, later to become the pastor of the famous People's Church in Toronto. The other brother also went into the ministry. [9]

The first meeting of the evangelists in the United States was in Philadelphia during the months of February through April. Preparations had been made on a large scale somewhat similar to the Melbourne Mission. Two large armories located in both the northern and southern sections of the city were remodeled for the campaign. The first month was given to the northern section; the final two months, to the southern. Frequently crowds of 9,000 daily poured into the armories—approximately 3,500 for the afternoon and 5,500 for the evening.

There was a particularly large response on the part of the businessmen of Philadelphia. Torrey always appealed to this class; however, the significant number reached was aided by two innovations. One was the revival luncheon conducted especially for businessmen in a hotel or restaurant. The program was simple—singing, testimonies from Christian businessmen and a few pointed remarks by Alexander. The other was the inquiry room suite located in the heart of the city. It was established to help those in spiritual need and was directed by William S. Jacoby, who had now joined the staff of the evangelist.

The evangelists also took a special interest in the college students and spoke in four colleges and three medical schools in the city. Torrey was also invited to speak at the University of Pennsylvania; Alexander, to Princeton University, where Woodrow Wilson was president. No doubt Torrey's most unusual meeting was with Theatrical Women's Sabbath Association at the invitation of Miss Bessie McCoy. Torrey never avoided meeting with any person or group although he declined their invitation to attend a theatrical performance.

Torrey's objection to the stage was sensible.

> The theater is an institution, and we must judge it as an institution, judge it as it really exists today. It is possible to imagine a stage of the purest and loftiest character, and to imagine plays that would be among the most elevating of all the influences in society; but the question is not of the stage, and the plays, as we can imagine them, but of the stage as it actually exists today.[10]

His cordial meeting with the ladies in no way mitigated his remarks concerning the theater. In fact, the theatrical managers of Philadelphia estimated that his meeting cost them over $60,000!

Some of the most interesting meetings were in the afternoon. These were more informal, and Torrey gave considerable time to the answering of Bible questions. In fact, on Saturdays he devoted the entire time to questions. The audience relished his answers—especially those directed toward objectors. Many used the occasion to vent their venom and even dared Torrey to read the question. But his reply was, "Read them? Why not? I am willing to read anything." He gave answers on almost every conceivable topic—including those two favorites, "Where did Cain get his wife?" and "How could the whale swallow Jonah?"

It was at one of those afternoon services that an interesting incident took place. During the previous evening in an unusually warm service Harkness stepped out for a breath of fresh air just as Torrey mounted the rostrum to speak. When Harkness returned and began his accompaniment for the close of the service, Torrey stepped down from the platform and met the young musician with the terse remark, "When I get up to preach, it is no sign for you to get up and walk out." The words were audible for some distance, and it amused the choir. Only the solemnity of the moment prevented outright laughter.

The next day Torrey, who undoubtedly felt he had been a little severe with his pianist, cheerfully approached Harkness about fifteen minutes before the afternoon service, "Bob, I want you to give a ten-minute talk."

"But what shall I say?"

"Tell them your experience. They have heard you play and have sung your songs. The people will appreciate a word from you."

When Torrey introduced "Bob," as he always referred to him, Harkness whispered, "What is your subject today? I want to say something in keeping with it." Torrey, who always approved of continuity of thought in a service, said, "What It Costs Not to Be a Christian," and further added, "Take all the time you like."

Then Harkness, thoroughly familiar with the sermon, proceeded to outline the message, giving two or three well-chosen sentences on each point, couched in the exact language of the evangelist. As his pianist descended from the platform a thoroughly nonplussed Torrey quickly called for Alexander, "Charlie! Charlie! Come here! Put on three songs. He has stolen my sermon, and I must get another ready." Alexander, convulsed with laughter, quickly "put on " three songs. At later times when the incident was resurrected in friendly conversation, Torrey always rejoined, "That wasn't a joke; it was a theft."[11]

The Philadelphia meeting was the longest of any in the United States, and was one of the most successful. There were nearly 5,000 converts during the meeting—a number of them leaders in the business and political life of the city. According to the *Chicago Daily News*,

> One of the most striking features of the movement has been the way in which local revivals have sprung up in large numbers of Philadelphia churches. Such large numbers of converts are uniting with the churches that it is not infrequent to hear of over 100 persons being received into a single church at one time.[12]

Torrey was especially gratified with this latter feature. "I think that is more to be rejoiced in than the great interest in the meetings in the armory." He further noted,

> In the souls won, in the interest aroused among professing Christians, in the churches which have been awakened and in the great wave of religious feeling which has gone all over the city, the mission has been a success. I have been happy in my work here and shall look back on it with greatest pleasure.[13]

In fact, Torrey was so happy in Philadelphia that he decided to move there from his summer home in Northfield.

The months of May and June were spent in Atlanta, Georgia, and Ottawa, Canada. Similar successes attended the meetings, particularly the latter. In both cities there was a remarkable decision of a well-known individual. In Atlanta it was the return to Christ of one of the South's most prominent evangelists, Rev. Sam Small. It had an electrifying effect on the Atlanta area. In Ottawa there was Alf Allen, champion middleweight boxer of Canada, who almost immediately began studies for the ministry at Moody Bible Institute.

Alexander had his most difficult time in Atlanta. The separation from his wife, who was still in Birmingham and now seriously ill, began to affect him. And although he was more of his old self in the Ottawa meetings, he longed to return to his adopted "Tennessee" in England. After the campaign he hurried to her side. Shortly after his arrival she had to undergo a very serious operation in which her life hung in the balance for several days. The doctor prescribed complete rest—perhaps a sea voyage—as necessary to her recovery. Thus Alexander discontinued his work with Torrey in order to spend his time with her.

Torrey wrote to friends in Birmingham, "It was a wonderful sacrifice on his part to leave her all these months, to follow the call of God and sing the Gospel in this country, but I could not consent to his being away from her now." He further added, "We are hoping that our separation may be short, and that we may soon be reunited in our work." [14]

During the summer Torrey kept busy, with hardly a break, in shorter evangelistic engagements and Bible conference work. He spent considerable time in the well-known conference grounds such as Mt. Hermon, California; Winona Lake, Indiana; and Northfield.

In the fall of the year Reuben enrolled in Lafayette College in Easton, Pennsylvania. It had been Torrey's desire for Reuben to attend Yale as he had, but the latter's going abroad would have necessitated his waiting an additional year to matriculate. Torrey felt Lafayette would give Reuben a solid education, and besides, it was close to their new home in Philadelphia. Edith, along with Blanche and young Margaret, resided at home with their parents.

Torrey did not feel fully ready for the campaigns in the fall. The heavy summer's work had taken its toll. He wrote to Fitt, "I need all the rest I can get before undertaking the work at Nashville. I have been shut out of my rest all summer." He further stated, "I am laid up with hay fever. Last night was the first night I have been in bed for over four weeks. I am not suffering much, but my cough keeps me awake, and I have to sit up." [15] It was that chronic hay fever trouble right on schedule in late summer.

A further complication concerned Alexander. The anticipated reunion did not take place. Alexander's absence was longer than intended, largely due to the accidental death of Mrs. Alexander's mother. This had necessitated another trip to England. Since Alexander could not give Torrey a definite committal, it became necessary for him to engage D. B. Towner of Moody Bible Institute as his songleader and Charles Butler as soloist. [16]

Neither Towner nor Butler, a baritone whom Alexander said "sounded like he had orange blossoms in his voice," could quite match the sunshine brightness and platform leadership of "Charlie." Their sterling worth as evangelistic musicians was quickly recognized, however, in the fall campaign in Nashville.

The Nashville meeting was difficult at the beginning. An indifference seemed to characterize the "Bible belt" audience so used to evangelistic campaigns. "What will it take to wake you up?" he exclaimed to his audience one evening.[17] But at the campaign's end the audience was sufficiently "waked up"—in point of fact the entire city was stirred. At the close of the meeting he was invited to address a memorial service for the late Evangelist Sam Jones in the famous Ryman Auditorium. The evangelistic party left for Omaha after the Nashville meeting and then began in Cleveland the first of the year.

Torrey wrote enthusiastically to Fitt about the Cleveland meeting, "I do not know when I have seen such deep feeling. . . .Cleveland has been called 'the graveyard of the evangelist,' but God is giving us great victory." [18] This despite the fact that rats ran through the hall among the audience, and hoodlums pelted the building with stones from the outside!

An interesting interview with Torrey was conducted by a reporter of the *Cleveland Press* as to the typical workday of the evangelist.

> I rise when I have slept enough. I exercise with dumbbells until the kinks are out of my muscles, and then I jump into a tub of cold water. Then breakfast. Diet? Oh, no. Whatever is put before me. I always manage to get in a brisk walk after breakfast. If I have time, I take a long jaunt. But before that I must dictate letters. This is my most perplexing duty. . . .After my walk I return to my hotel to study and think. . . .My day's work begins with the noon meeting, and from then on, except for brief intervals, I have no rest until nearly midnight.

> The strain is sometimes tense, but I do not resort to

stimulants to help me bear it. . . .For the rest I never
worry. I have always been strong and healthy. . . .God
has been good to me. [19]

The most remarkable campaign of the year, however,
was that of Buffalo. Torrey noted that the meetings
"eclipse anything we have witnessed in this country," and
further, "We have never dared to look for such splendid
results the first week." After a meeting in which 702 men
came to accept Christ, Bishop Berry leaned over to Torrey
and exclaimed, "Why, this is Pentecost!" [20] Torrey's
preaching had a thunderous impact upon the audience and
caused a Buffalo *Express* reporter to describe his preaching
as having the "relentless quality" of Cotton Mather,
Jonathan Edwards and Charles G. Finney.

At the beginning of the summer the "prophet with
honor" was awarded the Doctor of Divinity degree from
Wheaton College on June 20, 1907. It was given because of
"outstanding service in the fields of evangelism and
Christian education." [21] Actually Torrey had received
numbers of offers for an honorary degree; however, he felt a
doctor's degree was of no vital importance and had declined
them all.

His change of mind was due to a very practical situation.
Because of his rare Biblical scholarship and his graduate
work in Germany practically everyone referred to him as
"Dr. Torrey." In strict honesty he felt compelled to explain
that he did not own such a degree. This became annoying
in its frequency, so he finally relented and accepted an
honorary doctorate. He chose to allow Wheaton College to
confer the degree because of the school's strong evangelical
stand and also because of his warm friendship with the
president, Dr. Charles Blanchard. [22]

The summer of 1907 was busy as usual, but was marked
by two conversations, which were to have an important
bearing on Torrey's future ministry.

The first was with a friend of Minneapolis days, T. C.
"Daddy" Horton. Horton and a wealthy layman, Lyman
C Stewart, were contemplating the starting of a Bible

Institute in Los Angeles. Considering Dr. Torrey as the foremost authority on Bible schools, both men eagerly sought his advice. Dr. Torrey thought Los Angeles an excellent place for an Institute and agreed to help launch it with a three-month evangelistic campaign in January. Could Dr. Torrey have sensed a possible future connection with the Institute?

The other conversation was with Dr. John Murdock MacInnis, pastor of the First Presbyterian Church in Montrose, Pennsylvania. MacInnis had visited Northfield and was impressed with the great spiritual impact of the conference. He felt that another such conference ground should be established which was more readily accessible to the middle states. Knowing of Torrey's similar interest, MacInnis elicited his promise that he would not decide on a site until he had seen Montrose. Rather reluctantly Dr. Torrey agreed to stop by briefly on his way to Chicago in the fall.

[1]W. B. Riley, "R. A. Torrey as a Preacher," *King's Business,* XXVII (January, 1936), p. 6.

[2]Charles S. MacFarland, "New Attitudes Toward Evangelism," *Current Literature,* XL (February, 1906), p. 163.

[3]Edward F. Merriam (ed.), "The Torrey-Alexander Mission," LXXXI *Outlook* (December 2, 1905), p. 806.

[4]MacFarland, p. 164.

[5]Letter to A. P. Fitt, November 29, 1904.

[6]R. A. Torrey, "The Revival We Need," *King's Business,* VI (October, 1915), pp. 848,849.

[7]McLoughlin, Jr., p. 371. Torrey wrote to Fitt, speaking of the ministry of Gipsy Smith, "Of course, Gipsy's method of appealing constantly to the emotions is not my line, but I think it does good, provided those who are led by this to take a stand are wisely dealt with and led to an intelligent acceptance of Christ." Letter to A. P. Fitt, January 21, 1907.

[8]Davis, *Twice Around,* pp. 232,233.

[9]Oswald J. Smith, *The Story of My Life* (London: Marshall, Morgan and Scott, 1962), p. 20.

[10]Torrey, *Power,* p. 113.

[11]Harkness, pp. 72-75.

[12]*The Chicago Daily News,* May 3, 1906.

[13]Ibid.

[14]Mrs. Charles Alexander, p. 118.

[15]Letter to A. P. Fitt, September 8, 1906.

[16]Alexander was a perfect complement to Torrey in the latter's campaigns, but it is certainly seriously amiss to say, "Without Alexander, Torrey would never have been a successful evangelist." McLoughlin, Jr., *Modern Revivalism*, p. 374. Dr. Torrey carried on very significant campaigns for a number of years without Alexander. Alexander joined Evangelist J. Wilbur Chapman the following year for an around-the-world evangelistic tour.

[17]Dr. Torrey did not have as strong a personal appeal with Southern audiences. He was always more effective with Northern and Eastern audiences.

[18]Letter to A. P. Fitt, January 21, 1907.

[19]"How Torrey Lived," *Moody Memo*, X (February 3, 1956)

[20]Letter to the pastors of Scranton, Pennsylvania, July 28, 1908.

[21]Letter from Edward Coray, Wheaton Alumni Association, Wheaton College, August 28, 1964.

[22]Torrey, Jr., interview.

20. Sunset Knoll

The train chugged slowly, wending its way up the heavily-forested Blue Ridge Mountains. As Dr. Torrey gazed out upon the seemingly forbidding landscape, he mused, "Perhaps I shouldn't have made that promise to MacInnis. I have about decided on that other site for a conference ground!" [1]

Presently his reverie ended as the train came to an abrupt halt, some 1,700 feet high, in the picturesque little Pennsylvania village of Montrose. Its many white houses with green shutters reflected some of its historic New England charm. MacInnis was there to greet him and he promptly whisked Torrey up to the tract of land just before sunset.

The view from the top of the little hill was breathtaking. The rolling hills and rugged but scenic forests, decorated with autumn colors and bathed in the glow of the setting sun, prompted an enthusiastic, "This is the most beautiful site for a Bible conference I have ever seen." [2] Dr. Torrey knelt with MacInnis in prayer, and made a quick decision to purchase the property.

Many thoughts must have crossed the evanglist's mind about Montrose as he continued his journey to Chicago. For some time Torrey had keenly felt the need for a conference which would avoid the encroachments of liberalism and have a strong emphasis on Bible study and prayer. The main question had been "Where?" Now he began to formulate definite plans for a conference program. He thought to himself, "Would it be possible to begin next summer?" But for the present there was the Chicago meeting.

There were fond memories of Chicago. His work with Mr. Moody in both the Institute and the Chicago Avenue Church would never be forgotten. Here also is where the first stirrings of world-wide revival had begun some six years previous.

Torrey had been invited for the campaign, which lasted throughout the months of October and November, through the auspices of the Laymen's Evangelistic Council of Chicago. The Council had been formed earlier in the year because "a number of independent groups of businessmen, as well as the several denominational young men's organizations were all committed to some specific evangelistic endeavor." [3] Therefore some definite steps were taken toward the formation of a "responsible body of laymen for the promotion of the evangelistic effort in Chicago."

In all of Torrey's campaigns—as well as those of Moody—there had usually been at least one layman of wealth and influence at the head of the committees. For example, there were John H. Converse, head of Baldwin Locomotive Works, and John Wanamaker, wealthy department store owner, in Philadelphia. Asa G. Candler, wealthy Coca-cola magnat, led in the Atlanta meetings. Laymen had the principal charge of the meetings in Nashville, and the Chicago campaign was exclusively sponsored by laymen. Henry P. Crowell, president of Quaker Oats, was the guiding light in Chicago.

This shifting of responsibility to laymen was indicative of both the increasing concern on the part of laymen for evangelism and also of the difficulty in enlisting the cooperation of ministers in an evangelistic effort. Torrey had noted earlier that even in cases of direct sponsorship the "ministers seem to think that their duty is over when they come and sympathize." But the newer liberal attitudes toward evangelism now adversely affected many of the ministers. The campaign in Chicago, however, was greatly aided by a number of important ministers (there was a strong Minister's Advisory Council) and, of course, the students of Moody Bible Institute.

Large preparations were made for the meeting. A heated tent with a capacity of 5,000 was erected on a vacant lot near the center of the city for the evening meetings. In addition, the Great Northern Theater was engaged for three weeks of noonday meetings, primarily for businessmen.

The meetings proved highly successful. In an article in the *Chicago Tribune* entitled "3,000 Converted in Eight Weeks," it was stated that "statistics of the revival are said to demonstrate that it has been the most successful campaign of the kind ever held west of the Alleghanies." There were 2,048 who stepped forward publicly to sign decision cards in the meetings. The noonday meetings in the Great Northern Theater, in which Torrey lectured to strengthen Christians in the veracity of the Scriptures, were one of the signal accomplishments of the meeting. As usual, Torrey made quite an impact on the businessmen, and the Laymen's Evangelistic Association grew from its initial number of 60 to 275. Most of this was due to these noonday meetings. [4]

Dr. Torrey had looked forward with great anticipation to a three-month meeting in January in Los Angeles; however, the large building to be used for the meeting was condemned shortly before the scheduled start. Since there were no other suitable accommodations, the meeting had to be abandoned. The meeting had been designed to launch the new Bible Institute in Los Angeles. Despite this setback, however, the Bible Institute began as scheduled.

In the meantime, Dr. Torrey turned his attention toward the Montrose Bible Conference. While in Chicago he had called a meeting of close associates to discuss plans for the conference. Now he issued a call to evangelical Christians for the very next summer.

> I now invite all those who love the Word of God and believe God answers prayer and who are burdened concerning the present state of the church and the world to meet for Bible study, prayer and mutual conference at Montrose, Pennsylvania, from August 21 through 30. [5]

After his return to Philadelphia, he performed the

wedding ceremony of his daughter Blanche in December.
She had become engaged to Herbert Wiggs of Elberton,
Georgia. She had always been known as the "sunbeam" of
the family, and it was difficult to give her up. When her
father said, "Blanche, will you take this man. . .," he
choked up a bit and lost some of his usual composure.[6] The
happy couple made their home in Elberton.

The winter and spring months passed rapidly. Despite
the Los Angeles cancellation, Dr. Torrey managed to keep
busy in evangelistic campaigns in both metropolitan
centers (such as Detroit in March of that year) and lesser
cities. One of his experiences in the latter category is worth
recounting.

Dr. Torrey had accepted an invitation to a midwestern
rural city upon the terms that a 2,500-seat tabernacle
should be built for the meeting. Upon his arrival he found a
hastily-erected tent which would not seat a thousand. His
response to the situation and the inviting committee was
chilly. He charged, "You are dishonoring God by failing to
live up to your contract." On the spot he predicted that a
rainstorm would come the following day and ruin the
service. Despite retorts that it never rained at that time of
year, the unbelievable happened. The next day a downpour
drenched the audience and ruined both the tent and the
service. Services continued in one of the churches until the
tent was repaired and enlarged.

Dr. Torrey, however, with his deeply engrained sense of
obligation, could not resist frequently pointing out the
responsibility of the committee for the tragedy. Eventually
this nettled them to the point of withdrawing from the
meeting. Sensing his own fault in the matter, he had a
private session of prayer with his co-worker Harkness,
confessed the sin of criticism and asked for a great victory.
The entire course of the meeting changed, and the
committee praised the work highly at the close. [7]

Soon summer arrived and Reuben was home from
Lafayette College. The family spent their summer
vacation at Heart Lake, Wisconsin. The family

togetherness which had characterized the Torrey household over the years still remained. There was never a richer time of fun and frolicking and exhausting exercise than during the family vacation. And Dr. Torrey still always led the pack—sometimes too strenuously for the rest.

While the family vacationed at Heart Lake, an interesting incident took place. It was always the custom for the entire family to attend services on the Lord's Day. On one of the Sundays they went to a little nearby church and listened to a sermon which was decidedly inferior and not wholly enlightening. A little embarrassed, Reuben happened to notice that his father's attention was riveted on the pastor.

Knowing that his father was so much more accomplished as a preacher, Reuben asked him how he could be so attentive. He replied, "Reuben, I attend church to worship God—not just hear the preacher. Whoever is speaking, if your heart is receptive, you shall receive. Even some train of thought may be started which will help you." [8]

During the middle of the summer Reuben attended the Northfield Conference. While he was there, he signed a Student Volunteer to become a missionary. He had resisted the call to missions for years. It was his life's ambition to enter the field of medicine. His father had yearned to be a lawyer! Ever since the son was five years old he had been deeply impressed toward missions through hearing Hudson Taylor and others at the World Fair campaign in Chicago. Somehow he had the feeling that he was "doomed" to become a missionary. But when he finally yielded, it was a happy decision. His father rejoiced in the surrender and "wrote in a wonderful way about it although he never personally mentioned it." The truth of the matter is that the prospect of his son's going as a missionary had both a gladdening and a saddening aspect. Dr. Torrey yearned to have his son associated with him in some capacity.

During the summer the family moved from their home in Philadelphia to "Torrey Lodge," a red brick, two-story home on Locust Street near the center of Montrose. For several years this was to be their permanent year-round home although conferences were held only during the summer.

The Torreys united with the Montrose Presbyterian Church where MacInnis was pastor. This was a departure for Dr. Torrey. His previous affiliation with the Congregational denomination had been quietly withdrawn. And although decidedly interdenominational in outlook, he believed in a local church membership. He became a Presbyterian "because I believe a man ought to belong to and be responsible to some definite body of believers," [9] and the strong orthodox position of the Presbyterians appealed to him.

Dr. Torrey, however, did not major on denominational distinctions. He once stated,

> The old distinctions between Presbyterians and Methodists, between Baptists and Congregationalists, between Lutherans and Episcopalians. . .have lost all significance for me. To be more exact they never had any great significance for me. [10]

He believed that denominational fences should not only be low enough for persons to shake hands across but also to step back and forth. His interdenominationalism is reflected in his answer to the frequently asked question as to his church affiliation, "I am an 'Episcopresbygationalaptist'!" He oftentimes further explained that his mother was a Presbyterian and his father a Universalist. He was sent to an Episcopal school and a Congregational college and completed his graduate studies in two Lutheran universities. His baptism was by immersion, his first sermon was preached in a Methodist church, and he married an Episcopal wife! [11]

In line with his interdenominational spirit Torrey visited the various churches in Montrose shortly after his arrival. The family was visiting the local Methodist church, and the pastor requested Dr. Torrey to preach about five minutes before the service. Normally he declined such requests, but the pastor insisted. Much to Reuben's surprise, his father preached an extemporaneous message, very fine, but most unlike his usual sermons. After the service he asked, "How did you do that?" Dr. Torrey replied, "Reuben, my mind is like pigeonholes. I just tuck things away to use for the right occasion." [12]

Soon the time had arrived for the first Montrose Bible conference. Great interest was generated in the late August meetings, and nearly 2,500 people attended. The accommodations were somewhat rough unless one were fortunate to find lodging with some of the townspeople. A large tent, which would seat 1,800 people, was erected on the fairground.

Dr. Torrey was very careful to stress that the Montrose conference was not in competition with others as "the conferences already in existence were doing a grand work" but that "another was needed where more time should be given to waiting upon God and to free discussion of the great problems before the church at the present time."

Great care was exercised by Dr. Torrey in the selection of the speakers. He desired those of "excellent character with a sane, noncontroversial message." A newspaper report carried the following item concerning the first program. "Dr. R. A. Torrey, Clear, Strong and Bold. Dr. A. C. Dixon, Pointed, Vigorous, Eloquent. Dr. H. H. Gregg, Tender, Penetrating, Convincing. Dr. W. J. Eerdman, Quiet, Precise, Impressive." [13]

Services were held intermittently from 7:00 a.m. until 10:00 p.m. Large emphasis was given to prayer and missions. From the very outset the children's meetings became a solid feature of Montrose. These were directed by Dr. James Farrar, Rev. James R. Swaim, Jacoby and Reuben.

The conference was an immediate success. At the close of the conference the crowd marched up to what is now Conference Hill for a brief service. Dr. Torrey announced laughingly, "All seats are free." He then outlined plans for the Montrose conference the following year, and a large amount in pledges was given for the project. On that site the following year the large tabernacle, with the bold message, "Holding Forth the Word of Life," placed above the door, was erected. A spacious dining hall was also constructed. One missionary, who had attended all of the great Bible conferences, spoke of this one as "the queen of them all."

Almost immediately Dr. Torrey conceived a new program for Montrose to begin the very next summer. He established the Society for the Promotion of Evangelization. It involved an intensive three months of instruction during the summer. The ten-day August conference, already established, was to climax the sessions. The conference had as its specific aim "to develop in ministers the evangelistic gift and to help evangelists along sane and Biblical lines of evangelism." [14]

A further aim of the Society extended beyond the Montrose conference. It was to develop the evangelistic spirit in large cities. Dr. Torrey remarked:

> In almost every large city, a good number of the ministers are in favor of evangelization, but there are always two or three who are not sound in doctrine, and who discourage evangelization, and tyrannize those who believe in it, but if someone could be sent into a city to wisely develop the sentiment, these opposers can be snowed under. [15]

At great personal sacrifice Dr. Torrey engaged Rev. George Mahy to do this work nine months of the year. The remaining three months of the summer he devoted to the ministry at Montrose, where he served as the first executive secretary of the Montrose Bible Conference Association.

A key meeting set up by Mahy was in Scranton, Pennsylvania, not too far from Montrose. Dr. Torrey was delighted with the prospects of the Scranton campaign. He addressed the pastors of the area:

> In regard to an Evangelistic Campaign in Scranton, I will be glad if such can be arranged. I should like to have it this season because in a year or two I will be a familiar figure in this part of the world. At present, I am something of a novelty. You will understand what that means for the purpose of creating public interest. If Scranton has a building large enough to accommodate

four thousand or more people, there will be no difficulty
about crowding it every night. [16]

The meeting took place in January of the following year
in a "crowded" auditorium. In one great men's service 440
men responded to the invitation to receive Christ as
Saviour.

Paralleling the establishment of the Montrose Bible
Conference was a significant step of a different nature—Dr.
Torrey's resignation as superintendent of the Moody Bible
Institute. He had hinted at this as early as September,
1905, when he wrote to Fitt from abroad, "I fear I should
not be able to give much time to the Institute for some years
to come, even if I do not resign altogether."[17] The call to
evangelism had kept him away from the Institute almost
exclusively for four years, and his many engagements in his
homeland altered that position very little.

For similar reasons he had already tendered his
resignation as pastor of the Chicago Avenue Church some
two years earlier, however, his heart was still in the
Institute. Thus, despite the impracticality of the situation,
he continued as superintendent until the summer of 1908.
At that time he resigned this position as well as his
membership in the executive committee and the board of
trustees.

He had not originally intended to resign these latter
positions, but additional reasons prompted this decision.
While Dr. Torrey was away, Dr. Gray had become a leading
figure in the direction of the Institute, and the two had
differing views as to financial and administrative policies.
The principal issue which concerned Dr. Torrey was the
extent to which the school was running into debt. Further,
he believed the school should be run by one man—not on a
two-deanship plan which had been proposed for him and
Dr. Gray.

Although the executive committee made repeated efforts
to keep him, the majority of the board's sentiment on
financial policy coincided with Dr. Gray. Thus Dr. Torrey
resigned all connection with the Institute. He wrote to Fitt,

"The more I think of it, the more confident I am that Dr. Gray would be happier in his position if I withdrew." He further added, "I hardly need assure you that the Institute will still have a place in my prayer and love, and that you will all have such a place personally." [18]

His action was typical in such situations. As his son said in subsequent years, "He would state his position and convictions and then when he could not go along conscientiously with decisions or policies adopted, he would simply drop out of the picture." [19]   The separation was amicable, and he and Dr. Gray were warm friends throughout the remainder of their lives.

Dr. Torrey's high regard for Gray is reflected in his inviting him to be the featured speaker at the Montrose Bible Conference. Gray was very well received and in a note in the Torrey Lodge Guest Book, wrote of the August conference as "six days of quiet delight." His splendid teaching prompted Dr. Torrey to invite him subsequently for a more extended stay, noting a personal reason for his coming.

> I admit I have one selfish motive in this request. I want Reuben to be under you at least for one month. He is in Princeton Seminary now, and I am afraid he will not have time when he gets through the seminary to spend a year in the Institute. Nor could we spare him very well in the summer. [20]

Although Dr. Torrey was busily engaged in both evangelistic and Bible conference work, he also embarked once again upon a significant ministry in writing. His writing had been largely curtailed since he had entered the field of full-time evangelism. And although he was very fond of writing—he once said that he could make at least $40.00 an hour doing so—any tendency to become prolific was curbed by a sincere conviction. "I cannot preach and write too, and I believe I can do the most good to the greatest number by preaching."[21] Nevertheless, several volumes were produced.

Since the second year of his world-wide revival, there had been a demand for his sermons in print. *Revival Addresses,*

Talks to Men, and *Real Salvation and Wholehearted Service,* which were collections of these sermons, appeared. *Anecdotes and Illustrations,* key sermon illustrations used in his meetings, were also published. There were two small Colportage volumes, which proved to be very stimulating—*Difficulties in the Bible* and *Practical and Perplexing Questions Answered.* His most significant volume, however, was *Studies in the Life and Teachings of Our Lord.*

His approach to the Gospels was striking and unusual. With a thoroughly inductive procedure Dr. Torrey divided each episode of the Gospels into logical categories and treated them in comprehensive question form. For example, in the topic, "Jesus' Teaching Concerning Marriage, Divorce and Children," in Matthew 19:3-15, he asked sixty-six pertinent questions about the thirteen verses. He then classified the passage into five heads—Jesus Christ, disciples, marriage, divorce and little children—and drew important lessons from the text concerning them.[22] His method, which had first been proven in the classroom, was geared to stimulate the reader's powers of observation and to make him think for himself.

Dr. Torrey also edited an important polemical work, *The Higher Criticism and the New Theology,* including such important contributors as Gray, Eerdman and Lewis Meyer. Further, he was asked by A. C. Dixon to serve on the board of the newly formed "Testimony Publishing Company." This organization was responsible for the publishing of the well-known series of volumes called *The Fundamentals.*

Although it is a little-known fact, the system of paragraphing in the popular Scofield Bible was suggested to Dr. Scofield by Dr. Torrey. This feature consisted of breaking up the Biblical narrative into paragraphs at such points as seemed warranted and giving them clear subtitles. Thus it gave the reader an instant suggestion of the contents of the paragraph.

Another important item was the only piece of music to come from the hand of Dr. Torrey—the hymn, "Bless Thou Jehovah." A great lover of music, he had earlier compiled a volume of songs and hymns. But this was his own production. The music was written by Charles Gabriel, but unfortunately it proved to be a little difficult to sing and did not become well known. It has a very solid message and appears to speak of his own spiritual experience.

Oh, my soul bless thou Jehovah, God of love and grace art Thou;
Thou alone art wise and holy; At thy feet I humbly bow.
Thou, Thy Son hast freely given, All our sins to bear away;
On the cross He made atonement, Then to glory led the way.

He for us received the Spirit, Precious gift of love divine;
Shed Him forth upon Thy children; Now forever He is mine.
Jesus soon again returneth, Evermore with Him I'll be;
Like Him thro' the endless ages, Saved for all eternity.

Chorus:

Bless Jehovah, O my soul, Him extol;
Cry aloud! on Him call
Bless Jehovah! at His feet humbly fall,
And crown Him Lord of all.

With his many-faceted ministry, it hardly seemed possible to add further responsibility to an already intensive and rigorous schedule. Yet one of the most significant of all his ministries loomed on the horizon. There was that new Bible Institute out West.

[1]Interview with R. A. Torrey, Jr., December 22,23, 1965.

[2]Ibid.

[3]Brochure of "The Laymen's Evangelistic Council of Chicago," n.d.

[4]*Chicago Tribune*, November 30, 1907. This same article notes that "a unique development of the revival was that the men converts outnumbered the women three to one."

[5]Article, "Montrose Bible Conference," *Christian Life*, XX (August, 1958), p. 39.

[6]Letter from Mrs. R. A. Torrey to A. F. Gaylord, December 19, 1907.

[7]Harkness, pp. 25-30.

[8]Torrey, Jr., interview, 1965.

[9]R. A. Torrey, *Is the Bible the Inerrant Word of God?* (New York: Doran, 1922), p. 14.

[10]Ibid.

[11]Harkness, pp. 67,68.

[12]Torrey, Jr., interview.

[13]"Montrose," p. 39.

[14]Letter to Lyman Stewart, June 3, 1909.

[15]Ibid.

[16]Letter to pastors of Scranton, Pennsylvania, July 28, 1908.

[17]Letter to A. P. Fitt, February 18, 1905.

[18]Letter to A. P. Fitt, August 5, 1908.

[19]Torrey, Jr., personal letter, October 21, 1966.

[20]Letter to Dr. James M. Gray, November 21, 1910.

[21]"How Torrey Lived," *Moody Memo*.

[22]R. A. Torrey, *Studies in the Life and Teachings of Our Lord* (Chicago: BICA, 1907), pp. 214-216.

21. Bible Institute in the West

Lyman Stewart, enterprising young businessman from the East, had gone to the land of promise. Resplendent with nature's wonders, California boasted of vast expanses of colorful desert with blooming cactus, majestic snowcapped mountains, deep, forbidden canyons, stately palm and eucalyptus trees, acres of beautiful wild flowers and one of the most healthful climates in the world. It possessed all the freshness and vigor of the West.

Its history was steeped in adventure beginning with the original settlement of the Spaniards and then more recently the feverish gold rush of the mid 1800s. By the latter part of the century, the major economic interest had shifted to the cultivation of citrus fruits, particularly oranges, and the refining of black gold.

This latter consideration was what first prompted Stewart to come to California in 1882. Despite many disheartening failures in the search for oil, success finally came, and Union Oil Company was founded with vast financial resources.

Stewart was a devout Christian and a member of the Immanuel Presbyterian Church in Los Angeles. Intensely interested in the ministry, he promoted and supported the printing and distribution of tracts and New Testaments among the Spanish-speaking people, and began in 1901 the Los Angeles Bible Institute. The latter ministry lasted only two years; however, with the coming of T. C. Horton from Minneapolis as assistant pastor of Immanuel Presbyterian, the Institute idea was revived. On February 8, 1908, the Bible Institute of Los Angeles was formally established.[1]

It was in the summer of 1911 that the infant Institute began casting about for a dean. Dr. Torrey, who had been consulted previously about the founding of the Institute, was the prime candidate. Now that the school was firmly established and further expansion a reality, Stewart felt that he could better afford to invite someone of Dr. Torrey's stature.

The invitation came while Dr. Torrey was conducting a Bible conference in Denver. It was still in the heart of Dr. Torry to teach and train young people, and he felt that an institute on the West Coast offered large opportunities. Accordingly after a season of prayer, he accepted the deanship and began to make his preparations to go to the land of promise.

His acceptance, however, included two stipulations. First, he stated that a church should be organized to function in much the same capacity as the Moody Memorial Church had to the Moody Bible Institute. Second, and more important, the auditorium of the Institute and church should be able to accommodate at least 3,500 people for evangelistic services.

The reasons for these conditions were aptly stated by his son Reuben.

> He considered this essential for the more adequate training of the students as a practical laboratory, and also it would enable him to continue the evangelistic preaching mission to which he believed God had called him. It would also make possible a strong evangelical witness in the heart of Los Angeles and serve as a platform from which conservative leaders from around the world could be heard.[2]

He gained a most enthusiastic reception on the part of the Institute faculty and student body. The *King's Business*, official organ of the school, stated:

> The coming of Dr. Torrey to our Bible Institute marks a new era in the progress of our work. . . .When we felt the need and commenced to pray for a Dean, we asked of the Lord the *best man* available for such an important position, but we had not thought the Lord would give us the *biggest* as well as the *best*.[3]

THE EVANGELISTS AND A PARTY OF FORTY CAMBRIDGE UNIVERSITY STUDENTS

Two center figures—Mrs. Alexander, Charles Alexander. Two on right of Alexander—R. A. Torrey, Robert Harkness.

Dr. Gray of Moody felt that the call of Dr. Torrey to Los Angeles was "one of the most important events that has occurred for a long while in the history of the church in this country."

It was not possible, however, for Dr. Torrey to assume the reins of the Institute until the beginning of the following year. He had already scheduled a United Evangelistic Mission that fall in the various cities of England and Ireland.

The results of the Mission were very gratifying, and the mission in Dublin, Ireland, in particular, even exceeded the accomplishments of his earlier campaign. The 5,000-seat auditorium, which was twice the size of the hall in the first meeting, was overcrowded. In a letter to Horton from Bristol, England, he wrote, "People were amazed at the enormous throngs. It was said that at no meeting, political or religious, for years had such crowds been seen in Dublin; not since Mr. Moody's first mission there."[4] In the three weeks there, over 1,300 conversions were recorded, including a large number of the Catholic population. He also reported a fine 8-day meeting with Cambridge students sponsored by the Cambridge Intercollegiate Christian Union. Dr. Torrey still seemed to have that rare appeal to English audiences which had been exemplified on his earlier visit.

Dr. Torrey was especially pleased to meet so many who had been converted in his earlier campaign seven years previous. Many of these had turned from lives of deep sin and were now ministers and Christian leaders.

A large portion of these also were children who had been converted in the earlier campaigns, and were now actively engaged in Christian work. His meetings were often criticized—as they were also in this mission—because of the large stress given to evangelizing children. But Dr. Torrey firmly believed in the conversion of children and had the results to prove it. He wrote a short time later,

> Can young children be converted? Does not conversion imply an apprehension of Divine truth of which they are incapable? Our faith is, indeed, based on knowledge; it is

rational; it has depths too deep for angels to fathom. But its essentials are very simple, appealing to conscience and the affections. A sense of sin and sorrow for it, with a sincere turning from it, is a common experience of the child. To weep out its contrition on the breast of a loving and forgiving parent, and to taste the sweets of reconciliation and restored communion is familiar. To their trustful and imaginative hearts the fact that the great Father is unseen is no hindrance.[5]

Returning to America at the close of the year, Dr. Torrey began his new ministry in Los Angeles in January. To him, Los Angeles was a city of spiritual opportunity. Sprawling at the foot of the picturesque San Gabriel mountains, it was already expanding rapidly. Because of the soon-to-be completed Panama Canal and an inland harbor for the city, it gave clear promise of becoming the fastest growing city in the West. The population was typically Western—fluid, restless, eager and boasting an ample sprinkling of the fortune hunter, immigrant, thug, political and religious charlatan, and aspirant to motion picture fame. It was not unlike the earlier challenges of Minneapolis and Chicago.

The Torreys made their home in suburban Pasadena. It was one of the most enjoyable spots in which they had ever lived and Mrs. Torrey especially fell in love with it. Dr. Torrey enjoyed the invigorating climate of the Los Angles area and felt it greatly contributed to the recovery of his daughter Edith from a nervous condition of several years' standing. Teenage Margaret made friends easily and promptly launched a girls Bible class in the Pasadena High School.

Dr. Torrey plunged into his teaching responsibilities with the usual vigor. Dr. J. H. Hunter, fiery red-haired Scotsman and former colleague of Dr. Torrey, joined the faculty after serving seventeen years as a teacher at Moody. The other faculty members were J. H. Sammis, Leaman F. Peckham and Miss Ethel Higgins.

His administrative responsibilities with the Institute in no way lessened his rigorous schedule of meetings. During April through June a large campaign was held in his own area in the Temple Auditorium in Los Angeles. The meetings were not totally geared to an evangelistic end, because he gave much time to instruction in important Biblical truths. In addition, he established at the Institute a Friday night Bible class which became immediately popular with the people of the community.

Despite these encouraging features Dr. Torrey's first six months as dean of the young school also had disappointments. These were primarily due to a major change in the Institute plans after Dr. Torrey had been engaged as dean. Stewart had taken a trip to Chicago to study the work of the Moody Bible Institute and became convinced that the proposed site for the new building in Los Angeles was not spacious enough for future expansion. Unfortunately, this sudden change in property sites and some unforeseen financial reverses of Stewart's Union Oil Company seriously hampered building plans. It was June before the groundbreaking ceremony for the Hope Street location took place.

There had been temporary inconveniences already in the use of different rented buildings, which were often drafty and unsuitable. But even more disturbing was the prospect that such conditions might continue indefinitely. This almost cost the young school the services of Dr. Torrey.

In a lengthy, handwritten reply to a letter from Stewart, Dr. Torrey wrote from Montrose in July,

> I cannot tell you how much I regret to hear it hinted that there is to be another serious delay in the completion of the auditorium. I would hesitate to put in another winter under such conditions as last winter. Of course, I saw that was inevitable last winter, as much as I was disappointed with the slow progress made on the building.[6]

Upon suggesting that he spend most of his time away in meetings the coming year, Dr. Torrey said in a more personal vein,

> You know, Mr. Stewart, that I am fifty-seven years old, and while I feel that, if possible, I am even stronger than I was when I started around the world in 1901, still I cannot but know that my years of intense activity are

> limited: and I want to use my strength while I have it to
> the largest glory of God. . . .Our talents are a sacred
> trust, for which we must answer to our Master when He
> comes again.[7]

At that particular time the Moody Memorial Church in Chicago was urging him to return as pastor, offering as an inducement a new auditorium seating 5,000 people. Although the Chicago invitation had a strong appeal, Dr. Torrey had no clear leading to go. Further, he did not wish to drop out of the institute picture. What course of action should he take?

Stewart, sensing the possible loss of his dean, moved swiftly. He proposed to arrange evangelistic meetings for him on the West Coast and promised the soon completion of the 1,500-seat basement of the Institute auditorium. The evangelistic meetings pleased Dr. Torrey, but the basement plan was not as agreeable. "If you begin on the 1,500 basis, the community will size you up as a 1,500 man, and this, humanly speaking, will make it more difficult later on to gather crowds."[8] Despite this drawback Dr. Torrey continued on with his teaching and administrative duties, which increased with the editorship of the *King's Business*.

The Institute program was organized on the same pattern as that of the Moody Institute, which had been established some twenty-three years earlier. Students began on the "come when you can and leave when you must" basis. They spent approximately four hours in the classroom. The course was of two years' duration consisting of a fall, winter and spring term. A diploma was presented upon successful completion of the course of study.

In noting some of the philosophy of a Bible institute, Dr. Torrey had as his aim to give the students a thorough knowledge of the Scripture and its doctrines, to train them in aggressive Christian work and to develop their spiritual life and character. In Dr. Torrey's estimation a standard liberal arts education should not be included. Institute work was for students desiring specialized training in Biblical and practical studies. Such a program would appeal additionally to returned missionaries, pastors desiring refresher courses, college and seminary graduates desiring supplementary training, and laymen and women.[9]

Large stress was given to courses in individual Bible books, Bible Introduction, Bible Doctrines, Christian Evidences, Pastoral Theology, Homiletics, Sunday School Organization, Teacher Training and Personal Evangelism. In addition, extensive work was offered in instrumental and vocal music.

Further, the Institute sought to unite theory and practice in Christian work. Each student was assigned to some phase of Christian work and was required to give reports of his activity. Students regularly held meetings, engaged in personal work and passed out tracts at the Los Angeles harbor, the many oil fields, the shops and factories and on the streets. This in addition to the many Bible and Sunday school classes organized in various homes and the meetings held in the established churches of the Los Angeles area. Significant ministries were begun among the Spanish and Jewish peoples of the area.

Significant emphasis was also given to training in manners and character building. In Dr. Torrey's estimation "their dining room training is a very important part of their education at the Institute. That is the reason we have a dormitory and a dining room. We wish to teach the students good manners as well as good morals and right methods of work."[10]

Dr. Torrey kept a constant watchcare over the students. Erring ones who consistently disobeyed the rules and did not fit in with the aims of the school simply did not stay. A student recalls one tense morning assembly when Dr. Torrey delivered an ultimatum to several students who had repeatedly flouted the rules. After reading their names, he said, "Go to your rooms, pack your bags as quickly as you can, leave the school and do not come back."[11] The student body, knowing Dr. Torrey's sense of fairness and justice, did not question his decision. The unfortunate students had made their own choice.

Lest one think that Dr. Torrey was overly severe and unapproachable, it should be observed that he was always at hand to comfort a sorrowing student, to counsel concerning important decisions, to instruct in Christian work or to help in financial need. He gave vital counsel to students concerning marriage and the call to the ministry—what he considered to be the two most important decisions in the Christian life. His radiant optimism was contagious, and he soon established himself not only as a warm friend to the students but also as the peerless teacher.

The most popular class at the Institute was his own Bible Doctrines course which met three days a week. Students remember his rapid stride to the speaker's stand with Bible and doctrine book—his *What the Bible Teaches*—under his arm. He was always quick and deliberate, not wasting a minute of time. After calling the students to attention with a brief prayer for enduement and guidance, he plunged into the topic for the day. He followed the same rigidly inductive class procedure which had so signally characterized his ministry in the earlier years at Moody.

Knowing Dr. Torrey's insistence upon thorough class preparation, students rarely neglected their assignments. To do so could be most unpleasant and embarrassing. But perhaps Dr. Torrey began to mellow a bit in his manner. There was the case of one student who recited very poorly and was asked in the presence of the students to remain after class. The atmosphere was exceedingly tense as the poor fellow sank into his seat. After the confrontation of teacher-pupil, fellow students gathered around him, asking, "What did he say?" To their amazement—and to the pupil's—Dr. Torrey had told him that he was overworking himself and that he needed more sleep and sufficient exercise. It was a true but most unexpected estimate of the student's condition.

The school year passed quickly and summer, 1913, had arrived. Reuben had just graduated from Princeton Theological Seminary and was married in the month of June to Janet Slade Mallary. The marriage took place in Macon, Georgia, the home of the bride, and was performed by Dr. Torrey. Both were under appointment by the Foreign Mission Board of the Presbyterian Church, USA, to go as missionaries to North China in the fall. Reuben had had inclinations toward the field of China ever since, as a youngster in Chicago, hearing Hudson Taylor. Further, the bride's parents had been missionaries in China and Korea for forty-six years.

Later in August, Montrose had one of its greatest conferences. W. H. Griffith Thomas and A. C. Dixon were the featured speakers, and approximately 3,500 people gathered together in the tabernacle on the closing Sunday afternoon. Mr. Robert M. Honeyman, a former YMCA secretary and Mission worker, was appointed as the executive director of the Montrose Bible Conference Association. Mr. Honeyman carried on a program of rural evangelism in many of the neglected areas of Pennsylvania during the winter months. Dr. Torrey gave largely of his own means to support the work of Honeyman.

When the Torreys returned to Pasadena in the fall, Reuben and his young bride spent a short time with them before leaving for China. The evening they left was unforgettable.

The Torreys went to the station with them. After they had boarded and the train started, the jubilant father hurriedly escorted Mrs. Torrey into the car and beat the train to the first crossing. Reuben and Janet stood on the rear platform, and both waved until they could no longer see each other. Not a tear was shed.

Dr. Torrey later recounted in a graduation address,

> We did not say much that evening to one another, but when I got to bed I could hold in no longer, and lay there and sobbed and sobbed. Mrs. Torrey tried to comfort me, but I needed no comfort. Through my tears and sobs my heart was rejoicing with joy unspeakable and full of glory at the privilege of giving my only son to live for the God and Father who had given His Only Son to die for me.[12]

[1]James O. Henry, "Black Oil and Souls to Win," *King's Business*, XLIX (February, 1958), pp. 13-17.

[2]Torrey, Jr., personal letter, April 7, 1965.

[3]T. H. Horton, "The Coming of Dr. Torrey," *King's Business*, II (October, 1911), p. 173.

[4]T. H. Horton, "News From Dr. Torrey," *King's Business*, II (December, 1911), p. 259.

[5]R. A. Torrey, "Do Not Forget the Children," *King's Business*, IV (November, 1913), p. 508.

[6]Letter to Lyman Stewart, July 2, 1913.

[7]Ibid.

[8]Henry, p. 28.

[9]R. A. Torrey, "The Purpose and Methods of a Bible Institute," *King's Business*, III (May, 1912), pp. 101,102.

[10]Letter to Lyman Stewart, October 31, 1914.

[11]Mrs. Elsie Ferrell, personal letter, October 3, 1966. Mrs. Ferrell is a former student of Dr. Torrey and mother of the martyred Congo missionary, Irene Ferrell.

[12]Torrey, *Essentials*, p. 13. It had been Dr. Torrey's cherished ambition to have his son associated with him in his ministry at the Institute.

22. *The Fundamentals*

The dawn of 1914 witnessed the nations of Europe embroiled in conflicts with each other and poised for the possibility of war. The inevitable took place later in the summer on June 28 with the assassination of Archduke Francis Ferdinand of Austria. This act precipitated actual hostilities between the warring camps of Europe and plunged them into the awful holocaust of the First World War.

There was another serious conflict of a different nature which had been broiling for some time. It had become increasingly apparent to Dr. Torrey as well as to other spiritually discerning leaders and laymen that strong currents of unbelief were wending their way into the evangelical denominations. Impelled by the forces of destructive higher criticism, biological and social evolution, studies in comparative religion and idealistic German philosophy, modernism began subtly to rear its head and entrench itself in the orthodox Protestant churches. Gradually the evangelical, Biblical doctrines began to be displaced with liberal teaching which often radically reinterpreted Christianity in the light of current secular thought.

This state of affairs prompted the calling of a prophetic conference at Moody Bible Institute in Chicago on February 24-27, 1914. It not only had as a clear objective the defense of the faith against the skepticism of modern theology, but also the serious consideration of the neglected truths of eschatology.

A galaxy of sainted and distinguished Christian scholars and leaders attended the meeting. Dr. Torrey gave two addresses—"The Coming Kingdom of Christ" and "Our

Lord's Second Coming, an Incentive for Personal Holiness." In the latter sermon he stated a profound conviction. "One of the simplest rules I ever found to make it clear to me whether a thing was right or not was to simply ask myself this question, 'If the Lord should come this moment, would you like to have Him finding you doing that?' "[1] His address closed the conference on a high spiritual note.

One of the most significant results of the conference was the drawing up of a doctrinal statement by a committee of scholars present, including Dr. Torrey, which served as a basis for subsequent gatherings.

Earlier than this Stewart had been concerned about the inroads and dangers of modernism and had proposed the idea of editing a series of volumes by well-known, trustworthy Christian scholars to combat this threat of apostasy. A. C. Dixon, who agreed to assume editorial responsibility for the task, gathered about him a committee of trusted men composed of Dr. Torrey, Dr. Charles Eerdman, Dr. Lewis Meyer and Henry P. Crowell and formed "The Testimony Publishing Company." The committee adopted a plan to publish a total of twelve volumes which were to delineate clearly the fundamentals of the faith. With Stewart's financial backing these were to be sent free to all English-speaking Protestant ministers, evangelists, missionaries, theological professors, theological students and YMCA secretaries. These volumes were called *The Fundamentals*.

The first five volumes were edited by Dixon; however, when he left to pastor Spurgeon's Tabernacle in London, Dr. Meyer assumed the editorship. He completed the next five volumes, but ill health and his untimely death interrupted the completion of the project. Dr. Torrey then undertook the editorship and completed the final two volumes of the $300,000 project in the spring of 1915.

The Fundamentals covered a wide range of topics by sixty-four of the most well-known scholars on both sides of the Atlantic. Dr. Torrey contributed three articles: "The Certainty and Importance of the Bodily Resurrection of

Christ," "The Personality and Deity of the Holy Spirit," and "The Place of Prayer in Evangelism." *The Fundamentals* set a standard for theological conservatives of different denominations and helped to stem the onrushing tide of modernism. Those who adhered to the doctrines enunciated in these volumes came to be known as "Fundamentalists."[2] Dr. Torrey continued the stress of *The Fundamentals* as editor of the *King's Business*. Further, he carried on a ministry of writing which more and more took on the character of a defense of the faith.

Dr. Torrey's ministry widened with the completion of the Institute buildings and the establishment of the Church of the Open Door. The beginning of a church in connection with the Institute had been the aim of Dr. Torrey from the outset, but the slow progress of the building plans had considerably delayed its becoming a reality.

Thus approximately two and a half years after his arrival in Los Angeles the Church of the Open Door was organized on September 3, 1915, with eighty-six charter members. Dr. Torrey was unanimously selected as pastor; Horton, as assistant pastor.

Great care was exercised in the selection of the name for the new church. It was to be strictly interdenominational with no hint of competition with the established denominations. Further, it was not regarded as an "institute church." Its purpose was to reach the lost of Los Angeles. This aim is reflected in the choice of name for the new church, The Church of the Open Door. Dr. Torrey based it on two passages, John 10:9 and Revelation 3:8.

> The first passage setting forth the truth that the whole object of the church is to "present Christ to men as an open door for all that will enter." The second passage setting forth the truth that "Jesus Christ has set before our church an open door for service in reaching out after the unchurched of Los Angeles."[3]

The building of a great church in Los Angeles was not especially easy. At the outset there was a large element who disliked both Institute and Church, feeling that they

encroached on the existing denominational works. Further,
there were an unusually large number of people in the area
who followed the various religious meetings, but could not
be depended upon to stick with any. In a comment to
Stewart Dr. Torrey said, "I think there are more
benchwarmers in Los Angeles than any other city in the
world, at least any other city of its size."[4] But despite these
and other difficulties, signal successes began to attend the
ministry of the church. And these blessings continued.
There was not a Sunday service in all of his years as pastor
when there were not conversions.

One service, however, almost proved an exception. On a
cold, rainy Sunday night, Dr. Torrey preached and gave
out the invitation but found no response. Greatly
disappointed, he said, "This is the first Sunday night in the
Church of the Open Door that we have failed to see anyone
come to Christ." Immediately a man arose, walked down
the aisle and took the preacher's hand saying, "I want to
accept the Saviour." Several others followed, and a great
prayer meeting for praise was held after the meeting.[5]

The services of the Church were always impressive when
Dr. Torrey was there, particularly on Sunday morning.
Large crowds invariably poured into the auditorium. On
Easter Sunday mornings when he preached on the
resurrection of Christ he seemed to be at his best. One of his
students recalls hearing a police officer standing in the
vestibule on a crowded Easter Sunday, say, "If he were not
a good man, he could become one of the most dangerous
men of our day. What a tremendous power he has over
men."[6]

In the evening services Dr. Torrey would often lead the
congregation in his favorites—"Hallelujah for the Cross"
or "O Could I Speak the Matchless Worth." Dr. Torrey was
not a singer but loved and appreciated the ministry of
music. Further, he emphasized the importance of capable
musical assistance in the Church. Manually-operated
chimes were installed in the Church in a day when such
things were rare. He felt they would stimulate people to

think of the days when they were in church and heard the grand old hymns.

Dr. Torrey's leadership of the Church implanted a strong emphasis on evangelism, missions and the spiritual life. Seven of the eighty-six charter members went into foreign missionary service and four into home mission work. An active Sunday school and adult Bible classes characterized the Church. Dr. Torrey regularly taught the International Sunday School Lesson at the popular Friday night Bible class which drew scores of teachers and Christian workers.

That same fall there were several significant additions to the faculty and staff of the Institute. Dr. William Evans, who had been a pupil and warm personal friend of Dr. Torrey in Chicago, came from Moody to become associate dean. H. J. Baldwin of the editorial staff of the *Sunday School Times* became the superintendent of men. Then there was also the fine addition of Charles Marsh, who wrote the music to "One Day" and "Is It the Crowning Day?" He was both instructor in music at the Institute and pianist at the Church. A year later, J. B. Trowbridge, who had worked with Dr. Torrey at Moody, came to the Institute to head the music department. He also directed the music at the Church and assisted Dr. Torrey in a number of his campaigns.

The Institute buildings were magnificent. Built in a pleasing modern style, they were constructed as two buildings, thirteen stories high, with the auditorium in the middle. There was also in the basement of the men's building a large cafeteria—something of an innovation for a Christian school. In order to complete the buildings, however, the school found it necessary to float a $375,000 bond issue and incur a heavy indebtedness. This debt was a struggle the Institute was to have for some years to come.

The Institute began to expand in other directions. Not only was there an increase in the number of day students but a very successful night school was also begun with an average attendance of 1,200. The following spring saw their largest graduating class up to that time—thirty-nine.

The summer of 1916 was an eventful one. On July 5, Margaret was married to Joseph Parker of Athens, Georgia, in an outside ceremony at Montrose. Since Dr. Torrey had such a close attachment to his children, it was an occasion of some sadness as well as joy. Now there was only one stocking to fill on Christmas Eve—that of daughter Edith who never married.

The following April the United States entered the War. It was a momentous but not totally unexpected move. Dr. Torrey, who had served as a chaplain in the Spanish-American War, wrote much on the nature of the War in editorials in the *King's Business* and in two booklets, *What the War Teaches* and *Peanut Patriotism and Pure Patriotism*. His observations were always optimistic but realistic, even though the prevailing mood of the period was pessimistic.

The War gave added impetus to the significant prophetic conference in Philadelphia, May 28-30. The Academy of Music, the scene of some of the Torrey meetings a dozen years earlier, was filled to its 3,300-seat capacity for some of the sessions. The question of apostasy in the orthodox denominations was a major concern of the participants and prompted a subsequent meeting that summer.

A call was issued to a select group of evangelicals to meet at Montrose for the purpose of organizing into a world fellowship with a strong united front against encroaching liberalism. In addition to Dr. Torrey there were present Robert M. Russell, W. H. Griffith-Thomas, John Campbell, H. Wyse Jones, W. B. Riley, Dixon and Evans. The thrust of the meeting was to stem the tide of apostasy and to re-educate the church in the basic Biblical themes. In their planning it was considered imperative to establish militant Bible schools and conferences all over America to hasten that objective. [7]

Dr. Torrey carried out these objectives very faithfully in the Church and Institute. The annual Bible conference at BIOLA featured the most outstanding preachers and defenders of the faith in the country—A. C. Gaebelein,

George Truett, Mel Trotter, L. W. Munhall, Robert Dick Wilson, M. G. Kyle, Courtland Myers, Mark Matthews, J. Wilbur Chapman, William B. Riley and A. C. Dixon, to mention some of the most prominent. Church and Institute became outstanding centers for Biblical preaching and defense of the faith on the West Coast.

It became increasingly an aim of Dr. Torrey to indoctrinate his congregation in the basic doctrinal truths of Scripture. When Dr. Torrey announced a series of fifteen messages on "The Fundamental Doctrines of the Christian Faith," the largest Sunday crowds up to that time flocked to hear him. These sermons were preached over the radio—a new outreach in his ministry—and were published in one of his most significant volumes by the same title, *The Fundamental Doctrines of the Christian Faith.*

On November 11, an armistice was signed ending the World War. In the same month large crowds attended another prophetic conference in Carnegie Hall and the Marble Collegiate Church in New York City. Addressing the vast audience, Dr. Torrey sounded a note of warning to those who would make the world safe for democracy.

> Such hopes are delusive; they will end in disappointment and dismay. There may be a league of nations, but no peace will come from such a league except a temporary peace, and then the most awful universal war that this old world has ever seen will follow.

But he was not pessimistic.

> My heart is not heavy, not a bit. . . .The Lord is coming.[8]

Liberal critics, however, were greatly disturbed concerning this emphasis. Two scholars in particular, Shirley Jackson Case and Shailer Matthews, of the University of Chicago Divinity School, created the distinct impression that premillennialists were both theologically suspect and nationally subversive. The premillennialists were justly indignant.[9] These attacks provoked a scorching reply—somewhat "unTorrey-like"—by Dr. Torrey in his booklet, *Will Christ Come Again?* The brunt of his remarks were leveled against that brand of postmillennialism which sought to discredit the Scripture.

Although devoting much of his energy to a vigorous stand for Biblical Christianity, Dr. Torrey did not lessen his evangelistic engagements. In fact, during the recent war he had spoken many times to soldiers in various army camps across the country. At no time was he "more intent upon saving 'the fundamentals' than upon saving souls."[10]

The most outstanding of his meetings that year was in neighboring Redondo Beach. Dr. Torrey had invited "for old time's sake" Charles Alexander to lead the singing in a six-week campaign. The Reuben Torreys also joined in on the grand reunion. They were spending the last few weeks of their first furlough in Pasadena. It was a happy moment for both Torrey families to greet "Charlie" after such a long period of separation. Dr. Torrey relished their reminiscences of past victories, and laughed heartily at some of the "miscues."

As usual everyone seemed to respond to the effervescent "Charlie," and his splendid job of directing the choir reminded them all of the grand days of the world tour. The founder of the Pocket Testament League, he held noon meetings to promote this ministry. Dr. Torrey stressed the great doctrines in his daytime meetings, and preached evangelistically in the evening. The meetings averaged 1,500 nightly, and 230 salvation decisions were recorded in the meetings.

During the meetings Reuben and his family sailed for China. Dr. Torrey had asked his son to remain with him at the Institute as superintendent of men; however, Reuben's clear call to the Orient once again made it impossible to fulfil this fond hope of his father. Edith, who had matriculated earlier at Wheaton College, graduated in May and accepted a position as instructor in Bible at Wheaton Academy.[11]

That same month a tremendous conference was held in Philadelphia, May 25 to June 1. It drew approximately six thousand people from all of the forty-eight states, most of the Canadian provinces and several foreign countries. In line with the previous summer's conference at Montrose there was a major shift of emphasis from prophetic themes to a defense of the faith. Dr. Torrey, along with such spiritual giants as Riley, Griffith Thomas, Gray, Chafer and Munhall, played a vital role in directing the course of the Conference. A nine-point creed, similar to the earlier one in Chicago, was adopted, and large-scale plans to promote the cause of the fundamentals of the faith were effected.

Thus the World's Christian Fundamentals Association was born.

[1] R. A. Torrey, "Our Lord's Second Coming, an Incentive for Personal Holiness," *King's Business*, V (May, 1914), p. 254.

[2] The term is a twentieth-century expression of Protestant orthodoxy. Its roots, as stressing key doctrines, stem back to the earlier prophetic conferences in this country. The term "Fundamentalist," however, was first coined by Curtiss Lawes in an article in the *Watchman-Examiner* in 1919.

[3] Letter to Lyman Stewart, July 2, 1915.

[4] Letter to Lyman Stewart, March 29, 1915.

[5] O. E. Sanden, *God's Marked Man* (unpublished typescript, 1954), p. 6.

[6] Ibid.

[7] Ernest O. Sandeen, *The Roots of Fundamentalism* (Chicago: University of Chicago Press, 1970), p. 243.

[8] Sandeen, p. 235.

[9] Ibid., p. 236.

[10] McLoughlin, Jr., p. 366.

[11] Miss Torrey continued in this position until 1924 when she was appointed instructor in Bible at Wheaton College. She remained in this position until 1950, the year of her retirement. She was made an assistant professor in Bible her last year of teaching.

23. "A Tower of Strength"

With the advent of the "roaring twenties" BIOLA was a
firmly established Bible school, robust and debt-free.
Stewart happily announced to the board of directors that
the entire indebtedness, amounting to $430,000 in bonds,
had been liquidated. Stewart took further steps to insure
the financial security of the Institute by turning over to the
school 4,000 shares of his own Union Oil Company and the
major interest in his Western Machinery Company.
Inadvertently this latter benevolent act almost proved fatal
to the school in subsequent years.

As the years passed, the imposing figure of Dr. Torrey
continued to mold the Institute—so much so that it was
commonly known as the "Torrey Bible Institute." Lyman
Stewart commonly referred to him as "a tower of
strength."[1] And indeed he was. His influence was
manifold, but he was at his best as a teacher. He was not
only profoundly spiritual; he was also intensely practical.

In Dr. Torrey's homiletics class an enterprising preacher
named Rex Mitchell was speaking on the paralytic borne of
four. In the course of his message he picturesquely
described the scene, saying, "Who knows! Perhaps a piece
of plaster fell, almost striking one of the grumbling
Pharisees." Dr. Torrey interrupted, "Rex, don't say,
'perhaps.' Say 'a piece of plaster fell, hitting the priest right
on the head!' "[2]

He also had an almost uncanny ability, undoubtedly
God-given, to detect and predict the spiritual worth of a
person. One young student delivered his sermon on Cain
and Abel in homiletics class, and at its conclusion Dr.
Torrey sat for the longest time making notes and saying

nothing. The student, thinking the message was a failure, became more nervous with the passing of each second. Finally the teacher remarked, "God has some great work for you to do, Charles"—a most uncharacteristic statement but a remarkably true prophecy. The student was the late Charles E. Fuller, who for many years was known internationally as the minister and director of the Old-Fashioned Revival Hour.[3] Reuben once remarked that he knew of only one instance when his father made a mistake in his spiritual assessment of a person.

His affection for the students is represented in his commencement address to the class of 1920 when he said, in part,

> There is one word I wish to say to you for the whole faculty: We love you. We shall miss you. I shall miss you. They say I am a cold, unaffectionate man. They say my eyes pierce more than they attract. Do not believe it. I do not think you believe it. But I do love you, and I will be lonesome without you.[4]

But that Torrey exterior did sometimes repel. Dr. Bob Jones, Sr., once said, "The first time I met Dr. Torrey, I thought he was cold. And one day I got up to him and I think he had the warmest heart I ever knew." Dr. Torrey told him, "Oh, Bob, I wish I did not have this outward surface."

The "outward surface," however, was sometimes cast aside. For instance there was the senior party where, in the presence of a number of faculty, he cast aside his ordinarily dignified manner and proceeded to lie down flat on his back in the middle of the floor. He simply laughed at their shocked expressions and thought it was a good joke.

One of the most shocking things students saw him do, however, was to run up the full thirteen flights of the Institute building! Though now in his mid-sixties he still had that unusual physical vitality. A prowler learned that one night. The unwary criminal attacked Dr. Torrey in the darkened church auditorium, and was sent sprawling under the grand piano! The dazed assailant was held at bay by Dr. Torrey until the authorities arrived. He was a "tower of strength" in more ways than one!

Another of his strengths was his comfort to those in times of distress or sorrow. In the fall of the year he wrote to a sorrowing Mrs. Alexander concerning the death of the affable, smiling "Charlie."

> For you, dear child, for you seem almost like my child to me, what can I say? Everyone who knows you knows how you loved him, but very few knew all the romance of it, and the wondrous depth of your affection for him, as I do. I always regarded it as one of the most beautiful things I ever saw in all my life. I remember that I said, on the day when you were married, and Mrs. Torrey and I took the place of father and mother for Charlie, "You think you love one another today, but you do not know what love means, as you will when years have passed by." And I know you have found it so.[6]

His passing was a great personal loss to Dr. Torrey, who considered Alexander as "beyond a question the greatest Gospel songleader of his generation." He now assumed the presidency of Alexander's Pocket Testament League.

Dr. Torrey's interest in missions carried him to the Orient on two separate occasions in 1919 and 1921. These trips were not primarily evangelistic in nature, but were mainly for the encouraging of the missionaries and the re-emphasizing of the great truths of the Word of God. The greater part of his time on both trips was spent in China, particularly in connection with the work of the Hunan Bible Institute (a branch of BIOLA). His son traveled with him on most of his trips to the various places in China.

The latter trip in 1921 was fraught with danger. Dr. Torrey, after much prayer and a consciousness of the clear leading of the Spirit, determined to go into inland China. The trip was "daring," as Mrs. Torrey commented; but Dr. Torrey encouraged his party to rely on Philippians 4:6, 7. And although they were fired on, the party reached their destination, Nan Yoh in the Hunan province, without harm.[7]

At nearly all of the conference sessions his main topics were "Why I Believe the Bible Is the Word of God," "The

Baptism With the Holy Spirit," and "Why I Believe Jesus Is the Divine Son of God." He found the inroads of higher criticism and the social gospel very prominent in China, and he gave more time than usual to the exposure of such tendencies. His messages made a profound impression and resulted in new faith, dedication and power in the lives of both missionaries and the nationals, who attended in large numbers.[8]

It was a real joy for him to meet his warm friend, the well-known missionary Jonathan Goforth, who shared the conference platform with him. He also enjoyed the fellowship and assistance of his former student at Moody, Fred C. Dreyer, who was a most remarkable missionary.

Not long after his return to the States plans were put into effect for the holding of the annual World's Christian Fundamentals Association. The June 25-July 2 meeting was held in Los Angeles the following summer. A galaxy of speakers were invited for the occasion—Riley, Munhall, Matthews, Wilson and a comparative newcomer, Lewis Sperry Chafer. The 1922 meeting covered a variety of topics in the war against unbelief; however, the focus was very forcibly directed against the question of evolution for the first time.[9]

This emphasis occasioned some concern for Dr. Torrey. He did not view the issue of evolution as the vital point of controversy with the liberals. Further, he felt that the cause of Fundamentalism would be hindered if the major emphasis was given to more secondary issues.[10] He believed that the vital point for conservatives was the inerrancy and authority of Scripture. Indeed, he felt that it should be the one cohesive factor uniting all true Christians. In a subsequent interview Dr. Torrey stated:

> Personally, I think it would be desirable, if possible, that there should be a new alignment of Christians. The old denominational differences have lost their significance. The alignment should be along the line of whether people accept the Bible as the inerrant Word of God or not. Those that do not should get together, irrespective of present denominational connections, and

form a new denomination, and those who do should get
together and form a new denomination.[11]

His conviction centered in the fact that "there is in the
Bible the truth that will safeguard you against every error
of these times." This must be the cornerstone of the
Christian's defense of the faith. In answer to the liberals
who accused Dr. Torrey as a "bibliolater," note his further
words. "The Bible has no hocus-pocus power. It has power
only for the truth it contains."[12] That truth allowed for no
human additions. When once asked whether he believed
the Bible from "cover to cover," he replied, "No, only from
Genesis to Revelation."

It should be further observed that Dr. Torrey did not
concern himself with unrevealed "truths." On one occasion
Reuben asked him some things concerning Heaven. His
father replied, "I don't know." A little stunned, his son
exclaimed, "You don't know? What do you mean, 'You
don't know!'?"

"Reuben, there are some things that are not revealed. I
do not waste time on things not revealed. If God wanted to
reveal them, He would have done so. My opinion is no
greater than yours, and yours no greater than that baby,"
pointing to a grandchild in a crib nearby.[13]

As a forceful defender of the faith Dr. Torrey was
engaged in a number of controversies. There were some
skirmishes with Adventists, who were quite prominent in
California; however, the sharpest conflict was over the
question of premillennialism. His contention was with the
unbelieving brand of postmillennialism which sought to
deny not only Biblical teaching concerning eschatology but
the inspiration and authority of the Bible itself. One noted
liberal critic deliberately misconstrued a reference in one of
Dr. Torrey's sermons, "not Kaiser but Christ," to make
him teach a ruthless, materialistic reign of Christ on
earth.[14] Frequently in matters of controversy his opponents
engaged more in personal invective and misrepresentation
than in clear defense of their position.

The most personal of his controversies concerned Paul

D. Moody, son of evangelist D. L. Moody, and then president of Middleburg College in Vermont. Paul Moody contended in an article in *Christian Century* that his father would be in sympathy with the liberals of the day and even had liberal leanings himself. This Dr. Torrey knew to be utterly false and gave a very convincing reply to Paul Moody's allegations in an article in *Moody Monthly*.[15]

Strange as it may seem, Dr. Torrey was not a controversial person at heart. He would far rather at any time preach the Gospel of the matchless love of God than deal with controversial issues. He did not flinch, however, when it was necessary to defend the faith. His close friend, W. B. Riley, has given an interesting note on this side of Dr. Torrey.

> Dr. Torrey was as tender in spirit as he was bold in speech. On a few occasions I counseled him on matters that involved controversy between brethren, and he always amazed and delighted me. This man who seemed to preach with a doubled-up fist was as gentle as a woman when giving advice. He was not only anxious to be just, but ready to be generous always, toward even those with whom he did not agree.[16]

The close of the year 1922 was one of sadness for the Torreys. Their youngest daughter, Margaret, passed away. The lives of Joseph and Margaret had seemed marked with tragedy. Their first child was born dead; and after the birth of the second, Margaret Elizabeth, the mother contracted tuberculosis. She stayed in Pasadena with her parents for some time endeavoring to recuperate. But she never fully recovered and died on December 7 shortly after returning to Athens.

The following year on November 20 the death of another friend and close associate, Lyman Stewart, was also a keen personal loss. Dr. Torrey telegraphed Mrs. Stewart, "Deepest sympathy, I Thess. 4:13-18. Mr. Stewart was one of the greatest Christians I ever knew—a rare combination of strength and achievement, on the one hand, and a gentleness and humility on the other."[17] Stewart's death was to have a profound effect on the Institute. He had been

its financial wizard and prime supporter, and a serious
financial matter now faced the directors.

The Western Machinery Company, whose major interest
now belonged to the Institute, was floundering. The
directors felt they must borrow money to keep Western
going and save it from bankruptcy. Thus they thought to
insure the school's financial future. Dr. Torrey opposed
this plan, particularly the idea of borrowing for Western to
establish security for the Institute. Such a plan did not
seem wise from either the business or the spiritual
standpoint. The majority opinion, however, was to borrow,
thus the Institute incurred heavy indebtedness to save the
company.[18]

This action, coupled with the fact that a majority of the
administrators favored the expanding of the curriculum in
the direction of a college or seminary, was to affect the
future ministry of Dr. Torrey at the Institute. Dr. Torrey,
with a firm conviction instilled by Moody, felt the need for
a strictly *Bible* institute to meet a special need. Others in
the administration felt that more could be accomplished
with a liberal arts curriculum.

In the spring of 1924, Dr. Torrey conducted one of his
most significant evangelistic crusades in over a decade in
Winnipeg, Manitoba, Canada. Those British audiences
again! Crowds up to five thousand thronged into the
skating rink where the meetings were held, and very large
numbers of decisions were recorded. It was in the midst of
this truly great awakening that Dr. Torrey seriously
pondered his future.

He asked his good friend, Will Houghton, to come up to
his hotel room. "Will, I feel as though God wants me out
into open service again. I want you to join me in prayer."
Dr. Houghton thought he was in for no less than a two-
hour session of prayer! But after five minutes on their
knees in prayer, Dr. Torrey arose and said, "I've got the
mind of God." And Houghton hadn't prayed at all!
Houghton later recalled that it was one of the greatest
lessons he had ever learned in simplicity and surrender in
prayer.[19]

As for Dr. Torrey, there was no question. He must spend his remaining years in evangelistic meetings and Bible conferences.

[1]Mrs. Lyman Stewart, "As His Students Saw Him," *King's Business*, XXVII (January, 1936), p. 9.

[2]Sanden, p. 27.

[3]Charles Fuller, "Ten Words—My Teacher's Legacy," (June, 1967).

[4]Torrey, *Essentials*, p. 13.

[5]Bob Jones, Sr., "Judgment," *Sword of the Lord*, (April, 1946), p. 2.

[6]Mrs. Charles Alexander, p. 242.

[7]R. A. Torrey, "Facts From the Foreign Field," *King's Business*, XIII (January, 1922), pp. 26-28.

[8]Torrey, Jr., personal letter, September 15, 1966.

[9]This was to be a dominant stress in the remaining meetings of the association, reaching its peak three years later in the famous Scopes trial in Dayton, Tennessee.

[10]This shift of emphasis in the WFCA, coupled with his concern over a subsequent divisiveness and improper spirit on the part of many of the Association's leaders, led him to withdraw from active participation in the WFCA after 1922. Dr. Torrey however, carried on an unabated and militant defense of the faith throughout the remainder of his life. Letter from Reuben A. Torrey, Jr., October 21, 1966.

[11]"The Battle Within the Churches," *Homiletic Review*, MCMXXIII (September, 1923), p. 188.

[12]Torrey, *Inerrant*, p. 99.

[13]Torrey, Jr., interview, 1965.

[14]Keith L. Brooks, "Does Dr. Torrey or Does He Not?" *King's Business*, XIII (December, 1922), pp. 1245, 1246.

[15]Torrey, "Paul D. Moody," p. 2. Dr. James Gray and Fleming H. Revell, brother-in-law of Moody, concurred with Dr. Torrey's reply.

[16]Riley, p. 6.

[17]Telegram to Mrs. Lyman Stewart, November 20, 1923.

[18]The Institute went through a very serious financial pressure. Once the indebtedness had been eliminated in subsequent years the board made "a solemn resolution before God never to go into debt again." Henry, p. 41.

[19]Wilbur M. Smith, *A Watchman on the Wall* (Grand Rapids: Eerdmans, 1951), pp. 26, 27.

24. The Finished Course

Upon his return to Los Angeles Dr. Torrey resigned his connection with the Institute and the Church of the Open Door. He did not allow his differences with the administration to become a matter of controversy. Thus he maintained an excellent relationship with the Institute.

Dr. Torrey could look back over the some twelve years spent with the Institute with a sense of genuine satisfaction. In 1924, Dr. Torrey's final year there, there had been a total of 2,431 enrolled in the various courses, and 119 were in the graduating class. Over 60,000 persons were dealt with personally and approximately 9,000 made professions of faith in Christ. In many respects there was a more marked achievement in the fruitful years in Los Angeles than there were in the grand days with Moody in Chicago.

At the final commencement Dr. Torrey's words sounded a prophetic note, as they were to soon characterize his own life.

> Young men, and women, as you leave these halls and these friendships with the faculty and your fellow students, that have become so precious to you, you will have many lonely days and weeks. . . .But you need not see lonely days, you need not see a lonely hour, or a lonely minute. You may have the most satisfying of all companions, the Lord Jesus Christ.[1]

"Daddy" Horton, longtime friend and newly-appointed dean of the Institute, wrote a glowing tribute to his associate of about thirteen years at the school:

> Dr. Torrey is a peerless preacher and transcendent teacher, and has been used of God in moulding the lives of hundreds of students and strengthening the faith of

thousands of people. The prayers of his people follow him
in the new service to which he is giving his life.[2]

The words reflected the appreciation and esteem which
all the Institute faculty had for Dr. Torrey and his
significant contribution to the school.

On June 22 Dr. Torrey preached his farewell messages to
the church. They were typical of his ministry. "Farewell
Message to a Dearly-Loved Church—How to Study the
Bible" was his morning topic. In the evening he spoke on
"Goodbye to the People of Los Angeles—How to Get Joy
Unspeakable and Full of Glory."

The church bulletin of the same date says in part:

> The Church of the Open Door owes its existence and its
> fruitful life largely to your faithful service as Pastor.
> From a handful to many hundreds you had the joy of
> seeing its development. Through your faithful ministry
> thousands have heard the Gospel, and hundreds have
> been brought to knowledge of and faith in Christ. We
> shall miss you but we shall remember you.[3]

In his nine-year ministry at the Church of the Open
Door there had not been a Sunday without a profession of
faith, and there was a yearly average of three hundred
additions. The Torreys continued to make their home in
beautiful Pasadena until the following year when they
purchased a home in the picturesque Smokey Mountains in
Asheville, North Carolina.

Dr. Torrey maintained a very rigorous schedule. In
addition to his evangelistic meetings and Bible conferences,
for an extended time he assisted Riley, during the latter's
illness, at the First Baptist Church and the Northwestern
Schools in Minneapolis. He wrote to his former student, O.
E. Sanden, "I am in excellent health; I do not feel a day
older than when I started around the world in 1901.
However, the calendar says I am older. My body doesn't
seem to say it."[4]

It is not surprising to note his reaction to a letter from a
friend who commented that she hoped he was enjoying his
vacation. He briskly replied, "I am not taking a vacation. I
am very busy and expect to be very busy going from place to

place."[5] He then outlined his rather exacting itinerary!

For some of his campaigns Dr. Torrey engaged as a songleader Homer Hammontree. Hammontree was struck by the manner of the evangelist's invitations. There was little emotion or entreaty—almost a "take it or leave it." In some of his first services with Dr. Torrey no one came forward. After several such nights he asked him, "Dr. Torrey, doesn't it bother you when they don't come?"

"Bother me, Hammie? [he always called him by that name] Hammie, that's none of my business. It's my business to preach the Gospel in the power of the Holy Spirit. It's *His* business to bring results."[6] In a later service "Hammie" saw over one hundred people stand up and come forward in the invitation.

Early in 1926 he was engaged at the Columbia Theological Seminary and the First Presbyterian Church, Columbia, South Carolina. The meetings were chiefly for students who had little interest in evangelism or Biblical preaching. In his first sermon in the chapel he faced a flippant, indifferent audience at the outset, but the mood rapidly changed as he began to speak. He spoke on "Ten Reasons Why I Believe the Bible to Be the Word of God." He relished the challenge of a college atmosphere and was thoroughly at ease. His powerful, convincing message captivated his critical audience, who gave him prolonged applause at the conclusion of the sermon. The services at the church on Sunday were filled to overflowing with both townspeople and students.

The Torreys looked forward to the summer with great expectation. Reuben and his family were coming home on furlough. They stayed at Montrose from the middle of May to October. In a note in the Guest Book at Torrey Lodge, Reuben said:

> Words cannot express what these weeks at home, with you both, Father and Mother, in the midst of these beauties of scenery, have meant to us after the last seven years in China. How we thank you and God for the heaven on earth that these months have been.[7]

One of the joys of the Montrose summers was the

delightful time with the family. Ordinarily Dr. Torrey had little time to spend with his children and grandchildren, but he enjoyed watching them through the big bay window of his study while he was busy at work. Janet, noticing him rocking in his chair and looking through the window, teased him, "Doctor, you look mighty lazy." He looked up, smiled and replied, "I am writing *The Gist.*"[8]

At a meeting the following year at Lewistown, Pennsylvania, at the First Presbyterian Church, Dr. Torrey celebrated his seventy-first birthday. Reviewing some of the highlights of his long and active life, he said, "If I had my life to live all over again, I would spend less time in praying and more time feeding on the Word of God."[9] It was akin to the discovery of Moody, who used to say, "In prayer we talk to God, and in the study of the Bible God talks to us—and you had better let God do most of the talking!"

All of his life Dr. Torrey had been preeminently a man of the Word. Although there was a great breadth in his reading—he found "great recreation" in the repeated reading of literature and philosophy—it never superseded the Word of God. As he noted in one of his significant books of this period, *Christ of the Bible,* "I am glad that God makes me a practical man instead of a philosopher." He accepted the Bible because of its practical, down-to-earth nature, not because he understood its philosophy.[10]

He published two small books on the Bible during these years, but his two other works, *Soul-Winning Sermons* and *The Holy Spirit, Who He Is and What He Does,* have had a greater effect. This is especially true of the latter volume, which is a compilation of his series of sermons on the Spirit given during his evangelistic campaigns.

His last campaign of the year was held at the First Presbyterian Church, Orlando, Florida, November 28-December 11. It is interesting to note in the newspaper accounts of the meeting that his sermon titles were precisely the same as those of his world-wide evangelistic tour. He spoke three times daily including one large community effort in the new Municipal Auditorium with the cooperation of forty-five churches in the area. Attendances often taxed the large Presbyterian Church auditorium to capacity.[11]

It was while he was in Florida that Harkness guardedly ventured a suggestion concerning Dr. Torrey's preaching. He hinted at the need for a series of messages on prophetic themes. Somewhat surprised, Dr. Torrey replied, "What is wrong with the message I have given all these years? Isn't my theme true to the teaching of the Bible?" Though Harkness assured him that there was no question about his present messages, Dr. Torrey was distinctly unimpressed with the suggestion. "When God ceases to bless the message I am giving, I will change it."[12]

Meetings were scheduled for Chicago and Duluth at the very first of the year in 1928, but these had to be cancelled. Dr. Torrey had always said, "I don't expect to be sick. I expect to drop dead some day." But now he was experiencing a throat paralysis which began to grow progressively worse. The exacting strain on his voice over his many years in public speaking was taking its toll. It was an entirely new experience for Dr. Torrey, who had always enjoyed unusually good health. Now it was not only the calendar but also his body which indicated he had passed threescore and ten.

After a time he could not speak, and it became increasingly difficult even to swallow. He had to forego much of his normal diet, and his weight dropped from 225 to 150 pounds. During this trying time his wife, always so tender and sympathetic, said, "Poor Archie. You must be discouraged. Your poor throat." Her husband replied militantly with paper and pencil, "Discouraged nothing! I am resting in Philippians 4:6, 7. Romans 8:28 is more precious to me than ever before."[13] This was one of the "all things." He didn't especially relish inquiries about his health. His reply was always positive—"improving."

His son, Reuben, has given an interesting assessment of

these trying days:

> I cannot but feel that the months of declining health
> were given to Father to enable him to demonstrate the
> completeness of his victory in Christ Jesus.
> . . .Throughout the ten months of inactivity caused by
> poor health, a new experience for my father, he never
> once manifested the slightest impatience, although it
> seemed that there was excuse for impatience and
> discouragement. His beautiful smile persisted, his
> optimism never faltered, his faith and glad acceptance of
> God's will became more evident. He gave himself to
> almost continuous Bible study and prayer, and his very
> presence was a benediction.[14]

On the final Sunday afternoon of the family gathering at
Montrose, he suggested that the entire family drive up to
Sunset Knoll to see the sunset. After gazing upon the
breathtaking view for a time, Dr. Torrey asked that they
have a season of prayer. It was a fitting benediction to the
last time he would ever behold what he regarded as one of
nature's beauty spots. Perhaps he had some premonition of
the future, as he had requested this very spot as his burial
place.

It was difficult for members of the family to leave
Montrose this time, particularly for Reuben. He was torn
as to whether he should return to China just then, knowing
that it was very likely he would never see his father again.
His father inwardly yearned for him to stay, but would not
allow himself to stand in the way of his son's ministry in
China. He told Reuben, "If you *do* stay, I *will* die." As it
turned out, Reuben received a temporary appointment
with his mission board as a regional secretary in St. Louis,
which delayed his return to China for a time.

In the fall, the Torreys returned to their Asheville home.
On October 22 they quietly celebrated their forty-ninth
wedding anniversary. It gave them an occasion to
reminisce about the wonderful years they had shared
together. He quaintly wrote in his diary, for that day, "I
knew I was getting a prize when I married Clara, but I did
not know how great a prize she really was."[15]

After his return to Asheville, he had seemed to be

progressing and wrote several friends of his improvement. Although days were spent in comparative inactivity, he wrote in his diary, "God is giving me much more time for prayer these days." On Wednesday, October 24, however, he developed a high temperature. The doctor was called in and diagnosed his illness as a mild case of influenza. By Thursday morning the fever had abated, and there seemed to be no cause for alarm.

Dr. Torrey rested quietly during the day and read from several versions of Scripture in the afternoon. Feeling weary, he asked for evening prayers early and retired immediately after dinner. Mrs. Torrey placed some extra pillows under his head as he was having difficulty breathing and bade him good night. She looked at him several times during the night, and he appeared to be resting peacefully.

In the morning she arose, dressed quietly, had devotions and returned to inquire about breakfast. It was then she discovered that he had been called home, and she had bade him the last "good night." The faithful soldier had stepped quietly without apparent struggle into the presence of his Master to receive the promised reward. The date was Friday, October 26, 1928.

The newspapers across the land told the story, many eloquently, of the evangelist's life and death. A Chicago paper with the caption, "Torrey, Evangelist, Is Dead in Carolina," said in part:

> The Rev. Reuben Archer Torrey, well-known evangelist who preached in nearly every country of the world, bringing thousands to kneel in repentence. . .died last night at Asheville, North Carolina, in his 72nd year. He had served as an evangelist for fifty years and was known throughout the world as an apostle of rare power.[16]

The words "evangelist" and "apostle of rare power" seemed most fitting as a tribute.

Funeral services were held in Montrose at Torrey Lodge on Wednesday, October 31. Longtime friend, Rev. Will Houghton, pastor of the Atlanta Baptist Tabernacle, conducted the service. He had accompanied Reuben and the body on the train from Asheville. Houghton based his remarks on II Samuel 3:38, "A prince and a great man has fallen this day in Israel."

Dr. P. W. Philpott, pastor of the Moody Memorial Church in Chicago, spoke on behalf of the church; Dr. P. B. Fitzwater, a former student of Dr. Torrey, on behalf of the Moody Bible Institute. President Volney P. Kinne represented the Montrose Bible Conference Association. Dr. Torrey's favorite hymn, "O Could I Speak the Matchless Worth," was sung with real effect. Reuben described the simple funeral as a "meaningful service with a note of triumph."[17] The burial place was on Sunset Knoll—the exact spot where he and the family had prayed together that last Sunday afternoon in Montrose.

Dr. Torrey left but little of material things. His estate was comprised of a modest, simply-furnished home, a small library of selected books, a supply of well-worn clothing, and some small annuities and investments. The latter were just sufficient to provide for the needs of his wife and unmarried daughter. It spoke of his careful provision for his family.[18]

The epitaph on the gravestone just as truly described Reuben Archer Torrey as it did the Apostle Paul. Both were in the truest sense a "vessel unto honour."

Reuben Archer Torrey
1856-1928

"I have fought a good fight
I have finished my course
I have kept the faith"

[1]O. E. Sanden, unpublished papers on the life of Torrey.

[2]"Testimonials," *King's Business*, p. 171.

[3]Excerpts on the History of the Church of the Open Door (compiled by C. J. Multhauf, Church Historian), p. 3.

[4]Letter to O. E. Sanden. The letter was undated but written in the fall of 1926.

[5]Letter to Mrs. A. E. Taylor, November 2, 1927.

[6]Personal letter from Homer Hammontree, October 3, 1964.

[7]Entry in the Torrey Lodge Guest Book, October 8, 1926.

[8]Interview with Reuben A. Torrey, Jr., December 22, 23, 1965. For many years he wrote the *Gist of the Lesson,* a commentary on the International Sunday School lesson. He continued this ministry to the time of his death.

[9]Personal letter from Harold S. Laird, August 17, 1966.

[10]Torrey, p. 39.

[11]*Orlando Morning Sentinel,* December 3, 11, 1927.

[12]Harkness, pp. 81, 82.

[13]Hunter, "Steward," p. 10.

[14]Torrey, Jr., "Home," p. 69.

[15]Ibid.

[16]*Chicago Tribune,* October 29, 1928.

[17]R. A. Torrey, Jr., personal letter, April 7, 1965.

[18]Mrs. Torrey now made her residence with Edith in Wheaton, Illinois, until her death in 1953 at ninety-four years of age. After, Edith moved to Santa Barbara, California, where she died in 1959 at the age of 77. Elizabeth (Mrs. Herbert Wiggs), after a lingering illness of some years, died in 1936 in Elberton, Georgia, at 52 years of age. Reuben, Jr., after lengthy service as a missionary in both China and Korea, retired and gave much of his time and energy to the Montrose Bible Conference Association. He died in 1970 in Duarte, California, at eighty-four years of age.

Bibliography

Works of R. A. Torrey

(Page numbers have been included for all works except small leaflets.)

Anecdotes and Illustrations, New York: Revell, 1907, 185 pp.

The Baptism With the Holy Spirit, Chicago: Moody, n.d., 67 pp.
The Bible and Its Christ, New York: Revell, 1906, 189 pp.
The Bible the Peerless Book, New York: Revell, 1925, 43 pp.

The Certainty and Importance of the Bodily Resurrection of Jesus Christ From the Dead, Los Angeles: Biola, 1940, 20 pp.
The Christ of the Bible, New York: Doran, 1925, 285 pp.

Daily Meditations, (ed. by Chester Mann), Grand Rapids: Baker, 1963, 160 pp.
Death Defeated and Defied, Los Angeles: Biola, 1923, 46 pp.
The Deity of Jesus Christ, Los Angeles: Biola, n.d.
The Destiny of the Christless Dead, Glendale, California: The Church Press, n.d., 12 pp.
Difficulties and Alleged Contradictions in the Bible, New York: Revell, 1907, 127 pp.
Divine Healing—Does God Perform Miracles Today? Chicago: Moody, n.d. Revell, 46 pp.
The Divine Origin of the Bible, Chicago: Revell, 1899, 93 pp.

The Exact Truth Regarding an Eternal Hell, Los Angeles: Biola, 1918, 48 pp.

The Four Great Essentials, Los Angeles: Biola, 1920, 14 pp.
The Fundamental Doctrines of the Christian Faith, New York: Doran, 1918, 328 pp.

Getting the Gold Out of the Word of God, New York: Revell, 1925, 64 pp.
God Hath Spoken: Twenty-Five Addresses Delivered at the World Conference on Christian Fundamentals, May 28-June 1, 1919, Philadelphia.

The God of the Bible, New York: Doran, 1923, 246 pp.
The Gospel for Today, New York: Revell, 1922, 216 pp.
Great Pulpit Masters, Vol. III, New York: Revell, 1950, 256 pp.

The Higher Criticism and New Theology (ed.), New York: Gospel
    Publishing House, 1911, 284 pp.
The Holy Spirit in Personal Experience, Chicago: BICA, n.d.,
    31 pp.
The Holy Spirit, Who He Is and What He Does, New York:
    Revell, 1927, 201 pp.
How to Be Saved and How to Be Lost, New York: Revell, 1923,
    218 pp.
How to Bring Men to Christ, New York: Revell, 1893, 121 pp.
How to Grow in Grace, Los Angeles, Biola, n.d.
How to Obtain Fulness of Power, New York: Revell, 1897, 76 pp.
How to Pray, Old Tappan, New Jersey: Revell, 1970, 96 pp.
How to Promote and Conduct a Successful Revival (ed.), Chicago:
    Revell, 1901, 336 pp.
How to Study the Bible, New York: Oxford, 1909, 29 pp.
How to Study the Bible for Greatest Profit, New York: Revell,
    1896, 121 pp.
How to Succeed in the Christian Life, New York: Revell, 1906,
    121 pp.
How to Work for Christ, Chicago: Revell, 1901, 518 pp.

The Importance and Value of Proper Bible Study, New York:
    Doran, 1921, 113 pp.
Individual Soulwinning, Los Angeles: Biola, 1917, 31 pp.
Is the Bible the Inerrant Word of God? New York: Doran, 1922,
    185 pp.
Is the Present 'Tongues' Movement of God? Los Angeles: Biola,
    n.d., 12 pp.

Jesus, the Prophet, Priest and King, Los Angeles: Biola, n.d., 61
    pp.

The Last Word on Christ's Coming, Los Angeles: Biola, n.d.

The Missionary's Message—the Full Gospel, Los Angeles: Biola,
    n.d.

The New Birth, Los Angeles: Biola, n.d.

Ought Christians to Keep the Sabbath? Chicago: Revell, 1899,
    45 pp.
Outline Studies in I John, Grand Rapids: Zondervan, 1963, 84 pp.

Peanut Patriotism and Pure Patriotism, Los Angeles: Biola, 1918, 12 pp.

The Person and Work of the Holy Spirit, New York: Revell, 1910, 262 pp.

The Personal Return of Christ, James E. Hawkins, n.d., 22 pp.

Personal Work, New York: Revell, 1901, 186 pp.

The Power of Prayer and the Prayer of Power, New York: Revell, 1924, 246 pp.

Practical and Perplexing Questions Answered, Chicago: Moody, 1908, 129 pp.

The Real Christ, New York: Doran, 1920, 189 pp.

Real Salvation and Wholehearted Service, London: James Nisbet, Ltd, 1905, 267 pp.

The Resurrection of the Lord Jesus, Los Angeles: Biola, 1913, 31 pp.

The Return of the Lord Jesus, Los Angeles: Biola, 1913, 142 pp.

Revival Addresses, New York: Revell, 1903, 271 pp.

The Second Coming of Christ, Los Angeles: Biola, 1915.

The Shepherd Psalm, Los Angeles: Biola, 1915, 29 pp.

Soulwinning Sermons, New York: Revell, 1925, 485 pp.

Studies in the Life and Teachings of Our Lord, Chicago: BICA, 1907, 347 pp.

Talks to Men, New York: Revell, 1904, 138 pp.

The Treasury of R. A. Torrey, Westwood, N. J.: Revell, 1954, 254 pp.

The Uplifted Christ, Grand Rapids: Zondervan, 1965, 104 pp.

A Vest Pocket Companion for Christian Workers, New York: Revell, 1895, 118 pp.

The Voice of God in the Present Hour, New York: Revell, 1917, 255 pp.

What the Bible Teaches, New York: Revell, 1898, 539 pp.

What the War Teaches, Los Angeles: Biola, 1918.

Why God Used D. L. Moody, Chicago: Moody, 1923, 59 pp.

Will Christ Come Again? Los Angeles: Biola, 1918, 31 pp.

The Wondrous Joy of Soul Winning, Los Angeles: Biola, n.d., 90 pp.

World Renowned Hymns, (ed.), Los Angeles: Biola, 1909, 246 pp.

You and Your Bible (an Anthology of R. A. Torrey). Westwood, N. J.: Revell, 1958, 220 pp.

Books

Alexander, Mrs. Charles, *Charles M. Alexander,* London: Marshall Brothers, 1920.

Beardsley, F. G., *History of American Revivals,* New York: American Tract Society, 1912.
—————, *Heralds of Salvation,* New York: American Tract Society, 1939.
Bruner, Frederick Dale, *A Theology of the Holy Spirit,* Grand Rapids: Eerdmans, 1970.

Chapman, J. Wilbur, *The Life and Work of Dwight L. Moody.* Philadelphia: Winston, 1900.
Cole, Stewart G., *The History of Fundamentalism,* New York: Richard O. Smith, 1931.
Cross, Wilbur L., *Connecticut Yankee,* New Haven: Yale University Press, 1943.
Curtiss, Richard K., *They Called Him Mr. Moody,* Garden City, N. Y.: Doubleday, 1962.

Davis, George T. B., *Torrey and Alexander,* New York: Revell, 1905.
—————, *Twice Around the World With Alexander,* New York: The Christian Herald, 1907.
Day, Richard E., *Bush Aglow,* Philadelphia: Judson Press, 1936.
—————, *Breakfast Table Autocrat,* Chicago: Moody, 1946.
De Remer, Bernard R., *Moody Bible Institute: A Pictorial History,* Chicago: Moody, 1960.
Dollar, George, *History of Fundamentalism,* Greenville, South Carolina: Bob Jones, 1973.
Dunn, James, *Baptism in the Holy Spirit,* Naperville, Illinois: Alec Allenson, 1970.
Dwight, Timothy, *Memories of Yale Life and Men,* New York: Dodd, Mead and Co., 1903.

Feinburg, Charles F., *The Fundamentals for Today,* 2 vols., Grand Rapids: Kregel, 1958.
Ferm, Robert O., *Cooperative Evangelism,* Grand Rapids: Zondervan, 1958.
Findlay, James F., Jr., *Dwight L. Moody: American Evangelist, 1837-1899,* Chicago, 1969.
Finney, Charles G., *Memoirs of Rev. Charles G. Finney,* New York: Revell, 1876.
—————, *Revivals of Religion,* Westwood, New Jersey: Revell, n.d.
Fitt, A. P., *Moody Still Lives,* New York: Revell, 1936.

Furniss, Norman, *The Fundamentalist Controversy, 1918-1931,* Hamden, Connecticut: Archon Books, 1963.

Gasper, Louis, *The Fundamentalist Movement,* The Hague, Paris: Monton and Co., 1963.
Gee, Donald, *The Pentecostal Movement: Including the Story of the War Years* (1940-47), London: Elim, 1949.
Getz, Gene A., *MBI The Story of Moody Bible Institute,* Chicago: Moody, 1969.

Harkness, Robert, *Reuben Archer Torrey,* Chicago: The Bible Institute Corporation, 1929.

Infidels Answered by Three Immortals, Wheaton: Sword of the Lord, 1946.

Loud, Grover C., *Evangelized America,* New York: Dial, 1928.

MacClean, J. Kennedy, *Torrey and Alexander,* New York: Revell, 1905.
_____, *Triumphant Evangelism,* London: Marshall Bros., n.d.
_____, *Under Two Masters,* London: Marshall Bros., n.d.
McLoughlin, William G., Jr., *Billy Sunday Was His Real Name,* Chicago: The University of Chicago Press, 1955.
_____, *Modern Revivalism,* New York: Ronald Press, 1959.
Mann, Chester A. (ed.), *R. A. Torrey Yearbook,* New York: Revell, 1929.
Miller, Basil, *Ten Famous Evangelists,* Grand Rapids: Zondervan, 1949.
Moody, William R., *D. L. Moody,* New York: MacMillan, 1930.
Morgan, Jill, *Man of the Word,* New York: Revell, 1951.
Muller, George, *Life of Trust,* New York: Sheldon, 1878.

Pierson, George Wilson, *Yale College: An Educational History 1871-1921,* Vol. II, New Haven: Yale University Press, 1952.
Pollock, J. C., *Moody,* Grand Rapids: Zondervan, 1963.

Rice, John R., *Power of Pentecost,* Wheaton: Sword of the Lord, 1949, (now Murfreesboro, Tennessee).
Runyan, William (ed.), *Dr. Gray at Moody Bible Institute,* New York: Oxford University Press, 1935.

Sandeen, Ernest, *The Roots of Fundamentalism: British and American Millenarianism, 1800-1930,* Chicago: University of Chicago Press, 1970.
Seeley, J. R., *Ecce Homo,* Boston: Roberts Brothers, 1890.

Sellers, E. O., *Evangelism in Sermon and Song,* Chicago: Moody, 1946.

Smith, Oswald, *The Story of My Life,* London: Marshall, Morgan & Scott, 1962.

Smith, Wilbur M., *An Annotated Bibliography of D. L. Moody,* Chicago: Moody, 1948.

_____, *A Voice for God,* Boston: Wilde, 1949.

_____, *A Watchman on the Wall,* Grand Rapids: Eerdmans, 1951.

Talbot, Louis T. (ed.), *Traits and Tracts of Torrey,* Los Angeles: The Bible Institute of Los Angeles, n.d.

Taylor, Mrs. Howard, *Borden of Yale,* Philadelphia: China Inland Mission, 1926.

Torrey, F. C., *The Torrey Families and Their Children in America,* 2 Vols. Lakehurst, New Jersey: Williamsport Printing and Binding, 1929.

Trumbull, Charles G., *C. I. Scofield,* New York: Oxford, 1920.

Unger, Merrill F., *The Baptizing Work of the Holy Spirit,* Findlay, Ohio: Dunham, 1962.

Weisburger, Bernard, *They Gathered at the River,* Boston: Little, Brown and Co., 1958.

Whitesell, Faris D., *Great Personal Workers,* Chicago: Moody, 1956.

Winona Echoes, Winona Lake, Indiana: Winona Lake Institute, 1906.

Articles and Periodicals

Bailey, Faith Coxe. "R. A. Torrey's Most Persuasive Sermon," *Moody Monthly,* LVII (February, 1956), pp. 15-17, 39-41.

"The Battle Within the Churches," *Homiletic Review,* MCMXXIII (September, 1923), p. 188.

Brooks, K. L. "Does Dr. Torrey or Does He Not?" *King's Business,* VIII (December, 1922), pp. 1245, 1246.

Camp, Norman. "Dr. Torrey as a Man of Prayer," *Moody Monthly,* XXX (October, 1929), pp. 70,71.

Dixon, Mrs. A. C. "Dr. Torrey as He Was Known in Great Britain," *King's Business,* XXVII (January, 1936), pp. 10,11.

Evans, William. "Dr. Torrey as I Knew Him," *King's Business,* XXVII (January, 1936), pp. 7, 15.

Fitt, A. P. (ed.), *Moody Church Herald,* Volumes I-IV, 1900-1904.

_____, *The Institute Tie,* V (May, 1904).

Gray, James M. Editor's Notes, *Moody Monthly,* XXX (October, 1929), p. 57.
_____ Editor's Notes, *Moody Monthly,* XXXI (October, 1930), p. 51.

Henry, James O. "Black Oil and Souls to Win," *King's Business,* XLIX (February, 1958), pp. 13-17.
Horton, T. H. "The Coming of Dr. Torrey," *King's Business,* II (October, 1911), p. 259.
_____ Editor's Notes, *King's Business,* XV (September, 1924), pp. 550, 551.
_____ "News From Dr. Torrey," *King's Business,* II (December, 1911), p. 259.
_____ "Our New Dean," *King's Business,* II (August-September, 1911), p. 173.
"How Torrey Lived," *Moody Memo,* X (February, 1956).
Hunter, J. H. "Dr. Torrey as a Teacher," *King's Business,* XXVII (January, 1936), pp. 8, 9.
_____ "A Faithful and Wise Steward," *King's Business,* XXX (January, 1929), pp. 8-11.

The Indian Witness, XXXII (November 13, 1902), pp. 90, 91.

Jones, Bob, Sr. "Judgment," *Sword of the Lord* (April, 1946), pp. 1-3.

McFarland, Charles, "The New Attitudes Toward Evangelism," *Current Literature,* XL (February, 1906), pp. 163-165.
McLaurin, J. "Revival in India," *Missionary Review of the World,* XXVI (August, 1903), pp. 583-586.
McNaughton, Margaret. "A Giant Among Men," *Moody Monthly,* XLVIII (September, 1947), pp. 11, 12, 68.
Merriam, Edward F. (ed.) "The Torrey-Alexander Mission," *Outlook,* LXXI (December, 1905), pp. 806-808.
Millar, Elinor Stafford. "R. A. Torrey in Australia," *Moody Monthly,* XXXI (October, 1930), pp. 53, 54.
"Montrose Bible Conference," *Christian Life,* XX (August, 1958), pp. 39, 40.
Morton, Duncan A. "Dr. Torrey as a Friend," *King's Business,* XXVII (January, 1936), pp. 14,15.

Norton, Edith. "Reminiscences of Dr. Torrey," *King's Business,* XXVII (January, 1936), p. 12.

Outlook Illustrated Memento of the Torrey-Alexander Mission (August-September, 1902).

Pierson, A. T. "Year of Grace," *Missionary Review of the World,*
   XXVI (November, 1903), pp. 801-805.
Prichard, A. B. "Dr. Torrey as a Counsellor," *King's Business,*
   XXVII (January, 1936), pp. 13, 16.

"Reuben Archer Torrey," *The National Cyclopedia of American
   Biography,* XXI, 1931, p. 428.
Riley, W. B. "Dr. Torrey as a Preacher," *King's Business,* XXVII
   (January, 1936), pp. 6, 7.

Seville, George H. "And Some Evangelists," *Bible Today,*
   (February, 1947), pp. 608-616.
The Southern Cross, (June 5, August 5, and September 10),
   Special Souvenir editions.
Stewart, Mrs. Lyman and Whitwell, Cutler B. "As His Students
   Saw Him," *King's Business,* XXVII (January, 1936), p. 9.

"Testimonials to Dr. R. A. Torrey," *Moody Monthly,* XXIX
   (December, 1928), pp. 171, 172.
Torrey, Edith Clare. "If You Can Be Thankful," *Moody
   Monthly,* LVI (November, 1955), pp. 17, 85.
Torrey, Reuben A., Jr., "Dr. R. A. Torrey in His Home," *Moody
   Monthly,* XXX (February, 1929), pp. 68-70.
Torrey, Mrs. R. A. "Desiring God's Glory," *King's Business,*
   XXVII (January, 1936), p. 14.
Torrey, R. A. "China, the Land of Promise and Peril," *King's
   Business,* XIII (February, 1922), pp. 134-141.

Torrey, R. A. (ed.), *The Institute Tie,* I (October 30, 1892).

_____ "Do Not Forget the Children," *King's Business,*
   IV (November, 1913), p. 508.
_____ "A Great Soulwinner Goes Home," *King's Busi-
   ness,* XII (January, 1920), p. 4.
_____ "Making the Most of Life," *King's Business,* IX
   (November, 1918), p. 938.
_____ "Misinterpreting Prophecy," *King's Business,* VII
   (May, 1916), p. 387.
_____ "The Missionary Message," *King's Business,* IX
   (July, 1918), pp. 559, 560.
_____ "Our Lord's Second Coming, Incentive for Per-
   sonal Holiness," *King's Business,* V (May, 1914), pp. 253, 254.

_____ "Paul D. Moody's Gross Calumny of His Honored
   Father, D. L. Moody," *Moody Monthly,* XXIV (October,
   1923), p. 2.
_____ "Personal Work," *Moody Monthly,* XXXVIII
   (October, 1937), pp. 65, 66.

_____ "A Powerful Plea for Prayer for Revival," *Moody Monthly,* XXVIII (October, 1927), p. 11.

_____ "The Purpose and Methods of a Bible Institute," *King's Business,* III (May, 1912), pp. 101, 102.

_____ "The Revival We Need," *King's Business,* VI (October, 1915), pp. 848, 849.

_____ "The Second Coming of Christ," *King's Business,* V (August-September, 1914), pp. 423, 424.

_____ "Shall We Sacrifice Our Convictions for the Sake of Religious Unity?" *King's Business,* X (January, 1919), p. 7.

_____ "Stick to Your Proper Business," *King's Business,* VII (September, 1916), pp. 771, 772.

_____ "Was Jesus a Soul Winner?" *King's Business,* VII (May, 1916), p. 198.

Wadsworth, Ernest M. "R. A. Torrey as I Knew Him," *Eternity,* VII (March, 1956), pp. 12, 38.

Warren, William. "Genesis of the Australian Revival," *Missionary Review of the World,* XXVI (March, 1903), pp. 200-203.

Wright, Mrs. W. E. "Dr. Torrey's Sense of Fairness," *King's Business,* XXVII (January, 1936), p. 15.

Newspapers

Buffalo Express, March 9, 27, 1907.

Chicago Daily News, November 24, 1900; May 3, 1906.
Chicago Tribune, November 30, 1907; October 29, 1928.

Nashville Banner, October 29, 1906.

Orlando Morning Sentinel, December 3, 11, 1927.

Post and Mercury (Liverpool), January, 1905.

Wheaton Record, November 4, 1948.

Yorkshire Daily Observer, May 14, 1904.

Letters, Pamphlets and Other Materials, Published and Unpublished

Brose, Rev. Fred. Personal letter, October 27, 1964.

Charter of the Chicago Evangelization Society, February 12, 1887.

Congregational Church, Garrettsville, Ohio. Minutes, October 22, 1878, to October 15, 1882.

Coray, Edward. Personal letter, Wheaton Alumni Association, Wheaton College, August 28, 1964.

Crane, Mrs. Philip, Library Assistant, Yale University Library. Personal letter, October 12, 1965.

An English Mission, Impressions of an American Editor, (n.d.).

Ferrell, Mrs. Elsie. Personal letter, October 3, 1966.

Fuller, Charles. "Ten Words—My Teacher's Legacy," (June, 1967).
_____ Personal letter, September 11, 1964.

Hammontree, Homer. Personal letter, October 3, 1964.

Henry, Carl F. H. Personal letter, August 27, 1964.

Jones, Dr. Bob, Sr. Personal letter, May 26, 1962.

Laird, Harold S. Personal letter, August 17, 1966.

"The Laymen's Evangelistic Council of Chicago," brochure (n.d.).

"Montrose Bible Conference, Jubilee 1908-1958," brochure (1958).

Moody, D. L. Letters to R. A. Torrey, October 8, December 22, 1894.

Multhauf, C. J. (comp.). "Excerpts on the History of the Church of the Open Door," typescript.

Rice, John R. Personal letter, August 15, 1966.

Sanden, O. E. *God's Marked Man* (unpublished typescript, 1954).
_____ Unpublished papers on the life of R. A. Torrey.

Smith, Oswald. Personal letter, August 24, 1964.

Tindall, E. Abbey, *et al. Information About Dr. Torrey and Mr. Alexander.*

Torrey, Edith Clare. Letter to Mr. Gaylord Perry, November 14, 1958.

Torrey Lodge Guest Book, 1908-1928.

Torrey, R. A. Autobiographical notes, *Moodyanna* collection.
_____ Letter to Chicago Avenue Church, December, 1901.
_____ Letters to A. P. Fitt, February 18, March 4, November 29, 1903; November 14, 24, December 16, 1904; September 8, 1906; January 21, 1907; August 5, 1908.
_____ Letter to James M. Gray, November 21, 1910.
_____ "Historical Sketch of the Moody Bible Institute," Moody Bible Institute Catalog, 1924-25.

_____ *How God Answered Prayer* (Chicago: Bible Colportage Association, n.d.), p. 3.

_____ Letter to Miss Della McNeil, Chicago, November 25, 1901.

_____ "A Parting Message and Appeal From Mr. Torrey and Mr. Alexander," August 21, 1903.

_____ Letter to pastors of Scranton, Pennsylvania, July 28, 1908.

_____ "Prayer and the Ministry of the Word," February 1, 1917, (unpublished sermon).

_____ Letter to O. E. Sanden, Fall, 1926.

_____ Letters to Lyman Stewart, June 3, 1909; July 2, 1913; October 31, 1914; March 29, April 17, 1915.

_____ Telegram to Mrs. Lyman Stewart, November 20, 1923.

_____ Letter to Mrs. A. E. Taylor, November 2, 1927.

Torrey, Mrs. R. A. Letters to A. F. Gaylord, July 17, August 10, 1905; December 19, 1907.

Torrey, R. A., Jr. Interview, December 22, 23, 1965.

_____ Personal letters, April 7, December 14, 1965; October 21, 1966; April 7, 1969.

Torrey, R. A., III, Personal letter, December 20, 1974.

Wadsworth, Ernest. Interview, November 22, 1958, *Moodyanna* collection.

White, John Wesley. Personal letter, November 18, 1965.

Appendix A

"He Being Dead Yet Speaketh"

The life and ministry of Dr. R. A. Torrey has had a vast influence upon a multitude of outstanding Christian leaders. This holds true not only for his own generation but also for subsequent ones through his prolific writing ministry. One of the most striking features of his influence is its varied nature. It covers many doctrinal, practical and spiritual areas.

The author has assembled a number of quotes from well-known Christian leaders, each one representing some facet of Dr. Torrey's character, conviction or ministry which has been significant in its influence. These have been divided into two categories. The first deal with those whose major ministry was contemporary with Dr. Torrey; the second, with those whose primary ministry took place subsequent to his generation. Many of these are taken from personal correspondence.

The purpose of these quotes is not excessively to eulogize Dr. Torrey—a procedure of which he would not have approved—but rather to show how God has used a choice servant to touch lives for His glory. God still speaks to us today through Dr. Reuben Archer Torrey.

Probably no man in the past has influenced my life concerning the doctrine of the Holy Spirit as has R. A. Torrey. His teaching on the fullness of the Holy Spirit took me out of the theoretical and into the practical, out of the classroom and into the laboratory, and out of theology and into my life. —Dr. Jack Hyles, pastor, First Baptist Church, Hammond, Indiana; letter, July 23, 1962.

Dr. R. A. Torrey has had a very definite influence on my life. I refer especially to his teachings on the fullness of the Holy Spirit.

As I look back over my ministry of thirty-four years, I believe that my first contact with solid teaching on the fullness of the Spirit came through sermons preached or written by Dr. R. A. Torrey.—**Dr. Lee Roberson, pastor, Highland Park Baptist Church; Chancellor, Tennessee Temple Schools, Chattanooga, Tennessee; letter, December 20, 1962.**

Few books in my library have equaled the single source of inspiration and blessing that the works of Dr. R. A. Torrey have been to my life and ministry. Perhaps his books on prayer and the Holy Spirit have wrought the greatest influence of all upon my spiritual life. To Dr. Torrey, these themes were more than theological doctrines. They were vital spiritual practices and living experiences that enriched his life and enabled him to convey the radiance of Christ and the dynamic of the Spirit to preachers and laymen around the world.—**Dr. Bob Gray, pastor, Trinity Baptist Church, Jacksonville, Florida; letter, September 24, 1964.**

There was more of a logical content to his messages than was characteristic of much evangelistic preaching, and this lent special interest to his pulpit ministry across the Atlantic.—**Dr. Carl F. H. Henry, past editor,** *Christianity Today***; letter, August 27, 1964.**

He was an unusual combination of pastor, evangelist, teacher and writer. His books have blessed me greatly, and I remember hearing him speak on "Moody As I Knew Him." He was a Spirit-filled man with a world-wide ministry that still continues.—**Dr. Vance Havner, evangelist and Bible teacher; letter, September 19, 1964.**

When I was a student in the Bible Institute of Los Angeles over forty years ago I had the privilege of sitting under the teaching ministry of Dr. R. A. Torrey for nearly three years. I have been very thankful for that enriching experience in the early years of my Christian ministry, for he grounded me in the Word of God. I learned much from his method of teaching which I have used with great profit and blessing over the Old Fashioned Revival Hour. Dr. Torrey's deep insight into the Scriptures and his logical presentation impressed me very deeply at that time when he became my example and has remained so through all these years. I am deeply grateful.—**Dr. Charles Fuller, late director, "The Old Fashioned Revival Hour"; letter, September 11, 1964.**

The printed sermons of Dr. R. A. Torrey, who was so greatly used of God in a world-wide ministry of evangelism, have meant more to me personally than perhaps the printed sermons of any other great man of the past. The sermons of Dr. R. A. Torrey were directed primarily to the hearts of people, the area in which God works in His power of transformation, but they also were strong sermons from the standpoint of intellectualism. They were well-outlined, filled with Scripture; they were mellowed with tremendous illustrations.—**Dr. Tom Malone, pastor, Immanuel Baptist Church, Pontiac, Michigan; letter, January 2, 1963.**

I believe I am correct when I say that more agnostics, skeptics, Unitarians and destructive critics were confounded and set at naught and persuaded to give up their erroneous positions by the persuasive preaching and unanswerable statements of Dr. Torrey than by the preaching of any other man of the last hundred years. By his preaching from the pulpit and by his potent pen, light and strength and salvation came to many as they expressed faith in the Bible and in the Christ of the Bible.—**Dr. Robert G. Lee, pastor-emeritus, Bellevue Baptist Church, Memphis, Tennessee; letter, September 3, 1964.**

I have never known in my long experience as an evangelist any evangelist or any minister of the Gospel for whom I had more respect than I had for Dr. R. A. Torrey. He was one of the most understanding and fair-minded men I have ever met. He had a great mind. He was loyal to his friends. He knew the Word of God and knew how to use it; and he loved souls and won many to the Lord Jesus Christ.—**Dr. Bob Jones, Sr., evangelist and founder, Bob Jones University, Greenville, South Carolina; letter, May 26, 1962.**

At eight years of age I experienced my first awareness of conviction of sin and the need of receiving the Lord Jesus Christ as Saviour through reading *Questions and Answers* by Reuben A. Torrey. Without counsel from others, for there was none to help, I bowed in prayer and asked the Lord to blot out my sins and make me His child. Some years passed before assurance of salvation became mine, yet, I can point to that moment when the Spirit of God used the pen of R. A. Torrey to bring conviction and conversion.—**Dr. Wilbert Welch, president, Grand Rapids Baptist Bible College and Seminary; letter, October 13, 1964.**

I was converted under Dr. R. A. Torrey in 1906. He was one of the world's greatest evangelists. I thank God upon every remembrance of him. Dr. Torrey was not a sensational preacher, but he was a great preacher, sound, fundamental, evangelical and evangelistic. He and Alexander were real soul winners.—**Dr. Oswald Smith, former pastor, Peoples Church, Toronto, Ontario, Canada; letter, August 24, 1964.**

Dr. R. A. Torrey was in the forefront of American evangelicals throughout the first quarter of the twentieth century. An able student of God's Word, he was a most effective Bible teacher, preacher and evangelist. There was a quality in his ministry which would make him even more effective in this generation.—**Dr. Torrey M. Johnson, Youth for Christ International, Wheaton, Illinois; letter, September 26, 1967. He was named after Dr. Torrey.**

Dr. Torrey was one of the greatest men I've ever known! Like the Rock of Gibraltar! He was straightforward in his approach and was never "out for show" as an evangelist. He was a man of wonderful character. I thank God for my few meetings with R. A. Torrey.—Dr. Homer Hammontree, composer and songleader for some of the later Torrey campaigns; letter, October 3, 1964.

Many of my messages are flavored with Dr. R. A. Torrey's illustrations. He has been a great influence in my personal life, as his writings challenge me constantly to do the job of personal soul winning and getting others to do likewise. I believe the greatest influence he has had on my life is his constant use of the Word of God in his ministry; consequently, I have tried to do the same and many of my messages contain thirty to fifty verses of Scripture.—Dr. Glen Schunk, evangelist; letter, October 15, 1964.

I have the highest regard for the work he did in the field of evangelism and in the field of education. He was certainly a stalwart of the faith and although he was thoroughly prepared with formal education, he had a child-like faith in the Lord Jesus Christ and the verbally-inspired Word of God.—Dr. Monroe Parker, evangelist and president of Baptist World Missions, letter, August 24, 1964.

I find his books very concise, logical, well-organized; a very good and thorough study on the subject matter, and most helpful to everybody and anyone studying the Bible. His book on *What the Bible Teaches* is uniquely set up, very easy to study and acquaint oneself with just what the title says. I used it constantly in my early ministry in acquainting myself with the teachings of the Bible on a given subject.—Dr. Theodore Epp, director, Back to the Bible Broadcast, letter, September 9, 1964.

I've been greatly challenged by studying his books and reading of the late Torrey-Alexander campaigns; not only in our own beloved land, but in the regions beyond. I think his book on soul winning was the greatest challenge to me as a young Christian to start digging in and pointing men to Christ.—Dr. Jack Wyrtzen, director, Word of Life Fellowship, letter, August 31, 1967.

It would be impossible to overestimate the influence that Dr. R. A. Torrey had on my life and thought. After graduating from college, I went to the Bible Institute of Los Angeles and sat under his teaching for a year. My mind was filled with questions that had been instilled in it in college. I had not accepted the unbelief that had there been given but I did not know the answers. Dr. Torrey's splendid scholarship, his solid faith in the Word of God, and his remarkable ability as an interpreter of the Scripture, strengthened and solidified my convictions and had a permanent effect upon my life. I know of no single human being to whose teachings I feel more indebted.—**Dr. Allan A. MacRae, former president, Faith Theological Seminary; letter, September 9, 1964.**

Dr. Torrey was a giant among men, a giant in intellect, in preparation for the Gospel ministry, in his teaching and preaching, in his administration as dean of Moody Bible Institute and the Bible Institute of Los Angeles. He was a giant for God with the pen as well as in the pulpit. Most of all, he was a giant in the things of God, by understanding of the Scriptures and by Spirit-anointed evangelism and Bible teaching. He has left a great heritage to the people of God.—**Dr. V. Raymond Edman, late president, Wheaton College, Wheaton, Illinois, letter, August 24, 1964.**

Although I never saw Dr. R. A. Torrey nor heard him preach, his ministry has had a profound effect on my life.

First, his little book, *How to Pray*, came into my hands when I was a teenager, a young Christian, in the cattle country of West Texas. I would read and pray and read and pray. So, in that most impressionable time, I learned to take the Bible literally, learned to claim the promises and learned to pray. Doubtless the germ of my large book, *Prayer—Asking and Receiving*, came here.

Later, as a young preacher, there fell into my hands the large book, *Soul Winning Sermons*, by Torrey, as preached in his great campaigns. Then, the *Life of Charlie Alexander* by his wife, told the thrilling stories, with details and many pictures, of the Torrey-Alexander campaigns in Australia and England. I was tremendously impressed by the simple, logical outlines of sermons preached, with every point proved by the Scriptures, by the great sweep of Torrey's faith, and the possibilities of reaching the multitudes in evangelism.

Dr. Torrey was a tremendous scholar, a bold defender of the faith, the pattern and the teacher for thousands of preachers, a Spirit-filled giant soul winner. There were some weak-kneed Christians who shrank from Dr. Torrey's great insistence on the power of the Holy Spirit, his bold defense of the faith, his constant pressure on people to do personal soul winning. But his impact on America and on Christianity for good exceeded that of any other of the great evangelists saving Moody himself. And in the area of Bible-teaching and scholarship and defense of the faith, he exceeded Moody.—**Dr. John R. Rice, evangelist and editor of *The Sword of the Lord*, letter, August 15, 1966.**

Dr. Torrey, by his patient kindnesses, his preaching and teaching, his counsel, and consistent living, greatly influenced my life. I may say that under God I owe to R. A. Torrey the honor for being used of Him to get my life into usable condition for the Lord, not only in my ministry in churches, but in the office of the Great Commission Prayer League.—**Dr. Ernest Wadsworth, late director of the Great Commission Prayer League.**

There was a solidarity to the messages of Dr. Torrey that made the results of his evangelistic efforts abiding. He preached the Gospel with the Holy Ghost sent down from Heaven. He refused to descend to unworthy methods or motives. He relied in all his ministry on the use of the "Sword of the Spirit which is the Word of God."—Dr. R. V. Bingham, missionary, author.

Dr. Torrey was a great man. God made him great. He has been in Heaven for a number of years, but his influence still lives, and his influence will go on living so long as this world lives. When I think of this man, a verse comes to my mind: Daniel 5:11. There you read the words concerning Daniel spoken by the queen mother. "There is a man in thy kingdom, in whom is the spirit of the holy gods."—Dr. Louis Talbot, former Chancellor, Bible Institute of Los Angeles.

Reuben Archer Torrey (1856-1928), the successor to D. L. Moody in world evangelism, also rated high as a teacher, a writer, a champion of the faith once for all delivered to the saints, and especially as a personal worker. In the writer's opinion, Dr. Torrey did more to emphasize and promote personal evangelism than any other one man since the days of the apostles.—Dr. Faris D. Whitesell, writer and former instructor, Northern Baptist Theological Seminary.

While it is perfectly true to say that Bible institute work in America owes its existence to D. L. Moody, it is likewise true to assert that Bible institutes owe their development to Dr. Torrey. . . .The curriculum of the Chicago Institute, which is largely the basis of Bible institutes the land over, was conceived chiefly by Dr. Torrey. And some of the ablest Bible teachers around the world owe their inspiration to the studies this renowned teacher made possible.—Dr. Herbert Lockyer, Bible teacher, author.

Most of the phenomenal success of the Institute is due to his wise administration. He was very close to Mr. Moody during the later years. No man, really, had Mr. Moody's confidence more completely, and justly so, for no man could ever be more loyal to another than R. A. Torrey to D. L. Moody.—J. Wilbur Chapman, evangelist.

Dr. Torrey was. . .a personal soul winner, and to him, almost more than to D. L. Moody, does the Moody Bible Institute still owe its reputation for turning out men and women stimulated and equipped to deal face to face and heart to heart with human souls about salvation. Mr. Moody furnished enthusiasm for that work, but Dr. Torrey taught us how to do it.

Oh, Dr. Torrey, you are greatly missed far beyond your family circle! And you are greatly needed here today, as we poor mortals think. You knew God and His Son Jesus Christ. You were a true witness who delivered souls. You contended earnestly for the faith delivered once for all to the saints. You fought the good fight and were not afraid. And we know that there is a crown of righteousness laid up for you which the Lord, the righteous Judge, shall give to you in that day, and not to you only, blessed be His name, but to all them also who love His appearing.—Dr. James M. Gray, late president, Moody Bible Institute, author.

His was no uncertain message. His positive and uncompromising attitude upon evangelical lines was generally known and sometimes misinterpreted. At heart he was most sympathetic and helpful. As an organizer Dr. Torrey was gifted and successful. In business affairs he was precise and capable—but to those who knew him most intimately, his Christian character and his warm friendship were most genuinely appreciated. As an author Dr. Torrey has given guidance and inspiration to great numbers, and this influence will continue so that while the voice has been stilled, the work of his pen will continue to make the Book of books an increasing factor in fostering a better life and better service. We shall greatly miss him.—Fleming H. Revell, late publisher.

He was utterly sincere in his consecration to God, a single-minded zealous soul winner, clean in money matters, persistent in prayer and Bible study, and true to his family and his friends. His private life was the best endorsement of his public ministry.—Mr. A. P. Fitt, son-in-law to D. L. Moody and co-worker with Torrey. Fitt led his first soul to Christ through reading Torrey's *How to Bring Men to Christ*.

But those who knew Dr. Torrey more intimately knew him as a man of regular and uninterrupted prayer. He knew what it meant to pray without ceasing. With hours set systematically apart for prayer, he gave himself diligently to this ministry.—Dr. Will H. Houghton, late president, Moody Bible Institute. This was spoken at Dr. Torrey's funeral.

A day spent with Torrey cannot be forgotten! His faith, hope and love are contagious. He reads the Scriptures constantly in five languages, English, German, French, Hebrew and Greek. The merciless way he demolished the sophistries of some of the higher critics makes him unpopular with men of advanced views. They pronounce him cold, dogmatic, and unsympathetic, but in his own family, and among his friends, he is the soul of gentleness, courtesy and sympathy. He is the one man I have known to whom praise of his preaching seems positively painful, doubtless fearing that such praise may breed pride and its consequent weakness. His breath is prayer, and he is never too busy to spend a whole hour every day in the inner chamber with God.—Dr. A. C. Dixon, late pastor, Moody Memorial Church; editor, *The Fundamentals*.

There is no question but that, under God, Dr. Torrey was used to build the foundation on which most of the Bible institutes of America are built. . . .Anyone acquainted with educational methods who would look closely into the curriculum of the Institute as Dr. Torrey outlined it—with its combination of classroom work and practical Christian work assignments—would certainly agree that here was an able educator, a man who in many respects was before his time so far as educational procedure is concerned.—Dr. William Culbertson, late president, Moody Bible Institute.

Dr. Torrey was sincerely religious and deeply spiritual. I never knew a man who wanted God's best more than he did. And for it he would spend whole nights in prayer. . . .He was a most true and loyal friend—not loudly, sensationally, emotionally; but actually, and in the truest sense of the word "friend." He was not slow to tell you your faults face to face, but he would defend you and speak of your virtues behind your back. . . .I recall vividly that when I was a student under him, there came a great sorrow into my life. Dr. Torrey came to my room, counseled and comforted me; and there we stood with head on each other's shoulders—the great teacher weeping with his poor student; then we knelt and prayed. The memory of R. A. Torrey is enough to move the heart to tears and the life to devotion.—Dr. William Evans, late teacher and co-worker.

But Dr. Torrey was as tender in spirit as he was bold in speech. On a few occasions I counseled him on matters that involved controversy between brethren, and he always amazed and delighted me. This man who seemed to preach with a doubled-up fist was as gentle as a woman when giving advice. He was not only anxious to be just, but ready to be generous always, toward even those with whom he did not agree. This side of Torrey's nature was known only to those who enjoyed some intimate fellowship with him, but it was a prime factor in his domestic and fraternal relations. . . .Torrey was never appreciated, at his full value, until the rest of the world communicated its estimate of him to his homeland.—Dr. W. B. Riley, late pastor, First Baptist Church; president, Northwestern Schools, Minneapolis, Minnesota.

Faithful always to the obligation for service which he felt, never seeking the "limelight" so attractive to some, living a simple unostentatious home-life with the wonderful wife God gave him—this man of God was dominated by a sincere love for the Lord, for the Book, and for the countless multitude of unsaved in this and other lands to whom he was privileged to minister through soul-saving messages and by personal contact.—T. H. Horton, late teacher, Bible Institute of Los Angeles.

If I were not a Christian, the very consistency of my father's life would force me to become a believer. The testimony of friends of ours who were not spiritually in sympathy with Father's work was that they could not observe one inconsistency in his life.—Edith Torrey, eldest daughter.

What others considered domination in Dr. Torrey seemed to me merely the exercise of good judgment. All problems were thought and prayed through until God's guidance was clear. Then Dr. Torrey was firm as to the course he followed. My husband was a man of much prayer and Bible study. He denied himself social intercourse with even his best friends, in order that he might have time for prayer, study, and the preparation for his work.—Mrs. R. A. Torrey, wife.

Perhaps the most signal influence of all has been that upon his own children and grandchildren. Over ninety percent are engaged in full-time Christian work.

Appendix B

Ten Reasons Why I Believe the Bible Is the Word of God

By Dr. R. A. Torrey

I was brought up to believe that the Bible was the Word of God. In early life I accepted it as such upon the authority of my parents, and never gave the question any serious thought. But later in life my faith in the Bible was utterly shattered through the influence of the writings of a very celebrated, scholarly and brilliant skeptic. I found myself face to face with the question, *Why* do you believe the Bible is the Word of God?

I had no satisfactory answer. I determined to go to the bottom of this question. If satisfactory proof could not be found that the Bible was God's Word, I would give the whole thing up, cost what it might. If satisfactory proof could be found that the Bible was God's Word, I would take my stand upon it, cost what it might. I doubtless had many friends who could have answered the question satisfactorily, but I was unwilling to confide to them the struggle that was going on in my own heart; so I sought help from God and from books, and after much painful study and thought came out of the darkness of skepticism into the broad daylight of faith and certainty that the Bible from beginning to end is God's Word. The following pages are largely the outcome of that experience of conflict and final victory. I will give ten reasons why I believe the Bible is the Word of God.

I. On the Ground of the Testimony of Jesus Christ

Many people accept the authority of Christ who do not

accept that of the Bible as a whole. We all must accept His authority. He is accredited to us by five Divine testimonies: by the testimony of the Divine life He lived; by the testimony of the Divine words He spoke; by the testimony of the Divine works He wrought; by the Divine attestation of the resurrection from the dead; and by the testimony of His Divine influence upon the history of mankind. But if we accept the authority of Christ we must accept the authority of the Bible as a whole. He testifies definitely and specifically to the Divine authorship of the whole Bible.

We find His testimony as to the Old Testament in Mark 7:13. Here He calls the law of Moses the "Word of God." That, of course, covers only the first five books of the Old Testament, but in Luke 24:27 we read, "And beginning at Moses and all the prophets, he expounded unto them in *all the scriptures* the things concerning himself," and in the forty-fourth verse He said, ". . .all things must be fulfilled, which were written in the law of Moses, and in the prophets, and in the psalms."

The Jews divided the Old Testament into three parts—the Law, the Prophets, and the Psalms—and Christ takes up each of these parts and sets the stamp of His authority upon it. In John 10:35 Christ says, "The scripture cannot be broken," thereby teaching the absolute accuracy and inviolability of the Old Testament. More specifically still, if possible, in Matthew 5:18 Jesus says that "one jot or one tittle shall in no wise pass from the law, till all be fulfilled." A jot is the smallest letter in the Hebrew alphabet—less than half the size of any other letter, and a tittle is the merest point of a consonant—less than the cross we put on a "t,"—and Christ here declares that the Scripture is absolutely true, down to the smallest letter or point of a letter. So if we accept the authority of Christ, we must accept the Divine authority of the entire Old Testament.

Now, as to the New Testament. We find Christ's endorsement of it in John 14:26, "The Holy Ghost, whom the Father will send in my name, he shall teach you all things, and bring all things to your remembrance, whatsoever I have said unto you." Here we see that not only was the teaching of the apostles to be fully inspired, but also their recollection of what Christ Himself taught. We are sometimes asked how we know that the apostles correctly reported what Jesus said—"may they not have forgotten?" True, they might forget, but Christ Himself tells us that in the Gospels we have not the apostles' recollection of what He said but the Holy Ghost's recollection, and the Spirit of God never forgets. In John 16:13,14, Christ said that the Holy Ghost should guide the apostles into "all truth"; therefore in the New Testament teaching we have the whole sphere of God's truth. The teaching of the apostles is more complete than that of Jesus Himself, for He says in John 16:12,13, "I have yet many things to say unto you, but ye cannot bear them now. Howbeit, when he, the Spirit of truth, is come, he shall guide you into *all truth*." While His own teaching had been partial, because of their weakness, the teaching of the apostles, under the promised Spirit, was to take in the whole sphere of God's truth.

So if we accept the authority of Christ, we must accept that of the whole Bible, but we must, as already seen, accept Christ's authority.

II. On the Ground of Its Fulfilled Prophecies

There are two classes of prophecies in the Bible—first, the explicit, verbal prophecies; second, those of the types.

In the first we have the definite prophecies concerning the Jews, the heathen nations and the Messiah. Taking the prophecies regarding the Messiah as an illustration, look at Isaiah 53, Micah 5:2, Daniel 9:25-27. Many others might be mentioned, but these will serve as illustrations. In these prophecies, written hundreds of years before the Messiah came, we have the most explicit statements as to the manner and place of His birth, the manner of His reception by men, how His life would end, His resurrection and His victory succeeding His death. When made, these prophecies were exceedingly improbable, and seemingly impossible of fulfilment; but they were fulfilled to the very minutest detail of manner and place and time. How are we to account for it? Man could not have foreseen these improbable events—they lay hundreds of years ahead—but God could, and it is God who speaks through these men.

But the prophecies of the types are more remarkable still. Everything in the Old Testament—history, institutions, ceremonies is prophetical. The high-priesthood, the ordinary priesthood, the Levites, the prophets, priests and kings, are all prophecies. The tabernacle, the brazen altar, the laver, the golden candlestick, the table of shewbread, the veil, the altar of incense, the ark of the covenant, the very coverings of the tabernacle, are prophecies. In all these things, as we study them minutely and soberly in the light of the history of Jesus Christ and the church, we see, wrapped up in the ancient institutions ordained of God to meet an immediate purpose, prophecies of the death atonement, and resurrection of Christ, the day of Pentecost, and the entire history of the church. We see the profoundest Christian doctrines of the New Testament clearly foreshadowed in these institutions of the Old Testament. The only way in which you can appreciate this is to get into the Book itself and study all about the sacrifices and feasts, etc., till you see the truths of the New Testament shining out in the Old.

If, in studying some elementary form of life, I find a rudimentary organ, useless now, but by the process of development to become of use in that animal's descendant, I say, back of this rudimentary organ is God, who, in the earlier animal, is preparing for the life and necessities of the animal that is to come. So, going back to these preparations in the Bible for the truth that is to be clearly taught at a later day, there is only one scientific way to account for them, namely, He who knows and prepares for the end from the beginning is the author of that Book.

III. On the Ground of the Unity of the Book

This is an old argument, but a very satisfactory one. The Bible consists of sixty-six books; written by more than thirty different men; extending in the period of its composition over more than fifteen hundred years; written in three different languages, in many different countries, and by men on every plane of social life—from the herdman and fisherman and cheap politician up to the king upon his throne; written under all sorts of circumstances; yet in all this wonderful conglomeration we find an absolute unity of thought.

A wonderful thing about it is that this unity does not lie on the surface. On the surface there is oftentimes apparent contradiction, and the unity only comes out after deep and protracted study.

More wonderful yet is the organic character of this unity, beginning in the first book and growing till you come to its culmination in the last book of the Bible. We have first the seed, then the plant, then the bud, then the blossom, then the ripened fruit.

Suppose a vast building were to be erected, the stones for which were brought from the quarries in Rutland, Vermont; Berea, Ohio; Kasota, Minnesota, and Middletown, Connecticut. Each stone was hewn into final shape in the quarry from which it was brought. These stones were of all varieties of shape and size, cubical, rectangular, cylindrical, etc., but when they were brought together every stone fitted into its place, and when put together there rose before you a temple absolutely perfect in every outline, with its domes, sidewalls, buttresses, arches, transepts—not a gap or a flaw anywhere. How would you account for it? You would say that back of these individual workers in the quarries was the master-mind of the architect who planned it all, and gave to each individual worker his specifications for the work.

So in this marvelous temple of God's truth which we call the Bible, whose stones have been quarried at periods of time and in places so remote from one another, but where every smallest part fits each other part, we are forced to say that back of the human hands that wrought was the Master-mind that thought.

IV. On the Ground of the Immeasurable Superiority of the Teachings of the Bible to Those of Any Other and All Other Books

It is quite fashionable in some quarters to compare the teachings of the Bible with the teachings of Zoroaster and Buddha and Confucius and Epictetus and Socrates and Marcus Aurelius Antonius and a number of other heathen authors. The difference between the teachings of the Bible and those of these men is found in three points—

First, the Bible has in it nothing but truth, while all the others have truth mixed with error. It is true Socrates taught how a philosopher ought to die; he also taught how a woman of the town ought to conduct her business. Jewels there are in the teachings of these men, but, as Joseph Cook once said, they are "jewels picked out of the mud."

Second, the Bible contains *all* truth. There is not a truth to be found anywhere on moral or spiritual subjects that you cannot find in substance within the covers of that old Book. I have often, when speaking upon this subject, asked anyone to bring me a single truth on moral or spiritual subjects, which, upon reflection, I could not find within the covers of this Book, and no one has ever been able to do so. I have taken pains to compare some of the better teachings of infidels with those of the Bible. They indeed have jewels of thought, but they are, whether they knew it or not, stolen jewels, and stolen from the very Book they ridicule.

The *third* point of superiority is this: The Bible contains more truth than all other books together. Get together from all literature of ancient and modern times all the beautiful thoughts you can; put away all the rubbish; put all these truths that you have culled from the literature of all ages into one book, and as the result, even then you will not have a book that will take the place of this one Book.

This is not a large Book; I hold in my hand a copy that I carry in my vest pocket, and yet in this one little Book there is more of truth than in all the books which man has produced in all the ages of his history. How will you account for it? There is only one rational way. This is not man's Book, but God's Book.

V. On the Ground of the History of the Book, Its Victory Over Attack

This Book has always been hated. No sooner was it given to the world than it met the hatred of men, and they tried to stamp it out. Celsus tried it by the brilliancy of his genius, Porphyry by the depth of his philosophy; but they failed. Lucian directed against it the shafts of his ridicule, Diocletian the power of the Roman Empire; but they failed. Edicts, backed by all the power of the Empire, were issued that every Bible should be burned, and that everyone who had a Bible should be put to death.

For eighteen centuries every engine of destruction that human science, philosophy, wit, reasoning or brutality could bring to bear against a book has been brought to bear against that Book to stamp it out of the world, but it has a mightier hold on the world today than ever before.

If that were man's book it would have been annihilated and forgotten hundreds of years ago, but because there is in it "the hiding of God's power," though at times all the great men of the world have been against it, and only an obscure remnant for it, still it has fulfilled wonderfully the words of Christ, though not in the sense of the original prophecy, "Heaven and earth shall pass away, but my word shall not pass away."

VI. On the Ground of the Character of Those Who Accept and of Those Who Reject the Book

Two things speak for the divinity of the Bible—the character of those who accept it, and, equally, the character of those who reject it. I do not mean by this that every man who professes to believe the Book is better than every man that does not, but show me a man living an unselfish, devoted life, one who without reservation has surrendered himself to do the will of God, and I will show you a man who believes the Bible to be God's Word. On the other hand, show me a man who rejects the Divine authority of that Book, and I will show you a man living a life of greed or lust or spiritual pride or self-will.

Suppose you have a book purporting to be by a certain author, and the people best acquainted with that author say it is his, and the people least acquainted with him say it is not; which will you believe? Now, the people best acquainted with God say the Bible is His Book; those who are least acquainted with God say it is not. Which will you believe?

Furthermore, as men grow better, they are more likely to accept the Bible, and as they grow worse, they are more likely to reject it. We have all known men who were both sinful and unbelieving who, by forsaking their sin, lost their unbelief. Did any of us ever know a man who was sinful and believing who, by forsaking his sin, lost his faith? The nearer men live to God, the more confident they are that the Bible is God's Word; the farther they get away from Him, the more confident they are that it is not.

Where is the stronghold of the Bible? In the pure, unselfish, happy home. Where is the stronghold of infidelity? The gambling hell, the drinking saloon and the brothel. If a man should walk into a saloon and lay a Bible down upon the bar and order a drink, we should think there was a strong incongruity in his actions, but if he should lay any infidel writing upon the bar and order a drink, we would not feel that there was any incongruity.

VII. On the Ground of the Influence of the Book

There is more power in that little Book to save men and purify, gladden and beautify their lives, than in all other literature put together—more power to lift men up to God. A stream never rises higher than its source, and a Book that has a power to lift men up to God that no other book has, must have come down from God in a way that no other book has.

I have in mind as I write a man who was the most complete victim of strong drink I ever knew; a man of marvelous intellectual gifts, but who had been stupefied and brutalized and demonized by the power of sin, and he was an infidel. At last the light of God shone into his darkened heart, and by the power of that Book he has been transformed into one of the humblest, sweetest, noblest men I know today.

What other book would have done that? What other book has the power to elevate not only individuals but communities and nations that this Book has?

VIII. On the Ground of the Inexhaustible Depth of the Book

Nothing has been added to it in eighteen hundred years, yet a man like Bunsen or Neander cannot exhaust it by the study of a lifetime. George Muller read it through more than one hundred times, and said it was fresher every time he read it. Could that be true of any other book?

But more wonderful than this—not only individual men but generations of men for eighteen hundred years have dug into it and given to the world thousands of volumes devoted to its exposition, and they have not reached the bottom of the quarry yet. A book that man produces man can exhaust, but all men together have not been able to get to the bottom of this Book. How are you going to account for it? Only in this way—that in this Book are hidden the infinite and inexhaustible treasures of the wisdom and knowledge of God.

A brilliant Unitarian writer, in trying to disprove the inspiration of the Bible, says: "How irreligious to charge an infinite God with having written His whole Word in so small a book." He does not see how his argument can be turned against himself. What a testimony it is to the divinity of this Book that such infinite wisdom is stored away in so small a compass!

IX. On the Ground of the Fact That as We Grow in Knowledge and Holiness We Grow Toward the Bible

Every thoughtful person when he starts out to study the

Bible finds many things with which he does not agree, but as he goes on studying and growing in likeness to God, the nearer he gets to God, the nearer he gets to the Bible. The nearer and nearer we get to God's standpoint, the less and less becomes the disagreement between us and the Bible. What is the inevitable mathematical conclusion? When we get where God is, we and the Bible will meet. In other words, the Bible was written from God's standpoint.

Suppose you are traveling through a forest under the conduct of an experienced and highly recommended guide. You come to a place where two roads diverge. The guide says the road to the left is the one to take, but your own judgment passing upon the facts before it sees clear evidence that the road to the right is the one to take. You turn and say to the guide, "I know you have had large experience in this forest, and you have come to me highly recommended, but my own judgment tells me clearly that the road to the right is the one we should take, and I must follow my own judgment. I know my reason is not infallible, but it is the best guide I have."

But after you have followed that path for some distance you are obliged to stop, turn around and go back and take the path which the guide said was the right one.

After a while you come to another place where two roads diverge. Now the guide says the road to the right is the one to take, but your judgment clearly says the one to the left is the one to take, and again you follow your own judgment with the same result as before.

After you had this experience forty or fifty times, and found yourself wrong every time, I think you would have sense enough the next time to follow the guide.

That is just my experience with the Bible. I received it at first on the authority of others. Like almost all other young men, my confidence became shaken, and I came to the fork in the road more than forty times, and I followed my own reason, and in the outcome found myself wrong and the Bible right every time, and I trust that from this time on I shall have sense enough to follow the teachings of the Bible whatever my own judgment may say.

X. On the Ground of the Direct Testimony of the Holy Spirit

We began with God and shall end with God. We began with the testimony of the second person of the Trinity, and shall close with that of the third person of the Trinity.

The Holy Spirit sets His seal in the soul of every believer to the Divine authority of the Bible. It is possible to get to a place where we need no argument to prove that the Bible is God's Word. Christ says, "My sheep know my voice," and God's children know His voice, and I know that the voice that speaks to me from the pages of that Book is the voice of my Father. You will sometimes meet a pious old lady who tells you that she knows that the Bible is God's Word, and when you ask her for a reason for believing that it is God's Word, she can give you none. She simply says, "I know it is God's Word."

You say: "That is mere superstition."

Not at all. She is one of Christ's sheep, and recognizes her Shepherd's voice from every other voice. She is one of God's children, and knows the voice which speaks to her from the Bible is the voice of God. She is above argument.

Everyone can have that testimony. John 7:17 (R.V.) tells you how to get it. "If any man willeth to do his will, he shall know of the teaching, whether it be of God." Just surrender your will to the will of God, no matter where it carries you, and you will put yourself in such an attitude toward God that when you read this Book you will recognize that the voice that speaks to you from it is the voice of God to whom you have surrendered your will.

Some time ago, when I was speaking to our students upon how to deal with skeptics, there was in the audience a graduate of a British university who had fallen into utter skepticism. At the close of the lecture he came to me and said, "I don't wish to be discourteous, sir, but my experience contradicts everything you have said."

I asked him if he had followed the course of action that I had suggested and not found light. He said that he had.

Stepping into another room I had a pledge written out running somewhat as follows:

> "I believe there is an absolute difference between right and wrong, and I hereby take my stand upon the right, to follow it wherever it carries me. I promise earnestly to endeavor to find out what the truth is, and if I ever find that Jesus Christ is the Son of God, I promise to accept Him as my Saviour and confess Him before the world."

I handed the paper to the gentleman and asked him if he was willing to sign it. He answered, "Certainly," and did sign it. I said to him, "You don't know there is not a God, and you don't know that God doesn't answer prayer. I know He does, but my knowledge cannot avail for you, but here is a possible clue to knowledge. Now you have promised to search earnestly for the truth, so you will follow this possible clue. I want you to offer a prayer like this: 'O God, if there be any God, and Thou dost answer prayer, show me whether Jesus Christ is Thy Son, and if You show me His is, I will accept Him as my Saviour and confess Him before the world.' "

This he agreed to do. I further requested that he would take the Gospel of John and read in it every day, reading only a few verses at a time slowly and thoughtfully, every time before he read asking God to give him light. This he also agreed to do, but he finished by saying, "There is nothing in it." However, at the end of a short time, I met him again, and he said to me, "There is something in that." I replied, "I knew that." Then he went on to say it seemed just as if he had been caught up by the Niagara River and had been carried along, and that before long he would be a shouting Methodist.

A short time ago I met this gentleman again, and he said to me that he could not understand how he had been so blind, how he had ever listened to the reasoning which he had; that it seemed to him utterly foolish now. I replied that the Bible would explain this to him, that the "natural man receiveth not the things of the Spirit of God," but that now he had put himself into the right attitude towards God and His truth, everything had been made plain. That man, who assured me that he was "a very peculiar man," and that methods that influenced others would not influence him, by putting himself into the right attitude towards God, got to a place where he received the direct testimony of the Holy Ghost that this Bible is God's Word; and any one else can do the same.

Index

Some of Our Latest

Come Out or Stay In?

"Get it straight from the horse's mouth!" is wise counsel for anyone. Dr. Rice is caricatured variously along all lines of the theological spectrum today—all the way from being a rank modernist to a hell-raising, cantankerous isolationist. This comparatively recent paper-bound volume will set the records straight for anybody who is really interested in knowing the facts: not only as to what Dr. Rice's personal position is but, after reading this candid, impartial, unprejudiced presentation of the important issues involved, the reader will be thoroughly and properly instructed and informed on the Bible position that every honest Christian should want to take. 249 pages, **$3.95.**

Preaching That Built a Great Church

By Dr. John R. Rice. 29 stenographically reported messages used of God to build a church of 1,700 members, with over 7,000 professions of faith, in the midst of the bitter depression times—1932-1940. With such preaching as this, Dr. Rice, under God, founded and built the Fundamentalist Baptist Tabernacle, now the Galilean Baptist Church in Dallas, Texas. Young preachers, this is the kind of specimen preaching that will put the old-time fire in the bones—you ought to read them! Every Christian ought to read them, and would profit immeasurably when he does. A colossal paperbound volume with perfect binding, 585 pages, **$3.95.**

Sweet Family Ties in Heaven and Hell

By Dr. John R. Rice. In addition to the sermon that serves as title of this recent volume, there are other life-changing sermons preached in principal pulpits all over America. Some other titles are: "Come and See!" "All-Out Christians," "Helping Jesus Get a Man Saved," "Going Back," "Bold Preacher, Trembling Sinner," etc. There are 11 chapters in all. These are hot, extemporaneous messages, just as given from the pulpit, not cold addresses prepared in the private study. Each one has a message for saint and sinner alike. 222 pages, **$3.50.**

Observe usual postage rates ($2.00 to $4—25¢; $4.01 to $9.99—7%; $10 or over—$1) and order from—

SWORD OF THE LORD   Murfreesboro, Tennessee 37130